The

.ITTERING

..URY

such as the

V

# THE GLITTERING CENTURY

FREDERICK THE GREAT AMONG HIS PHILOSOPHERS

*From a painting by Menzel in the National Gallery, Berlin. The scene is the round-table room in the Potsdam palace of Sans Souci, which still exists. Frederick is in the center, back. On the left Voltaire, shown in profile, is leaning forward to speak to him*

# THE GLITTERING CENTURY

BY PHILLIPS RUSSELL, 1884-

ILLUSTRATED
*with Contemporary Paintings and Prints*

CHARLES SCRIBNER'S SONS · NEW YORK
*Charles Scribner's Sons · Ltd · London*
1 · 9 · 3 · 6

COPYRIGHT, 1936, BY CHARLES SCRIBNER'S SONS

PRINTED IN THE UNITED STATES OF AMERICA

*TO*
*E · A · M ·*

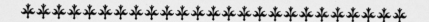

# FOREWORD

THE eighteenth century was very like our own. Preceding centuries seem to us remote, belonging, in thought and way, to the Middle Ages, which were concerned with the relation of man to God. But the eighteenth century steps forth briskly, speaking with our voice and accent.

It had the ideas, attitudes, vices, follies, which were the embryos of our own. Its thoughts were practical and objective rather than deep. Its concern was with the relation of man to man. Its men in wigs and breeches, its women with curls thrown over their shoulders, do not deceive us; we recognize in them our immediate ancestors.

Imposing figures cross the stage; for it was the century of the Louis's in France, the Georges in England, Frederick the Great in Germany, Peter the Great and Catherine the Great in Russia, Maria Theresa in Austria, Charles XII in Sweden, and George Washington, Benjamin Franklin, and Thomas Jefferson in America.

For kings it was not a good century. They lost their

power, their thrones, and even their heads. The commoner pushed them aside and became monarch in their stead. With him entered a train of new ideas, with which he made the world over in his image.

The movement of the story is something like a symphony. It begins with a stately measure. This, just as the middle of the century passes, is accelerated. Then ensues a rapid climax, ending in the clangor of three revolutions. The final note is one of relative tranquillity.

✳✳✳✳✳✳✳✳✳✳✳✳✳✳✳✳✳✳✳✳✳✳✳✳

# CONTENTS

## Part One

## Part Two

# ILLUSTRATIONS

# PART ONE

## CHAPTER ONE

## SUN KING

### I

At the very opening of the eighteenth century Louis XIV achieved a triumph which seemed to place him on a new pinnacle of glory. After several misfortunes his reign now seemed destined for heights more shining than any yet reached by any monarch of France, if not of the world; and he deigned to accept the applause of his courtiers with a graciousness in which there was no trace of his usual hauteur.

The success that brought to his veined complexion this glow of well-being was the placing of his grandson, the Duke of Anjou, on the Spanish throne as Philip V. The crowning of Philip in 1700 was the culmination of long maneuvers, of wars and intrigues. But to Louis the prize was worth it all: for his grandson was now lord not only of the Spanish peninsula, but of the Low Countries, of virtually half of Italy, and of what was more important, those gold and silver and gem-bearing provinces of New Spain overseas known as the Americas, or the Indies.

Dominion over Spain, for three hundred years France's rival, had been long desired because of the stream of wealth

3

which, though often emptied into the warlike maw of Europe, ever renewed itself and flowed without end from the mines of Mexico and Peru,[1] and from the trade-routes that circled the isles of the West Indies. To hold Spain and Spanish America was to have money. And abundant money was the one thing that Louis, now sixty-two years old, most craved; for too often had he been seriously embarrassed not only with regard to his most promising projects, looking toward world-dominion, but even in his personal exchequer. Colbert and his other ministers had done what they could to uncover new fields for taxation, but taxation, even when ingeniously devised and widely ramified, had at best pressed wealth only out of the pockets of peasants and traders and stingy townsmen. And it came in scant and halting streams and set up grumblings and resentments. What Louis needed were rivers, lakes, cataracts, of money flowing inexhaustibly from the very founts of the earth.

In his Grand Stables alone were 200 saddle-horses and 100 English hunters; in his Little Stables were 600 carriage horses; while his personal riding-horses kept at Versailles numbered 48, all wearing white bridles adorned with red ribbons. But although it is known that horses, whether in field or stall, eat their heads off, to keep kings on one's payroll is even more expensive. And had Louis not been compelled to maintain in proper style Charles II and James II of England, also freely bribing their ministers, meantime carrying on war upon war, not only upon enemies abroad but upon those at home, such, for example, as blue-nosed Protestants?

[1]"The mines of Mexico and Potosi furnished the means of buying the liberty of Europe." — Voltaire, *Age of Louis XIV*.

With Spain and its possessions now under his control France would be not only powerful but unimaginably rich, and in his exultation[2] Louis called his secretary in November, 1700, and dictated to Harcourt, his ambassador at Madrid, this message intended, of course, for passage to higher quarters:

The good of his kingdom will require one day that the king of Spain take measures to exclude the English and Dutch from the commerce of the Indies.[3]

## II

"To exclude" — that had ever been Louis's policy. It had been the policy, moreover, dictated by the theory which had governed his age not only in France but in Europe. Mercantilism made money and wealth identical. Mercantilism required in general that each nation should heed strictly its own interests, disregarding all others; specifically, it taught that each country should export goods copiously but import as little as possible, that it should sell constantly but buy rarely, and finally that it should accumulate and hoard the world's gold and silver and the other precious metals that determined the value of national currencies, to the end that one's own country should have all wealth and the others nothing. Although it created savage competitions which repeatedly soaked Europe in blood,

[2]This exultation was shared by the French upper classes. Joseph Addison, who was in Paris in 1700, wrote home to England that "the French conversation begins to grow insupportable; that which was before the vainest nation in the world, is now worse than ever." — *Life and Writings of Addison,* Edinburgh Review, July, 1843.

[3]Lavisse, *Histoire de France,* Vol. VIII, Paris, 1908.

the mercantilist theory remained virtually unquestioned for two hundred and fifty years. It was to Louis's particular interest at the time to exclude from the profitable commerce of the Indies, east and west, the traders of his neighbors, England and Holland. That policy had been taught him by his finance minister, Colbert.

It was characteristic of Louis XIV to regard a new idea with suspicion and to admit it to his mind very slowly, but, once he had accepted it, to hold it with an obstinate and crablike tenacity. It was so that he accepted and adopted this doctrine of Colbert. England and Holland had been troublous rivals; neither bribery nor war had prevailed over them. But Spain's power and riches joined to France's could not fail finally to dispose of them. Then indeed would Louis, who was France, be supreme in the world. Then indeed would he be *le Grand Monarque.* Then indeed would he be deserving of the title, the Sun King.

## III

To have, under God, no superior had from the first been Louis's ambition. When as a youth he had succeeded to the crown and ministers had come to him asking to whom they should now report, Louis had answered quietly: "To me."

*"To me."* Either shocked or amused, the ministers went away, certain that the young king had either not meant what he had said, or that he would soon tire of statecraft. On both counts events proved them mistaken. Louis not only took the reins of government in his own hands, but

kept them in an unrelaxing grip. He not only directed the government but himself became the government. Beside him there was in all France no authority, no force, no law.

Louis had no intention of dividing power with the nobles of the provinces, or of permitting them to trouble him as they had his ancestors. But as long as they remained in their provincial castles they were capable of forming leagues against the throne and of fomenting revolts as they had during the Fronde, memories of which still made him twitch in his sleep. Vestiges of this ancient feudal structure were everywhere found in rural France. To prevent any possibility of its rise, Louis, early in his reign, drew in his nobles from the provinces and required them to remain in constant attendance upon him at court. Thereafter they were called courtiers, but they were no better than prisoners constantly under Louis's eye, and under necessity of being unremittingly obsequious.[4]

Soon there remained in France no great estate whose owner was not hanging around Louis's court at Versailles. Those noble families whose poverty or circumstances compelled them to remain in the country fell out of favor and Louis let it be known they could expect no consideration.

"I do not know them," he said. "They are people I never see."

The result in rural areas was stagnation and deteriora-

[4]The Duke of St. Simon relates in his memoirs how, suspecting himself and his colleagues to be out of favor with Louis, he went to the king one day and assured him that "none of his subjects were more submissive to his will or more willing to acknowledge his supremacy in all things than the dukes." Louis, who had received him coolly, at once softened and replied, "that was how it was proper to speak and think."

tion; fertile acres went out of production and the peasants living on them, finding themselves ignored, produced only what they had to. At court the result was what might have been expected—the creating of a large body of a bewigged and satin-clad people who, having no employment except the competition for Louis's approval, surrendered themselves either to vicious amusements or a bottomless ennui. Sheer idleness made them base or feather-headed. Simply to pass the time they resorted to sexual intrigues, to gambling, and to details of eating, drinking, and dressing, or of inane diversions. In what survives of their memoirs and correspondence recurs one note—a boredom that became an affliction and a disease.

## IV

These provinces, thus depopulated of nobles, Louis governed through intendants, officials who were neither too able nor too scrupulous, and who were responsible to him alone. His ministers he chose not as counsellors but as assistants. Parliament, which had once summoned up the courage to demand the right to revise royal decrees, became under Louis an assemblage of grovellers accustomed to kicks and insults. Even the Pope was warned not to infringe upon the powers of the State, *i.e.,* of Louis. Convincing himself that France was his property, in every avenue and stratum of his kingdom he made himself absolute. He brought himself to believe, "that in considering the impost of the most searching taxation, all the wealth of his subjects was his, and that when he took it he only took what belonged to him," a hint given him by his confessor, Father Tellier. He attained a state of mind in which he could no longer bear in any particular to be crossed, or even annoyed. For example, there was the celebrated episode of the carp pond, the story of which was wafted throughout Europe.

When his son the Duke of Burgundy had brought home as his bride the young Princess of Savoy, Louis had been captivated with her. She was fresh, pretty, and roguish, and the king, in his delight, had accorded her liberties he granted to no other person. She alone could in public throw her arms around his neck, sit in his lap, explore his pockets, and even when he sat in council interrupt him without rebuke.

One day as the warmth of spring made itself felt Louis proposed that the court should adjourn to Marly, where he maintained a neat country residence, smaller than that at Versailles but still very comfortable, and orders were given out that all the ladies should prepare for the journey, including the Duchess of Burgundy. Uneasily the king's physician, Fagon, came to him and suggested that the young duchess, being in a certain condition, ought not to undertake any extended movements. Louis's face clouded over; he consented to postpone the trip to Marly, but only for a few days, and he refused to permit the duchess to remain behind.

Soon after arriving at Marly, the king, followed by his courtiers, was taking a walk near the carp pond when a lady came running from the palace to meet him. She said something to him and went away. For a moment the king said nothing but continued his walk around the pond. At

length he stopped and, without addressing any one in particular, said grumpily: "The Duchess of Burgundy is
hurt." The courtiers repeated these words in horror, and
one of them expressed the fear that she might not again be
able to have children.

"And if so," cried the king, "what is that to me?"

The courtiers stood still with amazement. But Louis
went on: "Has she not already a son? And if he should die,
isn't the Duke of Berry old enough to marry and have one?
What matters it to me who succeeds me—one or the
other?"

The courtiers scarcely dared to look up. They kept their
eyes upon the ground, and even the domestics and gar-
deners stood motionless, as Louis continued in an injured
tone: "Thank God, she is hurt, since she was to be so. I
shall be no longer annoyed in my travels and in everything
I wish to do by the pleas of doctors and the reasonings of
matrons. I can go and come at my pleasure, and shall be
left in peace."[5]

For several minutes a silence hung in the heavy air. It
was maintained until Louis himself broke it. When he
spoke again it was on the life, history, and habits of the
carp. He was leaning meantime on a balustrade, looking
down into the fish-pond. The courtiers having been petri-
fied into silence, the king tried to carry on the conversation with the servants, who hovered around with terrified
eyes. But they, unused to being addressed directly by royalty, were either too paralyzed or too little versed in the
natural history of the carp to sustain the discussion, which

[5]St. Simon, *Memoirs.*

languished and died. Enveloping himself, as he did on all critical occasions, in his dignity, the king stalked away, followed at a distance by his courtiers, who shrugged their shoulders or looked at each other without speech. Some among them could never afterward see a carp swimming sluggishly in a pond without thinking of pregnancy and Louis XIV.

## V

Brought up by a mother who was more attentive to her lover, Cardinal Mazarin, than to her slow-witted son, and reared in poverty and meanness, Louis on reaching the throne in 1661 early displayed, no doubt by a natural reaction, a craving for splendor and domination. Finding it relatively easy to override local and provincial rights and to set up a central absolutism, Louis's ambitions, fed by bowing ministers and courtiers, began to look beyond the borders of his domain. He craved to be master not only of France but the arbiter of all Europe.

Why not? Spain, become lethargic on her too sudden and too easily won wealth, and weakened by the expulsion of Protestants, Moors, and Jews — her most valuable workers — was now fit only to be hitched to Louis's train. Italy and Germany were helpless under the trampling feet of rival princes and factions. England, inhabited by a coarse people, lacked leaders with political skill and finesse. Holland, fed by her seamen and colonies, had grown fat and bumptious, but was too small to resist the weight of France. The other nations of the civilized world were too poor, remote, or barbarous to offer serious opposition. France then should be supreme in Europe and he, Louis, should be supreme in France.

For centuries the notion of a hegemony over Europe had been fostered in the minds of various monarchs by prodding ministers. Louis in his turn permitted the notion to make its home in his wig, and for a time it promised to be very nearly successful. To realize this ambition Louis had at hand the two great necessary instruments—a treasury and an army. An enriched nation and a staff of glory-worshipping generals were heritages handed down by Cardinal Richelieu; and they had been preserved fairly well by Richelieu's successor, Mazarin. History has given Louis both credit and blame for his restless militarism, his incessant toy-play with soldiers; it has paid less attention to the greater effectiveness with which, in attacking nations, he wielded the sinuous weapon of cash. "He bought and paid for the English nation," wrote Voltaire concerning Louis's bribes to Charles II; it was also French money that at times governed politics in Spain, Holland, Italy, Austria, and even far-away Sweden. Louis had no noteworthy sense of humor, but he could not help being amused by the avidity with which his bribes, nearly always generous, were accepted. He once said of James II of England, who had just pocketed a subsidy of 500,000 livres, "The king, my brother, is proud, but he loves French pistoles."

But French pistols and French pistoles—how could the quantity of them in the face of such demands be enlarged? That was the question that frequently worried Louis. To be splendid, to be dominant, to dictate to Europe—such things cost money. Where was more of it to be had? The answer was Colbert.

## VI

Jean-Baptiste Colbert was born in Rheims of a family of clothiers, and in all his attributes he was a true representative of an ambitious middle class. Colbert's rise from a clerical post under Cardinal Mazarin to the control of State finance brought upon the scene a figure new to civilization—the business man who exists only for business. As a young man Colbert would have been welcome in the head office of any great enterprise of modern times; he was cold, intelligent, hard-headed, and hard-working, loyal to his superiors, loved efficiency for its own sake, and he knew how to keep his mouth shut. In his own affairs he observed rectitude to a superlative degree, but could close his eyes to the manipulations of his superiors. Favored by Mazarin, he toiled upward under Louis XIV until at last there was nothing in his way except Fouquet, Louis's finance minister.

Fouquet was an office-holder of the old style—careless, lavish, believing in favors to friends and privileged groups, indulgent toward graft, and extravagant in feathering his own nest out of state money. He awarded generous pensions to whomsoever pleased him among the artists and poets—La Fontaine was one of his protégés—and at Vaux, south of Paris, he maintained a château where he entertained like a nabob and where the grounds were beautified by a thousand artifices in the manner beloved by the French; that is, the shaving, trimming, contorting, and massaging of Nature until the wildness and hairiness was completely gone from her and she resembled a rouged dame of the boulevards.

Fouquet was a member of the *noblesse de la robe,* the legal nobility, and Colbert, the little *bourgeois,* could not abide his heedless, wasteful ways. Fouquet's very expensiveness left his conduct of his office open to criticism, and Colbert found abundant opportunity to complain to the king about Fouquet's methods. Gradually he undermined Fouquet's prestige with the king until at last Louis's slow but tenacious Bourbon mind was convinced that Fouquet was a traitor. One day at Vaux the financier gave for the king a sumptuous dinner after which Molière's piece, *Les Facheux,* was played before 6000 courtiers and fashionables. Louis, who was astonished by such luxury, observed everything carefully — the graceful architecture of the buildings, the gardens and fountains, the avenues of trees, the green lawns and grottoes bearing the statues of nymphs. . . .

Sometime later Louis took Fouquet on a tour of inspection and at Nantes had him arrested. Fouquet was astounded; "I believed the king liked me as well as any one," he said. He was still bewildered when he was placed on trial, convicted, and sent to prison to pass twenty miserable years before he was to die forgotten. Sadly La Fontaine wrote an *Elegy to the Nymphs of Vaux,* while Colbert climbed eagerly into Fouquet's place.

## VII

There was in Fouquet's fall and Colbert's rise something symbolic. The nobility, though striving to retain its grip

LOUIS XIV AND HIS FAMILY

*The painting is by Nicolas de Cargillière. The monarch is seated. He is wearing the red-heeled shoes which set a fashion throughout the century*

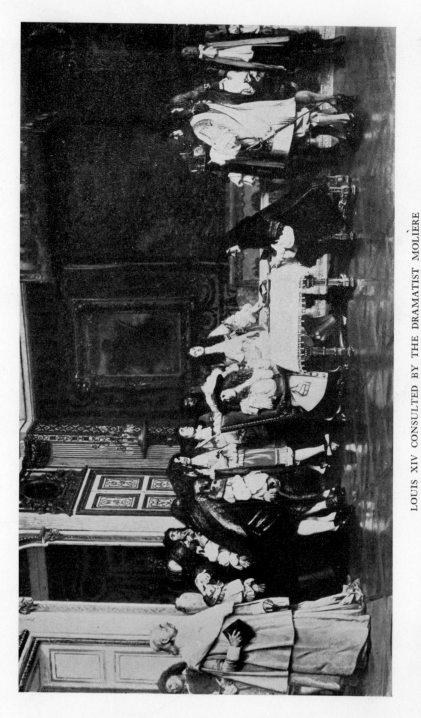

LOUIS XIV CONSULTED BY THE DRAMATIST MOLIÈRE

*In the arts as well as war and diplomacy Louis was the final arbiter. His is the figure, somewhat idealized, in the plumed hat. All the courtiers are uncovered*

on affairs with all its prehensile fingers, was decaying within. The French middle class, though long submerged, was slowly collecting and co-ordinating its powers. Since the middle of the sixteenth century its arteries had begun to feel a new strength. At that time the formation of a kind of clearing house in Lyons, intended to foster and regulate the business of the great post-medieval trade fairs, had led to a concentration of financial power which, to serve its own ends, often swayed or twisted the whole fabric of European political policy. The merchant and banker became so important that monarchs began to serve them and even court them. Louis XIV himself, prompted by Colbert, became the agent of the French commercial classes, and in his bitter need for money was sometimes compelled to smile upon and defer to that ranking monarch of the middle class — the banker — with the obsequious flattery which he himself was accustomed to require from his courtiers.

In fact, all the time that Louis XIV was dazzling Europe with his splendor and power, challenging rulers, defying popes, snubbing ambassadors, and reducing his courtiers to silence with a lift of his chin, the real monarchs of France, as of all Europe, were sitting on their thrones elsewhere — in their counting-houses or before their bullion-vaults. We can easily see who were the actual rulers of France from this episode related by the Duke of St. Simon in his memoirs:

The royal treasury was in one of its dismally empty stages when Desmarets, Louis's financial director, came to him and confessed that the situation was disquieting; he had knocked on every financial door in vain; only one hope remained—Samuel Bernard. Somehow he must be reached. Bernard had already been appealed to, but he would do nothing, although he was the richest banker in Paris, if not in France, having acquired a reputed fortune of 33,000,000 livres.

Desmarets offered to invite Bernard to dinner at his pavilion at Marly, where the king was then in residence, and proposed that Louis walk in on them as if by accident. Bernard, he hinted, was a man of strange whims. Believing that his career was somehow bound up with that of a black hen, Bernard was having this fowl treated with the most distinguished consideration; he was also imbued with an enormous vanity; it was the key to his coffers; if that vanity could be properly used . . . well, Desmarets would leave it to His Majesty to do what seemed best to him. The dinner was duly held and at the right moment the king walked in upon the two financiers. Affecting great surprise, Louis exclaimed to the banker:

"You are just the man never to have seen Marly—come and see it now. I will give you up afterwards to Desmarets."

Bernard followed the king into the gardens where Louis showed him all the sights and curiosities, introduced him to one of his marshals, Bergheyck, and walked along between the two, conversing affably as if with familiars. Bernard was enchanted; he observed that he, a *bourgeois,* was being received by the king as an equal, walking by his side while the nobles were kept back in the train of courtiers; his emotions were touched; and he returned to Paris declaring he would rather ruin himself than leave in embarrassment a prince of such gracious manners. The subsequent effect on the treasury was so beneficial that even Desmarets was satisfied.

"I wondered," wrote St. Simon, who was an eye-witness of the scene, "and I was not the only one, at this species of prostitution of the king, so niggard of his words, to a man of Bernard's degree."

Well might St. Simon wonder. Although he secretly disliked Louis XIV, this note-taking duke was inordinately jealous for the integrity of courts, and he could not fail to suffer in his inmost instincts when he saw the most glittering monarch of his age playing the part of a smirking courtesan toward a fat little bourgeois banker. St. Simon was a careful observer, but no more than the most stupid scullion in Louis's kitchen could he perceive that the victory of Louis's blandishments over Bernard merely marked one skirmish in the long battle of the eighteenth century in which the world's middle classes sought dominion over kings and nobles.

The struggle wore various disguises. At one time it was political, and parties fought each other for the offices of power; at another time it was nationalistic, and armies trampled back and forth over borders; again it was religious, and persecution, exile, and fagots followed. During this tug-of-war, royalty and nobility remained mostly conservative, land-holding, ritualistic, and Roman Catholic; while the middle class became gradually radical, adventurous, commercial, urban, and Protestant.

## VIII

The overthrow of Fouquetism by Colbertism was no
accident. Only a manager with bourgeois virtues could
have rescued Louis XIV from the abyss toward which
Fouquet had been pushing his régime. When Colbert came
to power he perceived that his primary task was, by breaking down the trade rigidities inherited from the Middle
Ages, to provide Louis with more money. A stream of
revenue was already flowing from faithful French labor as
applied to fertile French land, but at a thousand places it
was being intercepted. Colbert's first blows were aimed at
the interceptors. Grafting officials and thieving tax collectors were driven from office. A careless and chaotic financial structure was overhauled. The tax system was reformed, the more indirect and imperceptible taxes were
increased, and administrators were appointed who con-
formed to Colbert's new and startling ideals of efficiency
in the public service. He himself worked sixteen hours a
day.

"Is it best," asked a hopeful young man one day, "to
work in the morning or in the afternoon?"

"It is necessary," said Colbert, "to work in the morning
*and* the afternoon."

The results were pleasing; that constant stream of wealth
flowing from French labor and land, which had been so
long diverted, began to patter and then to gush into the
royal treasury. Louis looked upon Colbert and beamed.
Colbert, encouraged, took another step. He revised French
tariffs upward, to the end that France might sell much but

buy little and keep her gold and silver at home. This policy
was at the time called Colbertism, but was later recognized
as a mere facet of mercantilism, which is a theory constructed around the belief that a nation must regard solely
its own welfare and can maintain a national prosperity
only at the expense of its neighbors—a theory that was still
dictating the actions of governments during the first third
of the twentieth century, when economic nationalism was
the guiding policy of all.

One of the first fruits of Colbert's high tariffs was a war
with Holland; but at the time the connection was not
seen, and France continued to plunge into war after war
without realizing how many were due to Colbertism.

Determined that France should keep pace with such
commercially developing neighbors as Holland and England, Colbert's next step was to provide nourishment for
nascent French industry. Perceiving that the world's markets, already being fought for by bristling nations, were
being flooded with cheap stuffs and gewgaws known as
"trade goods," Colbert decided that France's products
should stand for quality rather than quantity. To this end
he instituted an exacting system of centralized regulation,
compelling manufacturers to conform to standards of quality and uniformity. Where they failed to do so, he set up
model factories known as *manufactures royales,* which subsequently became famous for their tapestries, silks, glass-
ware, and china.

Colbert made industry his pet; for agriculture he had
less sympathy. He fostered the breeding of better cattle,
horses, and sheep; he started canals and works of drain-

age; but he made the mistake of forbidding, because it would aid France's neighbors, the export of grain. The result was an injury to the world market which did vast hurt to the French peasantry and subsequently brought on famines which were felt even in the palaces of Paris, Versailles, and Marly.

At first, however, these reforms fattened the royal revenues, and Louis in his delight gave one important post after another to Colbert and finally made him controller-general. Colbert, encouraging in Louis the notion that all these activities would enhance the splendor of his reign, then launched upon his most spectacular project—the creation of a French navy and merchant marine sufficiently formidable to meet those of France's rivals—Holland, England, Spain, and Portugal. In a few years, through subsidies and tariffs, Colbert was able to present Louis with a powerful fleet which had its havens in the new ports designed by the ingenious military engineer, Vauban. Colbert's purpose was to make France the dominant commercial and exporting nation of the world and to give it the means of controlling the great markets opening in India and the Americas.

Colbert in so doing was following in the footsteps of the shrewd Richelieu, who in 1603 had encouraged Samuel de Champlain to go out to Canada and found a French colonial empire. Other interests had diverted Richelieu, and then in 1673 Louis Joliet, the Canadian-born trader, and the French Jesuit, Père Marquette, had discovered the Mississippi.

To Colbert the news was rousing. Ever since the first

bulky Spanish galleons had ferried over from the New World their cargoes of gold and silver, other nations had envied Spain and tried to imitate her example. The metallic stream flowing from Mexico and South America had made Spain the world's most formidable power; it had also enormously raised prices throughout Europe and set in motion consequent convulsions; and the trader and commercial adventurer had begun to lay the foundations of a new metallic age. Every maritime nation began to dream of owning gold-yielding colonies. Disillusion occurred when none of the hasty North American settlements yielded so much as an ounce of precious metal.

A revival of interest took place, however, when it was seen that northern North America was yielding products much more valuable than chimerical gold mines—skins and furs. It was perceived, moreover, that although a colony might furnish no gold to its mother country, it could be made into an outlet for her surplus goods and her surplus population. There ensued a general European race for more colonies and more markets. In this race the weaker nations soon succumbed or had to be satisfied with leavings, and at length only two strong competitors remained —France and England.

## IX

The discovery by Frenchmen of the Mississippi was exciting to Colbert for two reasons: the great river might furnish the means of extending southward French posts in North America so as to cut off the English and confine them to the narrow strip of land lying on the Atlantic coast between the mountains and the sea; and it might open to France an empire having a protected all-water route to Mexico, where lay one source of Spain's river of silver.

In 1682 Robert René Cavelier, Sieur de La Salle, was despatched from France to report to the French governor at Quebec, Count Louis de Buade Frontenac, and then to explore the massive river revealed to Europe by Joliet and Marquette. Louis XIV's letters-patent authorized La Salle to "endeavor to discover the western part of our country of New France . . . through which it is probable that a passage may be found to Mexico."

How hard died that old dream of a passage to Mexico! La Salle found it, but such a passage was not what Louis had dreamed of. With an energy which causes us to wonder where lay the source of its secret springs, La Salle overcame a thousand difficulties, and in April, 1682, found himself inhaling the salt breezes of the Gulf of Mexico. He had successfully descended the Mississippi, which Louis Joliet, in honor of the Virgin, had named *la Riviere de la Conception;* which Joliet wishing to honor the Canadian intendant, had called "La Buade"; but which La Salle, in honor of Louis XIV's first minister, immediately named the "Colbert." The river, with its main stream 2503 miles long, with its vast basin and all the territory drained by its tributaries, he seized and took possession of in the name of Louis XIV, naming it, in honor of his sovereign, Louisiana. It was an empire greater in area than all modern France, Germany, Austria, Hungry, and Italy combined.

And it was subsequently sold to the United States for

Copyright 1903 by The Singer Mnfng Co

LA SALLE AT THE MOUTH OF THE MISSISSIPPI

*Louis XIV, for whom the territory was named, thought that this might be a short route to the gold and silver of the Americas, for which he envied Spain*

A PRODUCT OF GOVERNMENT REGIMENTATION UNDER LOUIS XIV

*From an etching by deClerc. The Marquis de Seignelay visiting the Royal Gobelin Manufactory, one of the first industries set up in pursuance of a policy of mercantilism*

$15,000,000. If France had held it, if all that part of North America lying north of the St. Lawrence River and west of the Alleghanies had remained French, how might not the course of history have been diverted? . . . but let us pass on. Enough to say that traders and sailormen, non-descript adventurers and runners of the forests and seas, virtually all members of an energetic and ambitious middle class, did find and seize for France great possessions in America, the West Indies, India, and Africa. To foster and administer these colonies, Colbert placed them under the control of great corporations, stock in which was held by Louis, his courtiers, and his women; and Colbert even induced Louis XIV to preside at Versailles regularly over a kind of early Chamber of Commerce; but the ignorance, paternalistic fatuity, and greed of Louis and his bureaucrats eventually permitted France's colonial empire to disintegrate; and as fast as great pieces fell away, England was there to engulf them.

Colbert could not induce the king to maintain any enduring interest in navies or colonies. Louis loved to play with soldiers, and preferred to dazzle Europe, and the women of his court, with resounding and costly military feats on land; and at last Colbert, seeing the fruit of all his labors and meticulous planning decaying or passing into other hands, while Louis's expenditures were mounting higher and higher, gave up, sickened and died.

"If I had worked for God," he remarked when near the end, "one-half as hard as I worked for Louis, I would be surer of my soul's salvation."

## X

Colbert died in 1683, in the midst of an important period for Louis. It was the period in which he had been able, after defeating Spain and then Holland, to rest and divert himself with the completion of Versailles and its palaces; a period in which he had put the Pope in his place by notifying him that in France he was to have only a spiritual power; in which the queen had died and Madame de Maintenon had come to soothe and rule him; and in which he had been at last able to bring to pass what he had regarded as one of the principal achievements of his reign — the Revocation of the Edict of Nantes. By this act he had crushed the Huguenots and made life so unbearable for Protestants that they fled from France by the scores of thousands, dispersing to all points of the compass — to England, to Holland, to Germany, even across the seas to America, there to find new homes and to set up new trades and industries. Louis was too fatuous to comprehend that in ridding France of its Huguenots he was depriving it of one of its vital elements — an industrious and frugal portion of the rising middle class containing artisans and thrifty traders, apt in the utilitarian arts and in commerce.

But the revoking of the peaceful edict laid down by the liberal Henri IV, Louis's grandfather, was probably a stroke inspired by a secret fear. The Revocation was royalty's blow at a fast-rising section of a burgeoning middle class. This class was finding Protestantism better suited to its desires and aims than the Catholicism which to Louis, for all his disputes with its popes, was the one true religion, and certainly the only one fit for a person amorous of riches and beauty. The Reformation had enabled men to give less attention, and particularly less material tribute, to Rome; to pay smaller heed to centralized authority; and to rely on themselves more and on interceding saints less.

The consequence was a nascent individualism in which the middle class mind rejoiced. But Louis XIV hated such individualism with his whole instinct. It threatened the very sills of his absolutism. He used all the powers of his government to dragoon it, to hunt it down, to expel it, and to stamp it out under the red heels which his commanders, aping Louis, wore on their shoes. He hated England for the Protestantism which, cloaking middle class ideals, had showed its head in Cromwell and William III. But above all Louis hated Protestantism for its skepticism, its questioning of all the old dogmas, traditions, and authoritarian opinion which, despite the Reformation and the Renaissance, had hung over from the obedient Middle Ages.

"Nowhere," wrote Brooks Adams, "has faith withstood the rise of the mercantile class."[6] But Louis could not foresee the consequences of the rise of this class in his own realm. To his mind there was something indecent and subversive in the raillery, the mockery, sometimes to be detected in rationalistic writings; and when skepticism in religion was linked with Protestantism, it became doubly repulsive. When his judges sent Huguenots to Colbert's newly built galleys in the Mediterranean, Louis deemed the punishment all too light for heretics who in another age

[6]*The Law of Civilization and Decay,* New York, 1895.

would have been roasted alive. And yet skepticism continued to mount and spread; a perfect fountain of it was maintained in Holland, another of those little countries in which Protestantism and commerce and the middle class were all cemented together.

# CHAPTER TWO

# FATHER OF IDEAS

## I

"It was Bayle who began it all." So Frederick the Great once remarked to Voltaire. Frederick was speaking of this very spirit of skepticism, of a realistic and canny rationalism, which pervaded so much of the eighteenth century. Pierre Bayle has been called the father of the eighteenth century and his *Philosophic Dictionary* its bible. His writings influenced some of the strongest and cleverest men of the age. Frederick the Great, who did not admire all philosophers, regarded Bayle's books as so precious that he not only stocked his library with them, but edited and published selections from them, particularly the *Dictionary,* which Frederick pronounced the "breviary of good sense." Voltaire, in one of his bursts of enthusiasm, found Bayle to be the "greatest dialectician who has ever written" and "the eternal honor of the human reason." In England, Germany, Sweden, and Holland, as well as France, Bayle gained a following among savants, teachers, philosophers, and even clergymen writers. Free thinkers and rationalists bestowed titles on him such as "the master of doubt" and "the athlete of skepticism."[1] Louis XIV deemed his opin-

[1]Robinson, *Bayle the Sceptic,* N. Y., 1931.

ions so abhorrent that in 1683 he ordered a book by Bayle, *General Criticism of the History of Calvinism by M. Maimbourg* (Maimbourg was a Jesuit priest), to be publicly burned. Bayle ever deprecated such attentions, being satisfied to remain a dry little bachelor snugly hidden away in his lodgings at Rotterdam, where he lived happily, as he once said, "in exile, indigence, and freedom."

## II

Bayle belonged to that restless, rationalizing middle class which throughout the eighteenth century troubled the dreams of monarchs and absolutists. He was born in 1647 at Carla in the county of Foix, now the department of Ariège in southern France. In that region, well removed from the centers of religious strife, there was no artificial stirring up of Catholic against Protestant, and because the Jesuits were even then famed as thorough teachers, Bayle at twenty was sent, although the son of a Protestant minister, to a Jesuit college. Almost at once he was converted to Catholicism, and almost as promptly he recanted. For fear of persecution by Louis XIV's agents, he fled to Switzerland. For six years he taught at a Protestant academy in Sedan, and then in 1681 the royal decrees, by which Louis strove to keep France Catholic, feudal, and reactionary, closed all Protestant schools. Bayle found refuge in Rotterdam, where he passed the rest of his life writing, reading, teaching, reflecting, and writing again, living alone and gazing from his bedroom out upon a world whose antics both angered and amused him.

Bayle was a member of that early *intelligentsia* which, reacting against civil and religious absolutism, instinctively devoted itself to the tearing down of the decaying ideologic fabric left over from feudalism and the Middle Ages. Bayle's was the first exposition on a large scale of the tolerant ideas with which a liberal *bourgeoisie* sought to imbue the world. He was a child of the Humanists, the father of the *philosophes* and nature-praisers of the eighteenth century, and a spiritual relative of a great company of reflective writers which, as now gathered in some elysium, probably includes Erasmus and Montaigne and Hume and Lessing and Frederick the Great and Benjamin Franklin and Thomas Jefferson. Locke, indeed, was a contemporary, and so were Leibnitz and Leuwenhoek and Fontenelle, and Newton and Spinoza: all belonging to that band whose mission it was to free the mind from mediæval scholasticism and superstition and to enable the sons of merchants to roam the new world of ideas as freely as they were roaming the new world discovered by Columbus.

When Bayle first arrived in Rotterdam, Holland was still in its golden age, ruled by an alliance between descendants of the old nobility and members of the new merchant and banking class; which alliance desired peace and decorum to reign in order that commerce and prosperity might be fostered and expanded. But Bayle was to learn that toleration no more swayed the Dutch Reformed Church than it guided the Church of Rome in France. Seven years before the opening of the eighteenth century Bayle was accused of "nourishing dangerous opinions" and was deprived of his Dutch professorship. He accepted his dismissal tranquilly.

To a solitary teacher approaching middle age, the loss of 500 guilders as salary was afflicting. But he congratulated himself upon having a "natural patience, joined with the habit of meddling only with books, of going little out of one's study, and avoiding as the plague those turbulent men . . . who busily thrust themselves into all affairs."

All loss becomes somehow gain, and of one thing Bayle was now glad: he was at last free to sit down before his table and, unburdened by demands from the world outside, give his whole attention to a project he had long nursed—the preparation of an encyclopædia which should do for secular knowledge what the *summas* of the old theologians had done for religious belief—collect, coordinate, and summarize. And finally to publish it alphabetically arranged in the national language, so that all could follow, comprehend, and use. In short, Bayle proposed that knowledge should no longer be the diversion and luxury of the aristocracy, but should be made available as the useful tool of the common man: that is, the man of the middle classes, for few men of the lowest classes could read.

Bayle carried out his purpose; his *Historical and Critical Dictionary* was published in two huge volumes in 1697, on the very threshold of that century whose ideas, on the Continent at least, he to a degree shaped and governed. Voltaire, who later in the century encountered Bayle's dictionary, was charmed with it, pronouncing it "a sort of dictionary of reasoning, the first work of this kind where one could learn to think." Civilization had already been favored with encyclopedias, or summaries and arrangements of knowledge, but such works had merely disclosed facts or enjoined dogmas; Bayle's was the first which favored thinking. The world had never seen any dictionary like Bayle's, nor has it seen any like it since. To the Baylean mind knowledge does not consist of ponderous absolutes to be put up, piled, and conveyed about in solid cubes, but is made up of airy relativities, lightly massed, and easily detachable in pocket-sizes which can be handled and turned over. His most weighty information was often embroidered with a gay and fecund wit, to which he gave fullest play in copious and erudite footnotes. It was Bayle, indeed, who sported with knowledge in the manner of a juggling comedian which Voltaire later adopted and carried to extravagance.

With things Bayle's dictionary dealt very little. He was much more interested in persons. He had learned from Plutarch and Montaigne the ingenious use of anecdotes, and these he employed, always documented, with such fascinating results that his two great tomes soon earned a second printing and established themselves in the favor of discerning persons throughout Europe. Bayleism and biography were thus inseparably linked. For example, in his discussion of Queen Elizabeth of England he brought in a quotation to show that at her audiences she used repeatedly to pull off and put on her gloves, with the object of calling attention to her hands, of which she was very vain. Bayle also indulged in occasional scandalous references, particularly in dealing with the great. This habit drew upon him the reproof of high personages, but did not lessen his readers.[2]

It is evident that Bayle, while compiling and writing his dictionary, thoroughly enjoyed himself. Over each morsel of learning he lingered with the delight of an epicure. He arranged his material as he pleased, blandly disregarding the principles of proportion. In his discussion of Eve, his footnote on the nature of the serpent that deceived her is longer by far than the main text dealing with the mother of all living; his treatment of King David was such that his critics complained he had "made a scoundrel of the greatest saint of the Old Testament"; and yet he wrote no articles at all for such great names as Galileo, Copernicus, Cicero, or even Montaigne.

His admirers called Bayle a philosopher; but he constructed no system and left none behind. His mission was to destroy the medieval débris of superstition and of conventional thought that still cluttered European minds. In the field of ideas he began the work carried out later by Voltaire, Diderot, and Rousseau. He was the spiritual father of a host of men whom we shall meet later in this volume.

## III

Louis XIV, whose habits set the tone for all European monarchies, had little respect for writers, philosophers, or teachers except as they paid him court and anointed his deeds with the flattery of which he never tired. In Europe

[2]For example, he wrote in one of his footnotes that, according to Monsr. Juricu, Pope Sixtus V, speaking of Queen Elizabeth, once said he believed if he could have one night with her, a new Alexander the Great would be created. — *Dictionaire Historique et Critique*, 5° ed., II, 352.

there was but one man who made him nervous and uneasy. This was the dour Dutchman who had become William III of England. Between Louis and William existed polar antipathies. William represented everything in life which to Louis was most abhorrent, and as men are afraid of what they do not understand, so Louis feared William.

Where the French king was avid of luxury, splendor, and power, the English king was hard, dry, self-locked, and single-minded. Where one was autocratic, the other was liberal. Where one was Catholic the other was Protestant. A lifetime of losses and frustrations had left the Protestant William III with a single ambition, which grew and burned as all other aims dropped away — to isolate Catholic France and to beat Louis XIV. Being called to the English throne pleased him most because it gave him an opportunity to unite Holland and England against Louis; and defeats, petty or large, had not altered his opinion that "it is not necessary to hope in order to undertake, or to succeed in order to persevere."

French armies had done much to defeat William's purposes, but much more hampering to the Hollander had been Louis's money. Throughout William's domain had trickled the stream of gold which Louis and his agents had with a hundred ingenious screws pressed out of France's producing and trading classes. Louis's gold had bribed ministers, suborned generals and admirals, bought off parliamentary measures, and nullified William's most careful plans. But William had pushed on through the massed bodies of soldiers and bribed politicians, and even though wretched health, of which a racking cough was the incessant signal, had reduced his cold energy, he in time, helped by Louis's fatuity, virtually isolated France and concentrated the attention of all Europe upon her as the most arrogant, ruthless, and dangerous power in the world.

## IV

The year 1700, then, found Louis XIV resting tranquilly at Versailles, that resort which had cost the taxpayers of France the equivalent of $120,000,000; where through his spies and informers he could see and hear and direct everything, and where everything reached him except the truth.

After several misfortunes in war and diplomacy—the war of 1692 in Flanders was ruinous and the Peace of Ryswick in 1697 was, because it destroyed the foundations of the commerce which Colbert had so laboriously built up, even more so—Louis had a right to feel almost serene. Among the rivals of France, Spain was now under his control; Holland was quiet; and England had momentarily been bribed into silence. He could not have deluded himself, however, into believing he had finished with the English, for they were Protestant, parliament-governed, ocean-roaming, and commercially aggressive. In this very year of 1700 William III was forging the links of a grand alliance of England, Holland, and the Germanic Empire against France; and Louis's ministers came to him to advise that it be forestalled.

In the furious commercial struggles between France and Spain, and France and Holland, the French mercantile class had long had an eye fixed upon the great trading ports of the Netherlands, and in particular had dreamed of extending French control along the North Sea as far as Antwerp. Such control, now that France had tied Spain to her apron-strings, seemed quite possible, and commercial Europe was instantly alarmed. In England the old saw was recalled that possession of Antwerp "means a pistol pointed at the head of England," and the Dutch knew that if Louis XIV spread his boundaries it would be at Holland's cost.

The forebodings of those who dreaded Louis's unsated ambitions came true. The crowning of a Frenchman as king of Spain was followed by the movement of French troops across the Netherlands border into Flanders and Brabant, provinces of the Spanish Netherlands. Here lay a line of forts which the Dutch, in fear of France, had garrisoned at their own expense. As fast as Louis's army moved against them, these troops fled or remained to be captured. This aggression was exactly contrary to Louis's promises as made in the Treaty of Ryswick, signed three years previously.

The results were the formation by William III of the second grand alliance against France, signed by Holland, England, and the Austrian emperor, and the breaking out of a new war. It was called the War of the Spanish Succession, but it was only one of a series of commercial struggles that, as the trader and merchant and banker fought for power, had racked Europe since the close of the Middle Ages. It lasted for ten years and well-nigh wrecked every participant. And one of the wrecking penalties fell upon Louis XIV and his administration.

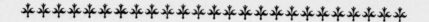

## CHAPTER THREE

## BEWILDERED QUEEN

### I

WHILE a half-strangled France was thus slipping and stumbling, there was across the channel a rekindling of energy. Holland, so long England's chief rival, was no longer formidable; Spain was enfeebled; hence a glittering vista opened before the eyes of England's trading classes: command of the seas, control of markets, ownership of colonies, and a general English supremacy.[1] All this seemed the more possible when the news came that while Marlborough had been marching to Blenheim, Gibraltar had been taken, August 4, 1704, from Spain with ridiculous ease. The fortress was guarded by only fifty men, who had just one cannon that would fire. The Dutch assisted in the capture, but the flag that went up over Gibraltar was English.

[1]Early in the century Defoe wrote in *The Review*, VI, 143: ". . . were England so full of people . . . that they could neither sow their own corn nor feed their own cattle, it would still be the richest, and be the greatest nation in the world. . . . All the world should be your breeders and feeders; all your neighbors should be your ploughmen, your hewers of wood and drawers of water."

At the moment the noise of the triumph at Blenheim[2] drowned the victory at Gibraltar, and it was not until some years later that it was realized that the capture of the straits fortress had been the more important. It gave England command of the Mediterranean, helped to insure her supremacy on the Atlantic, and assisted her to climb rapidly to the position of arbiter of Europe in place of Louis XIV.

The war rumbled on until all the nations involved in it became sick of it. In France a party of peace-at-any-price became so strong that Louis was induced to humble himself before the allies and pray them to stop the war. In England the landowners, who saw themselves being ruined by it, wished to accept his terms, which became so abject that he tried to bribe Marlborough, and even offered to desert and sell out Philip V of Spain, his own grandson. His pleas were not listened to; the trading classes were in control and were enjoying the profits from loans, deals, sales, and speculations.

But a war-tired country threw out the Whigs; Queen Anne wearied of Sarah's habit of inserting her relatives into every vacant post and quarrelled with her; Marlborough fell out of favor;[3] and a Tory ministry came in which

---

[2]Godolphin, Queen Anne's minister, subsidized Joseph Addison to celebrate the victory with a poem. The fame and revenue that thus came to Addison enabled him to found the *Tatler* and *Spectator*.

[3]In 1712 a commission charged that Marlborough had received from contractors for bread and other supplies a total of £282,366. The general replied that whatever perquisites he had got were no more than those commonly allowed to commanders-in-chief; which was true. A new morality, however, was being born, and Marlborough was so unfortunate as to be one of its first victims.

was willing to make a secret treaty with Louis XIV's agents. This ministry was led by Robert Harley, later the Earl of Oxford, belonging to the country gentry and by religious inheritance a Noncomformist.[4]

In September, 1711, Harley was made governor of a company of merchants "trading to the South Seas and the other ports of America, and for encouraging the Fishery." Among its directors were his fellow ministers, St. John (Viscount Bolingbroke) and Benson. Scarcely thirty days later these men obtained from France preliminary articles which relinquished to England the *Asiento* or slave-contract trade by which France had been enjoying a monopoly of supplying Negro slaves to the Spanish colonies in America. This trade had been one of Louis XIV's chief sources of revenue in his more prosperous days. The Protestant traders in England had long envied him for it and had resolved to take it away from him.[5] The Harley ministry now refused to negotiate a peace with Louis unless he gave up to them this profitable traffic in Negroes, and Louis assented to the deal with Harley's company, in which Queen Anne had a fourth interest.[6] The transaction was completed two years later at the signing of the Peace of Utrecht.

[4]"It is said he sometimes takes a bottle," wrote Wodrow, historian of the Covenanters, "but otherwise he is moral, and never fails to pray with his family at night."

[5]Ownership of slaves was common in Queen Anne's England, black pages being especially favored by ladies of rank. All such slaves wore a collar as the bridge of servitude. Slaves who ran away were advertised for in newspapers, this establishing customs which were preserved by American slave-owners until the nineteenth century.

[6]Burton, *The Reign of Queen Anne,* III, 218

## II

This year, 1711, was noteworthy also for an attempt to weaken the French grip on Canada. While these ponderous campaigns were being carried on in Europe, fighting on a much smaller but fiercer scale was going on almost continuously between the French traders and English settlers in America. Such warfare was particularly embittered because of the presence on both sides of Indian rivalries, usually heated by draughts of official rum.[7] The prize being disputed for was the fur trade, from which great companies, backed by European capital, were taking enormous profits.

At length the English traders began to press against the French. In June, 1711, a British expedition including twelve men-of-war and forty transports was sent over to Boston to prepare for an attack on Quebec. Its commander was Jack Hill, brother of Abigail Hill, who had succeeded Sarah Marlborough as Queen Anne's favorite. At Boston a larger force of New Englanders were to be taken aboard, but when it was found that no provision had been made for feeding them on the ships, the troops were marched overland to the St. Lawrence River, where the fleet met them. No sooner were they on board than eight of the transports, blinded by fog and storm, got on the rocks and sank, carrying down 800 men. Not knowing what else to do, the fleet, without even a fist shaken at Quebec, sailed

[7]Count Frontenac refused to prohibit the sale of liquor to Indians in Canada on the ground that French commercial interests would be harmed. His action caused frequent quarrels with the clergy.

for home. On reaching England, one of the warships blew up, destroying more than 400 men and decimating a throng of visitors who had come on board to celebrate the return.

## III

War consists of a series of blunders; that side wins which commits the fewest. England had not yet produced an efficient navy;[8] in the whole of Europe it was still believed that a nation's chief weapon was its army. Even after it had acquired sea-power, England used it haltingly and stupidly. But when the importance of colonies and overseas trade was more fully realized, England, because it had the ships, learned in time to dominate that body of water over which the world's trade-lanes were developing—the Atlantic ocean. The securing of the balance of trade led to the holding of the balance of power in Europe.

Of the contending nationalities in North America the Indians most disliked and feared the British, because the British were always seizing their lands. With the French, who wanted only furs, the Indians were much more friendly. But with British prices the French traders could not compete; the French were hampered by the rules of royal monopoly and by lack of communication with France, and in time they lost control of the fur trade and of the Indians. The English colonies hugging the Atlantic coast, after the experiences of a century (Virginia having been settled in 1607 and Massachusetts in 1620), began to

[8]In 1707 Admiral Sir John Norris reported "there is two butts of stinking beer with a small quantity of damnified oat-meal on board her Majesty's ship *Adventure*." — Burton, *Reign of Queen Anne*, III.

thrive, to stir and expand. Queen Anne's War, as the Americans called the war of the Spanish Succession, was only one of several which they used as means to squeeze out the French.

A war so ruinous could not continue indefinitely and in 1713 it came to an end with the Treaty of Utrecht. By it France lost Newfoundland, Acadia (Nova Scotia), and control over the fur-yielding Hudson Bay region; England won a stronger foothold in North America, won control of the Atlantic and Mediterranean, and of their trade routes; and finally won the financially fat slave trade. The Asiento contract provided for the delivery of 4800 Negroes annually to Spanish America, where the native Indians having become exhausted, rebellious, or decimated, it had been found necessary to replace them with cheaper and more docile Africans. The Old World thus presented to the New an organized supply of black men in chains, one end of which was around the necks of the slaves; the other gripped the necks of their owners, a situation which culminated in the American Civil War of 1861–65.

So was France beaten and Louis XIV forced to give up the naval and colonial dreams fostered by Colbert. Queen Anne called the settlement a victory for British trade and then died, August 1, 1714. Harley, whom she had just deposed, wrote sadly to his friend, Dean Swift, a stanza of what he called "an imitation of Dryden," the last line of which was: " 'Tis fatal to be good." In these five words was summed up the philosophy of the early eighteenth century in England.

## IV

It is not to the literary Addison, with his air of elegance
and suavity, to whom we must look for an accurate picture of English life under Queen Anne; for the genial and
useful Addison, as a writer hired and kept in office by the
politically powerful class, naturally looked upon the world
as a fair one, and he loved best to write about gentlemen
and their clubs and coffee-houses, and of ladies and their
fashions and gallantries; it is rather the journalistic Defoe,
with his plainness and his ability to see what was before
his nose, who furnishes what appears to be a more convincing if not gracious portrait of the times.

From his periodical, *The Review,* which the academies
have ignored in favor of the politer *Tatler* and *Spectator,*
we learn that drunkenness, somewhat abated since the
Revolution of 1688, revived rapidly under Queen Anne
(perhaps due to the cheapness of gin, the manufacture of
which was encouraged by the landed interest); that clergy-
men of the Church of England were not respected for
their morals and were so free with their oaths that they
made the exclamation "God damn" popular; that elections
took place amongst scenes of the grossest debauchery; that
in political life corruption was the expected thing; and that
the streets of the great towns were full of aggressive beg-
gars by day, and at night of robbers and thugs. It was also
the era of the well-dressed "Mohawks," capable of mobbing
a man for the love of it.

In general, we get an impression of a people gross, vulgar, and brutal, and yet full of energy and an abounding

health, perhaps owing to the cheapness of food, the price of which had begun to fall near the end of the seventeenth century. We recognize their portraits in the paintings of Hogarth: their coarse, protruding features; their knowing and cynical expressions; their stocky limbs and thick necks; their love of obscenity, ribaldry, and the infliction of pain.

In Hogarth's pictures of children and young women, there occasionally appears a face or pair of eyes of rare delicacy and beauty, but it is the beauty of a stag or heifer. In it there is often grace, but never tenderness, never imagination. It is a beauty in youth only; in old age it becomes, beneath Hogarth's brush, coarse, red-faced, swollen-veined, and malicious.

These are the people of whom Swift, cloaking his sensitive nerves with an outward coldness, was thinking when in *Gulliver's Travels* he created his hated Yahoos;[9] and it was by the accepted manners and principles (or lack of them) of the times that Bernard Mandeville, the Hollander who became an Englishman, was no doubt affected when in the course of Queen Anne's reign he wrote and published the witty *Fable of the Bees,* devoted to the thesis that vice (which, however, he did not make synonymous with evil) often redounds to and contributes to public prosperity.[10] One attribute often ascribed to the British as

[9]"I have ever hated all nations, professions, and communities," wrote Swift to Pope in 1725, "and all my love is toward individuals. . . . Principally I hate and detest that animal called man. . . ."

[10]At one time it was the fashion to regard Mandeville as a monster. But subsequent generations, although they read him less, have been kinder to his memory and see his seemingly outrageous views as reflecting only the prevailing social creed. Mandeville was one of those clever men of the period who had been affected by the skepticism of Pierre Bayle, to whom

a nation had, however, not yet taken firm root—hypocrisy. That vice had, owing to the relatively small development of the profit motive under commercialism, risen and enlarged only with the rise of what Renan called *l'homme intéressé*—the man with an axe to grind, who, finding it impossible to reconcile the spirit of individual gain with the teachings of Jesus,[11] contented himself with public smirks in the direction of virtue.

## V

Not all was good in the reign of "good Queen Anne." The driving of the laborer, through enclosure acts, from the land and his concentration in the cities had brought one person in every five to the edge of pauperism. Offenses against property were punished ferociously; the theft of goods valued at £2 brought death by hanging, and young boys were sometimes executed for trifling robberies. Prosecutors rode in the death carts of condemned men, reviling them on the way to the gallows, and the last

he often referred. Mandeville saw all morals, all civilized usages, all religious practice, as being a mere rationalization of selfishness. He ridiculed idealism and the belief in absolutes. He perceived the gap between mercantilism and Christianity, and laughed at the difference between public preaching and private conduct. National wealth, he averred, consists in having "a Multitude of laborious Poor," whose poverty "it is a Prudence to relieve, but Folly to cure." Mandeville sometimes wrote in order to annoy the bourgeois, but many of his pages contain shrewd observations. Mandeville was a man of his time in his belief, which accorded with the teachings of Locke, the philosopher of the period, that all human knowledge is *a posteriori* and comes from experience—that is, contact with cold facts.

[11]"Religion was not meant to curtail the enjoyments of the rich, but to keep the poor in their places, and to prevent the lower ones from rising above their stratum in life."—Herbert Paul, *Queen Anne*, London, 1806.

Ludovicus Victor et Pacator.

LOUIS XV

*Whose reign was characterized by boredom, extravagance, and the loss of France's prestige*

MERRY ENGLAND IN THE EIGHTEENTH CENTURY

*Rowlandson's impression of a bachelor drinking party*

AN ELECTION ENTERTAINMENT

*A satire by Hogarth on the disorder and corruption of the times*

struggles of the victims were greeted with raucous jeers from disorderly mobs. Men imprisoned for debt grew old in filthy cells, and the insane or mentally unbalanced were regarded as devils and treated as such.[12]

If the common people had been degraded by poverty and brutal customs to Yahoodledum, the gentry were but little better. In his advice to the waiting-maid in great families, Swift, who loved to mingle with the great, wrote cynically: "If you are handsome, you will have the choice of three lovers: the chaplain, the steward, and my lord's gentleman. I would advise you to choose the steward; but if you happen to be young with child by my lord, you must take up with the chaplain."[13]

Swift was not alone in his cynical view of the times. John Gay in *The Beggar's Opera* wrote:

> When you censure the Age,
>   Be cautious and sage,
> Lest the Courtiers offended should be;
>   If you mention Vice or Bribe,
>   'Tis pat to all the Tribe,
> Each cries, "That was levell'd at me."

The corruption that took the form of political bribery was due to the hidden struggle between the two upper classes for supremacy. On one side was the aristocracy of the land, on the other were the merchants of the towns.

[12]The prevalence of debt and petty crime caused so great an overcrowding of prisons that measures were taken to send felons to America (which term also included the West Indies). The Virginia and Pennsylvania assemblies protested in vain. "It would be safe to reckon the total of involuntary emigrants sent forth from Old Bailey alone as less than 10,000 between 1717 and 1775." — J. D. Butler, *Am. Hist. Review,* Vol. 2, No. 1.

[13]*Directions to Servants in General.*

The rural nobility and gentry, who had been in the saddle ever since the Norman conquest, could not bear to share power with the up-coming traders; but the latter, driven by their business interests to seek political representation, bought their way into parliament where they could not beat their way in; thus revealing, as Swift put it, that *"power, which, according to an old maxim, was used to land, had now gone over to money."*

But under Queen Anne the battle of land-owner against town trader for political and social control was only begun; it continued throughout the eighteenth century until in horror the combatants beheld across the channel the smoke of the French Revolution. Shrinking back appalled, lord and merchant fell into each other's arms; whatever the cost, they must keep that thing out of England.[14]

## VI

It was the strife between land-owner and trader which lay at the bottom of the difficulty in securing the union of Scotland with England, and of the endless oppressions inflicted on Ireland. In each case the bone of contention was the wool trade. The Scots, in negotiating for the union, demanded complete free trade between the two kingdoms. The English wished to except wool and sheep, and to bar Scotch ships and goods from the American colonies. All goods going to or coming from these plantations must first be landed in England, so that the English middle-man might take his toll.

It was out of the determination to monopolize the

[14]See the speeches of Burke at this period.

woollen business that England forbade Ireland to manufacture or export cloth made wholly or partly of wool, and ordered the Irish to turn their attention to the cultivation of flax and the manufacture of linen, in which English growers and traders had no interest. Such enactments were in perfect accord with the mercantilist belief that if a nation wished to make itself rich, it must make its neighbor poor. It was the pursuit of this policy which, before the century had ended, had cost England its most valuable American colonies.

## VII

For the time being, however, the profits of mercantilism were fat, and the merchant class and those who ministered to it with ideas grew constantly stronger and bolder. Luxuries, once confined to the land-holding aristocracy, became easily accessible to the urban middle class, and rivers of wealth flowed into England in the wake of ships from overseas bearing cargoes of coffee and sugar from the West Indies and tobacco from Maryland and Virginia. The plenty and cheapness of these commodities and the increase of leisure made possible the rise of the London coffee-house where a gentleman might linger all day around an open fire, while at home his wife lay abed all morning and spent her afternoons adorning herself. This is the life smiled at by Joseph Addison and sneered at by Jonathan Swift.

The energy of a class which was rising to mastery found vent in literature, philosophy, and science. In literature its ideology was expressed by Addison, Pope, Swift, and Defoe; in philosophy by Locke; and in science by Newton. The scientific spirit, the craving to get and organize knowledge, had just begun to burgeon; but already, as the middle class came nearer and nearer to the top, a breath of that atmosphere which we love to call modern was perceptible; and there was among successful people a disposition to rely upon reason rather than authority; to discard absolutes for relativities; to think of the present and future rather than the past; and to assert the right of the individual, so long as he had cash and influence, to do as he pleased.

Gross and hard as was this rising class in many of its manifestations, particularly in the cities, where the competition for bread or position was fiercest, it was full of vigor, and occasioned defeats only increased its determination to know, to expand, and to rule.

## CHAPTER FOUR

# ENIGMATIC WOMAN

### I

*Our father who art in Versailles, unhallowed is thy name, thy kingdom is no longer great, thy will is no more done on earth, nor on the wave. Give us this day our daily bread, which everywhere is lacking. Forgive our enemies who have beaten us, but not those generals who let them do it. Lead us not into the temptation of Maintenon and deliver us from the evil of Chamillart.*

THIS MOCKING prayer circulated in Paris might, if he had heard it repeated, have acquainted Louis XIV with the feelings of his people after his diplomats had returned defeated from Utrecht.[1] It is possible that, despite the efforts of his spies, courtiers, and physicians to keep him ignorant of everything disagreeable, he did overhear some of the ditties chanted even under the walls of Versailles, such as:

> Le grand-père est un fanfaron,
>   Le fils un imbécile,
> Le petit-fils un grand poltron.
>   Ohé! la belle famille![2]

At any rate, after the wretched ending of the War of the

[1] Lavisse, VIII, 459.
[2] The grandfather is a swellhead, the son a fool, the grandson a coward. O what a family!

Spanish Succession, which he had begun with such vain-glory, Louis was no longer the pompous Sun-King. He was only a disappointed old man of seventy-six years, in need of money, and having a thousand servants but no friends. He leaned more than ever on the companionship of Ma-dame de Maintenon, whose views and hints he accepted so often that it was said that he had removed his crown and left it in Madame's lap.

## II

History has not been able to make up its mind as to the character of this woman, who has been called a "trans-parent enigma."[3] On the one hand she has been regarded as a cold-hearted schemer; on the other hand a self-sacrific-ing saint. At the court of Louis XIV, where an immense power flowed into her protesting hands, she became indis-pensable by virtue of her ability to soothe, tranquilize, and stabilize things.

To her position in the most closely watched court of Europe she rose by degrees from her home in a jail at Niort, where her father, a wastrel, was a prisoner. As a child she had been taken by her parents to the West Indian island of Martinique, and on that account was often called "the Américaine." A convent education and omnivorous reading had cultivated an already considerable intellect and as the orphan girl, Françoise d'Aubigné, she coolly deter-mined, on her return to Paris, what her way of life should be: not to oppose, or to struggle, but to accept, to wait, and to serve. Above all she determined, possibly after she had

[3]Sainte-Beuve, *Causeries du Lundi*, July, 1851–Sept., 1851.

discovered that her head would always be superior to her heart, that she would strive to be not so much loved as honored. With affection, since her emotional gifts were so meager, she could dispense; but honor, esteem, elevation —these she must have.

In keeping with her policy, when the crippled Scarron, wit and writer, offered to marry her, she accepted. To him as a wife of only seventeen years, slender and pretty, she was devoted; and Scarron returned her care with uniform kindness and consideration. At his death Mme. Scarron had made so many friends, especially among women of rank, by deferring to and serving them, that they brought her to the attention of Mme. de Montespan, the king's chief mistress, who was having trouble in managing her children by Louis. An arrangement was made by which Mme. Scarron took the children under her care, leaving Mme. de Montespan free to wage war upon her rival, Mlle. de Fontanges. Confessing herself beaten, la Montespan once exclaimed to Mme. Scarron: "The King has three mistresses—me in name, this *fille* (Fontanges) in fact, and you in heart."[4]

Louis at first, however, disliked Mme. Scarron, possibly because he was afraid of her erudition. Subsequently, recognizing her gifts for management, he brought her into the royal household, where she gradually became his confidante, counsellor, and chief executive. At Versailles she became the friend of all and the manager of all. Night and day she was at Louis's beck. For his sake she even refused to have a screen placed around her chair, although the

[4]Sainte-Beuve.

palace was in winter full of chilly draughts (and sometimes, says the historian Lavisse, of smoke and bad smells).
For his sake she endured a thousand trials, a million tedi-
ums, without losing her self-control — she once remarked
that for twenty-six years she had not permitted a vexatious
word to escape her. Her outward fortitude was based on an
unshakable faith in the Church. (She was often accused
of having instigated Louis's persecution of the Jansenists
and of Protestants, but of this there is no cogent proof.)

Devoted as she was to her duties, this is no evidence that
she had any affection for the monarch to whom she ministered so long. While he lay unconscious but not dead, she
left Versailles and withdrew to St. Cyr, where she maintained a school for friendless young girls, and seemed no
longer interested in what became of Louis XIV. *"I had to
perish in symmetry,"* she once said of her life with him,
and perhaps was she so tired of living geometrically — that
is, according to perfect form — that Louis's death was, as
Sainte Beuve suggests, a relief to her.

It is possible now to see Mme. de Maintenon as no waxen
saint on the one hand, and no unscrupulous plotter on the
other, but as a creature of the eighteenth century — guided
by reason, having constant good taste but no enthusiasm,
skeptical of emotion and fearful of a surrender to feeling,
and shedding a uniform kindness that more resembled
light than warmth.

### III

While the king's ministers were running around trying
to patch up a crackling empire, Monseigneur, heir to the

throne and Louis's only son by the queen, was seized with smallpox. This son was a man of fifty years, amiable, idle, and stupid. His good humor and lack of snobbishness had made him a favorite among the tolerant, however; and while he lay ill a delegation of fishwives came to his bedroom to kiss his bedclothing and pray for his recovery. The news of his son's critical condition was kept from the king until the last moment. At Monseigneur's death his father collapsed and shed tears, but next day was able to attend to his usual business.

As heir or *Dauphin,* a title then used for the first time, Louis named Monseigneur's oldest son, the Duke of Burgundy, whose wife was the vivacious heroine of the carp-pond episode. In less than a year this merry young woman, in whose charm Louis had delighted, was dead of a mysterious fever. A few days later the duke, her husband, was also dead. This couple left two male children; the older, the Duke of Brittany, when made Dauphin, was almost at once smitten with a fever, and all the bleedings and infusions given by the royal physicians could not save him. In the confusion the doctors overlooked his brother, the Duke of Anjou, and this pale, sad-eyed infant survived to become Louis XV, the succeeding king of France.

## IV

The sudden loss of his son and his grandchildren, and above all of the gay Duchess of Burgundy, who, the gossips said, was the one person whom Louis had ever adored, made the king feel the weight of his years and loneliness.

Instead of taking his daily outing he began to sit silently in his cushioned chair. For the first time in his life he seemed to take no interest in affairs around him, and did nothing to quell the rumors of scandals that filled the back-corridors of Versailles. He waved aside the report that the dead Dauphin had been poisoned, and ignored the open whisper that his grand-daughter, the Duchess of Berri, was daily drunk at dinner and was carrying on an incestuous intrigue with the reputed poisoner, his nephew, the Duke of Orleans.

The long repression which Louis had wielded over the court now broke asunder. The tedium was dissolved by an outburst of scandal, accusations, intrigues, and barely concealed hysteria. It appeared for a time that Louis's apathy would permit the court to get altogether out of hand; but he was saved by his dignity. Indeed, in his death-hours Louis XIV was more admirable than in his life. He learned that in London bets were being laid on the days of life yet remaining to him. He knew that he was soon to die; but he accepted the news tranquilly, remarking that dying was a less unpleasant business than he had been led to believe. To his weeping valets he said: "Did you think then that I was immortal? For myself I have never thought so." To his officers he gave a last audience saying, "Adieu, messieurs; I hope you will remember me sometimes." To the Dauphin, then five years old, he is said to have given this advice: "Do not imitate me in my love of buildings nor in my love of war. Try to keep peace with your neighbors. Give to God what is due to him."

The immediate cause of Louis's last illness was described

*The bookcase shown above was a part of the
Dournovo collection in Russia*

FURNITURE OF THE LOUIS XIV PERIOD

*Characterized by extreme dignity with a touch of the pompous and a fondness for orna-
ment in classical style. These pieces are by André Charles Boulle (or Buhl), famous for
his inlay work and his use of bronze, ebony, and tortoise shell*

*From an engraving by Robert Nanteuil*

COLBERT, LOUIS XIV'S MINISTER

*He determined that French goods should stand for quality and enforced rigid rules to that end*

as "sciatic gout," believed to have been brought on by over-eating, for which the Bourbons were famous over Europe. Elizabeth Charlotte, Duchess of Orleans, wrote in her memoirs that she had seen the king eat at one sitting "four platefuls of different soups, a whole pheasant, a partridge, a plateful of salad, mutton hashed with garlic, two good-sized slices of ham, a dish of pastry, and afterward fruit and sweetmeats."

That Louis was able, despite such meals, to keep himself in good condition[5] was due perhaps to his refusal to worry, his abstention from alcohol, his regular habits, and his fondness for the open air. In the palace at Versailles it was often remarked that the king was comfortable in temperatures that gave his courtiers gooseflesh.

In Louis's final attack, spots appeared on his feet and legs. Fagon, the royal physician, treated him with bleedings, infusions, and sweat-baths, but the spots persisted and became gangrenous. Fagon realized too late that his patient was suffering from blood-poisoning, and all his panicky measures failed. Louis repeatedly lost consciousness, but suffered little pain. On a Friday Mme. de Maintenon left him, not to return. On the Sunday following he died, September 1, 1715. In three days he would have been seventy-seven years old. He had been king of France seventy-two years, and for a great part of that time he had been the arbiter of Europe, although he could scarcely read or write and was almost completely ignorant of even the bases of

[5]Saint-Simon remarks that after Louis's death an autopsy showed his intestines were healthy and that he might have lived "beyond his hundredth year."

history.[6] Within a few years legends began to gather about him as the Great Louis, King Sun, and so on; and Frenchmen easily persuaded themselves that in Louis XIV they had been governed by an illustrious if, on occasions, faulty monarch; yet at the time the news of his death was received with relief and even rejoicings. Saint-Simon wrote: "Paris, tired of a dependence which had enslaved everything, breathed again in the hope of liberty. . . . The provinces which had been in despair at their ruin and their annihilation breathed again and leaped for joy. . . . The people ruined, overwhelmed, desperate, gave thanks to God, with a scandalous *éclat,* for a deliverance." And Voltaire wrote that along the road to Saint-Denis, on which the king's body passed, he saw tents in which the people were laughing and drinking and singing.

## V

The age of Louis XIV has sometimes been cited as one of the golden ages of French history; yet after his death it was revealed that Louis had bankrupted France while his agents had made of her body a kind of honeycomb of looted cells. The most conspicuous monument he left behind him was his palace at Versailles, ornate, florid, and draughty; built according to the tastes of a nabob newly enriched; a palace that was at once imitated by all those little princes of Europe who dared to give their taxpayers another twist of the screw.

However, since no evil is absolute, it is possible to dis-

[6]Louis XIV's court was filled with nobles who read a book as seldom as they bathed.

cover in Louis's reign a measure of positive accomplishment. The regulations imposed by him and his ministers at least had the effect of partly breaking down the hoary feudalism, with its suffocating restrictions, that had persisted as vestiges of the Middle Ages. Not only were the nobles herded at court, where they could be watched and controlled, but under Colbert the masters and workmen of the trades and guilds which had restrained production and suppressed competition were steadily undermined.

All this redounded to the interest of the middle class which on the one hand hated the arrogant nobility of the provinces and on the other detested the rigid rules of the town guilds. This middle class was chafing to go into business, to trade, to manufacture, to compete, to destroy limits and rules; in short, as it defined it, to be free.

Louis XIV's age was the age of Corneille, Racine, Molière, Pascal, Bayle, La Bruyère, La Fontaine, Bossuet, and La Rochefoucauld, whose cynical maxims expressed the spirit of the age under Louis just as Mandeville's fables, on the other side of the channel, expressed the spirit of the age under Queen Anne. These prosateurs, dramatists, poets, painters, musicians, and philosophers, shed a lustre upon Louis's reign which he easily appropriated for himself. His heart, however, lay entirely in devices for external show; for such devices he blandly and pompously brought France to the edge of ruin. And that ruin threatened the safety of all the peoples of the Continent; for during his life Louis XIV had extended the secret hand of French diplomacy over virtually the whole of Europe. Louis had held the balance of power; English governments gradually took it away from him; but if that balance should be upset a new chaos would impend.

Louis had gripped his people in an intellectual strait-jacket. They could amuse themselves as they liked, but they were not permitted to explore ideas or enjoy doubt. The intelligentsia could only look enviously across the channel at the figures of Robert Boyle and Isaac Newton who had in an exciting way mingled, without interferences, theological speculation with scientific investigation. The French intellectuals therefore received the news of Louis's death with relief. It seemed to them that France was about to enter upon a new, free, and joyful era.

## CHAPTER FIVE

## BRED FOR WAR

### I

ONE OF the kingdoms in Europe which had been in the secret pay of Louis XIV was Sweden.[1] At one time Sweden had the most formidable army in the North. It had been built up by Charles XI.

Charles XI was one of those monarchs who, like Louis, had fettered the nobility. In order to strengthen the throne and put his nobles in their place, he had attacked them at the source of all feudal power — possession of the land. Where Louis had separated his seigneurs from the land by moving them to Versailles, Charles created a separation between lords and land by removing the land into the control of the royal treasury. But the struggle between crown and nobility, so familiar elsewhere in Europe, went on until his son, Charles XII, came to the throne.

To him the nobles, bishops, and gentry looked for relief, for this straight-nosed youth had shown more interest in drilling soldiers than in political affairs; but no sooner had

[1]In 1672 France began to pay Sweden an annual subsidy of 600,000 crowns for the use of 16,000 Swedish soldiers at need, particularly against the German provinces. — Hill, *History of Diplomacy*, III, 99.

Charles XII become king than he turned on his feuda-
tories a cold and freezing face, as if to bid them keep their
distance. Indeed, at his very coronation he took the crown
from the astonished hands of the archbishop and calmly
crowned himself. This was regarded as an omen. It was.

From the first, Charles XII ignored all activities in favor
of war. Indeed, except for some attention to mathematics,[2]
he had no interest in anything except military affairs. He
had been bred for war as a greyhound is bred for racing.
To exercise his peculiar gifts he got ample opportunity; for
Sweden, with her great possessions and her determination
to control the Baltic Sea and its fast-rising commerce, lay
across the path of other nations with restless rulers.

Wearing his high boots and his gauntlets of reindeer
hide, Charles began when only a youth a series of campaigns that soon altered the face of northern Europe. Leading his toughened Swedish peasants, used to cold and
hardships, out into icy plains or snow-crusted forests, he
subdued Frederick IV of Denmark in six weeks; he captured Thorn and Dantzig and defeated Augustus, Elector
of Saxony; installed Stanislaus Leczinsky as king of Poland; and then, at the opening of the eighteenth century,
he invaded Russia and attacked the thick but disorderly
legions of Peter the Great.

His spectacular victories, repeated many times, gave
Charles a resounding fame. In their first encounter Charles
with 8000 Swedes routed 40,000 Muscovites; and Europe,
perceiving France's decay, began to look to this blue-eyed

[2]Charles XII is said once to have recommended that 64 be substituted
for 10 as a counting unit, because 64 contains both a cube and a square
and is easily divided.

chieftain, Protestant and ascetic, to succeed Louis XIV as the arbiter of continental affairs. Charles went on beating the Russians, and at length, waving aside the cautions of his ministers, announced he intended to plant the Swedish banner in the heart of Moscow.

It was a rash resolve, as rash as was Napoleon's similar and later resolve. Cold and famine wore down Charles's army until it was weakened both in numbers and stamina. Peter the Great had meantime cheerfully accepted tremendous beatings from the Swedes as the price of acquiring better methods and better arms. At length in 1709, in a winter[3] so cold as to "freeze birds on the wing," Charles, who believed his own genius invincible, attacked at Poltava a Russian army twice larger than his own. Peter's moujiks, by now trained by imported officers and equipped with improved weapons from western Europe's factories, out-maneuvered, out-charged, and out-shot the Swedes, enveloped them, wiped out their infantry, and captured all their cavalry. Charles XII, wounded and stripped of the army with which he had intended to walk over the face of Europe, took refuge in Turkey.

The crash at Poltava was heard throughout the continent. Charles's prestige was dimmed, and as Sweden's position fell from that of cock of the north to a minor rank, Russia rose as suddenly out of the darkness, and its hairy, grinning face was for the first time in history seen staring through "the window of Europe," the Baltic Sea. For two centuries and a quarter the memory of that face has not died from European chancelleries, and even today the sight

[3]Its effect in France under Louis XIV has been already described.

of it (for it is still there, although no longer grinning) produces uneasy visions.

The news that Sweden was out and Russia in caused a vertigo in cabinet closets. Particularly depressing was it to Louis XIV, who, from the peak of a very mountain of power, had fallen into a valley of humiliation so low that his own subjects were mocking him with secret placards and his envoys were begging peace from England and Holland. Charles XII, like so many other monarchs, had been on the French pay-roll; Louis had subsidized him to exercise a police surveillance over the German states and to maintain France's power in the north. Intimations were brought to Louis that Czar Peter was willing to do business with him on the same terms as Charles XII had accepted; but to Louis this notion was revolting. Hence control of the situation in the Baltic, as well as that in the Mediterranean and Atlantic, was lost to French commerce. The Polish crown was restored to Frederick Augustus, the Saxon elector; and the alliance of Poland, Denmark, and Russia against Sweden was renewed, and the way cleared for new alignments, new rivalries, new wars.


## II

Charles XII remained in Turkey in the hope of stirring up his hosts against Poland and Russia, but eventually tiring of his presence and double-dealings, the Turks forced him out. When Charles returned to Sweden, he had been absent from it the first fourteen years of the eighteenth century. He found his country well-nigh ruined. He had tried to govern it from an army tent; levies of horses and men had exhausted the peasants; high taxes had crippled the trading classes of the towns; the nobles, whose estates had been reduced, were sullen; and the French subsidy having been lost, there was little hope of help from England, that country having been offended by interference with her commerce in the Baltic.

So desperate did Charles become that he signed a paper permitting von Görtz, his financial minister, to borrow money or to sell his king's military services anywhere, on any terms, he could. Failing, von Görtz tried a spectacular inflationary move, by which copper money was raised to the value of silver by government fiat. This brought down on von Görtz the angry fears of the commercial classes, who were not long in having him hanged, drawn and quartered. Charles stumbled on, still dreaming of conquests that would give him the mastery of northern Europe, and still taking part with his soldiers in reckless attacks; but in an invasion of Norway he was struck in the head by a ball[4] and killed. He was not yet thirty-seven years old.

It was the end of absolute monarchy in Sweden and of the extreme forms of feudalism, and the nobles swarmed back into power. They set up an oligarchy in which, however, they were forced to make room for a middle-class party which called itself "the party of freedom and parliamentary government."

Europeans, even before the century was old, were taught to regard Charles XII as a genius rivalling Alexander the Great, partly because of an admiring biography of him by

[4]Rumor had it that this bullet came from behind.

Voltaire; but although he was no doubt a gifted militarist, Charles's reign in Sweden was regarded by certain classes of his people as a pestilence and a destruction. He had lost many thousands of healthy young soldiers who had been needed as farmers; he had lost Sweden's commercial domination of the Baltic and most of her possessions bordering on that sea; he had lost for his country her prestige as the chief military and economic power in the North, a position given to her by the labor of Gustavus Adolphus; and he had left little behind except poverty, debt and disease, and the memory of a coldly conducted tyranny.

Charles XII of Sweden was one of those kings who, like Louis XIV of France, made the traders and bankers and other taxpayers of Europe ask themselves: How much longer can we afford to maintain these men who imagine they are next to God?

## CHAPTER SIX

# RUSSIAN AXMAN

### I

THE ISSUE at Poltava which must have been, despite his iron control of himself, so depressing to Charles XII, was to Peter the Great correspondingly exalting. To the captured Swedish generals the Czar, after the battle, went around, a delighted smile widening his face under that mustache which with its spreading hairs looked so much like a cat's whiskers.

"Thank you, thank all of you, good sirs."

"For what, Your Majesty?"

"For being such good teachers, aha! Yes, yes, truly you have taught us well. It is to you, indeed, that we owe the victory."

And then he clapped them on the shoulder. Also, some of them (although the historians do not say so) he probably kissed. For Czar Peter was emotional and showed his feelings, not masked like the diplomats of eastern Europe, who believed in nothing and in nothing delighted, but openly like a child. Also, it would not have been surprising if the Czar had followed his kiss by grinding his fist against their noses or kicking them from behind, for he was given to fantastic humors and to violent changes in demeanor.

He might be smiling genially when without warning his face would alter. Fearful jerks and contortions would run over his features; his eyes would glare like a beast's, or glaze like a dying man's, and a spasm would rack his body. In a moment the convulsion would be past, and the Czar would resume the business in hand as if, although his companions might be sick with fright, he had felt or seen nothing extraordinary.

This *tic* or tendency to epileptic spasms was supposed to have been a consequence of the shock suffered by Peter when as a child, a mild and affectionate one, he was compelled to witness the cutting to pieces of his mother's advisers by a mob having at its head the Strieltsi, the soldiers of the Moscow garrison; but he may have inherited the weakness from his father, Czar Alexis, or from his grandfather Michael, founder of the Romanoff dynasty, who died after many years of melancholia.

At any rate Peter suffered throughout his life from acute neuroses, which often dissolved or exploded in astounding manifestations. He grew up, however, physically strong, energetic, and playful. His toys were chiefly tin soldiers, wooden ships, or metal gadgets imported from Germany — playthings borne on those streams of influence which had been for years gradually converging on Russia from various parts of western Europe. The guardian of Peter's mother was Matveyef, whose wife was a Scotch woman; teachers and cunning workmen from Europe had often been brought into Russia for special purposes; and such a taste for western things did Czar Peter acquire that as a young man he was sometimes reproached for spending so much time in the foreign quarter or "German suburb," as it was called, that lay between Moscow and Preobrazhenskoe, his home in the country.

As Peter reached his late 'teens two of his most admired companions were an army quartermaster, General Patrick Gordon, one of those emigrating Scots who have carried war, business, and the Presbyterian religion to the remotest parts of the earth, and a well-dressed young Swiss adventurer named François Lefort, son of a druggist in Geneva.

From the very first Peter was vastly impressed by the ingenious Lefort. The Swiss completely embodied the hairy young Czar's idea of what a gay young European gentleman should be like. Lefort dressed fashionably, he knew several languages, he could select good wines and music, and he could tell smutty stories and devise dissipations whose fantastic humors enchanted the Czar. And he wore under a supercilious nose a thin little upturning mustache that Peter at once copied; only on Peter's lip it insisted on taking the shape of a cat's whiskers and would never look like anything else.

Lefort's stories of the wonders of the West engraved themselves upon an imagination that had been already worked upon by European influences, and suddenly Peter announced that he wanted some fifty or sixty picked young men to depart for Holland and England, also for Vienna and Venice, to learn shipbuilding, navigation, the art of fortification, and other western ways and devices. On the heels of this, another thought struck him and he made a second and more sensational announcement: he would go to Holland and England himself.

## II

Once he had decided upon this expedition into the heart of civilization, Peter prepared for it with zest. Although he was to travel as plain Peter Mikhailov, a carpenter, he took along some 200 people, of whom some 50 were personages, and about 70 were tall and imposing soldiers. The rest were servants, dwarfs, and buffoons. Thirty-two vehicles were needed to haul this imperial circus, the strangest that had ever come out of the East to penetrate the body of Europe. Two persons were important: Lefort, now an Admiral-General, who carried his own orchestra; and Menshikov, a young army sergeant whom the Czar called "child of my heart."

Two things Peter packed with extra care: One was a stamping seal (he was fond of engraving), showing a workman among his tools and bearing the legend: *I, a pupil, seek a master.* The other was his own pet and private drum. All his life Peter loved to beat, to roll, to pound the drums. Music he looked down upon until he learned that all good orchestras have drums. Instantly he approved Lefort's carrying his musicians into Europe; but he would have liked them the better if they had all carried drums. He would have liked to be able to make his first Russian imperial passage from middle Asia into Europe with a big bass drum strapped to his own shoulders and to see himself pounding it: *boom* for Poland, *boom* for Germany, *boom* for Sweden, and for Holland, France, and England *boom, boom, boom.*

## III

In the spring of 1697 the Russians cross into Swedish territory by way of Riga, scattering insults but no gold (for Peter is no waster of his substance), dropping pearls from their fur hats and lice from their coat-tails. At Koenigsberg Peter gets a chance to take out his drum; he plays it for Frederick, the Elector of Brandenburg. He wishes to go to Hamburg by sea, but is stopped by one of Colbert's French squadrons, which is cruising off Dantzig. He hurries through Berlin and is at last in Holand. He arrives at Zaandam on a Sunday, and, bursting with impatience, on Monday buys a set of carpenter's tools, dresses himself in the red blouse and white trousers of a Dutch workman, hires a room in a blacksmith's house, and goes to work in a shipyard.

Here he is content to be known as Peter Bas, Master Peter. He builds a frigate, delighting in the callouses on his hands, and has a look at mathematics, astronomy, physics, surgery and dentistry.[1] He visits and studies shops, factories, schools, museums, canals, and bridges. Everywhere he makes notes, drinking in information with the same thirst he brings to workingmen's beer. At Utrecht he meets and converses with William III. In all these activities he is completely happy and voices his satisfaction

[1] At Leyden Peter visited a dissecting room, where he made members of his suite bite the muscles of a dead body. He also procured a set of dental instruments and watched his aides for aching teeth. Oudard, *Peter the Great,* N. Y., 1929.

in a pious letter, in the style of St. Paul, to the Patriarch
back home:

> Being of Adam's line, we labor. We do not work of necessity
> but of good will for the sake of our sea routes, in order that
> having complete experience, we can, in the name of Jesus Christ,
> be conquerors, and liberators of the Christians.[2]

"For the sake of our sea routes" — thus did Peter proclaim himself the agent of those merchants and bankers
who in their struggle for the control of the world's commercial traffic were transforming society, were transforming even Russia, for so long the darkest land in Europe;
and who all believed themselves to be, even while they
waged the twenty major wars of the eighteenth century,
the servants of a greater good.

## IV

All this time Peter was trying to induce Holland to help
him build a great Russian navy and begging the Dutch to
lend him artisans, architects, designers, and engineers.[3] The
Dutch, however, at war with England and still in fear of
Louis XIV of France, hesitated to lend any of their care-

[2]Graham, *Peter the Great,* N. Y., 1929.

[3]Holland, owing to the development of its dyke and windmill system,
had then the foremost engineers in Europe, and Peter was fascinated with
their inventions, which were chiefly devices intended to pump water or
harness the wind. The painter, Jan van der Heyden, was at this time trying to improve his "fire-engine," which was a steam pump somewhat akin
to the crude engines devised later in the seventeenth century by Papin in
France and Savery in England. It was in Holland that the Czar first encountered the machine age, and he was alert enough to realize that unless
improved tools, weapons, and methods could be carried into Russia, he
could not keep pace with his rivals in the Baltic region or drive out the
Turks in the South.

fully conserved strength even to so promising a customer as Peter; and the Czar, convinced that England had better shipbuilders anyhow, suddenly left Holland in 1698 and accepted William III's invitation to cross the channel and be England's guest.

## V

In England Peter was provided with the best that the land afforded, and he and his small suite of twenty-one persons were not slack in enjoying it. One of their breakfasts is on record—half a sheep, nineteen pounds of lamb, ten pullets, one dozen fowls, and three quarts of brandy.[4] As a pre-breakfast appetizer they had already been served with seven dozen eggs with salad. Peter was even provided with an English mistress, although he was accustomed only to servant girls. When she complained of the smallness of the honorarium she received from him, Peter remarked:

"Ha! What I had from her was not worth even that."

At Deptford he was supplied with every facility for studying shipbuilding and designing. Near the river here was Sayes Court, the splendid home of John Evelyn, gentleman and diarist. Its pride was the garden, which Evelyn, who was a lover of the sciences as well as the open air, had constructed and maintained with meticulous care. The house had been let to Admiral John Benbow, who sublet it to Peter and his suite.

This English house, soberly elegant in its furnishings, the Russians converted into a gymnasium, night-club, and playground. In the beds they had pillow-fights, they

[4]Graham, *Peter the Great,* N. Y., 1929, p. 81.

wrenched off doors and sections of fence for firewood, they soiled the carpets and spilled grease on the rugs, they smashed furniture and pictures. They broke 300 window-panes while cavorting and throwing bric-a-brac at each other.

When Evelyn's gardener returned, he could only look at the lawns, the trees, and the flower-beds; and groan. Chief pride of his master had been a "close hedge of glittering holly." The Czar had used this portion of the garden for footraces in boots; and, in search of new sensations, had seated himself in a wheelbarrow and been driven, shouting and laughing, at full speed through the hedge. At this novel sport, which exhausted onlookers with laughter, three wheelbarrows had been broken. Soon afterward Oxford University made Peter a Doctor of Law.

At Deptford Peter not only caroused with might but so labored. He visited everywhere, inspected everything, questioned everybody. He even went to the Quaker meeting-house and waited on the Spirit. Twice he had conversations with William Penn and several times he quitted the rioting in Evelyn's house to go and listen at Quaker services. For Peter, when not taking a holiday with Venus and Bacchus, believed himself to be the agent of Heaven, and he might get a message from on high even at a Quaker meeting.

When he returned to Holland he had engaged 500 Englishmen, experts in all occupations, to come to Russia and teach his people the new ways; and for £20,000 he had sold the monopoly of tobacco in Russia to an English firm. In only one desire did he fail: he could not induce the

Powers to join him in a coalition that would drive the Turk out of Europe. Monarchs and diplomats were already pre-occupied with the approaching War of the Spanish Succession, and at Vienna Peter was treated with a shortened courtesy. At Venice he cancelled the rest of the trip and hurried back to Moscow, for he had had sudden tidings thence.

## VI

At Moscow the Strieltsi, the garrison troops of bullies and reactionary strong-arm men, had mutinied. The local commandant had put them down and sent 1700 of them into exile. Peter had them recalled and, mounted on a scaffold in Red Square, received them as they were brought up. They came in bundles with their arms tied behind them. Flourishing a headsman's axe, Peter himself began to chop their heads off. He afterwards boasted that he has thus disposed of 200 rebels in one day. Tiring, he summoned his nobles and ministers to the task, and jeered as they hacked feebly at tough and dirty necks. Other Strieltsi he caused to be broken on the wheel, leaving them to die slowly. Of the victims he had 195 bodies hung in the courtyard of the convent where his enemy and sister, the ex-regent Sophia, was confined. Three of them he caused to be suspended for five months before the single window of her cell. Each corpse held a petition in its stiffened hands.

## VII

On his return from western Europe, Peter wielded not only the axe but the shears. When ministers came to present their respects, he seized them and with his own hands cut off their beards. The *ukaz* went forth: *No more beards in Russia.*

The order shocked Peter's subjects, who for centuries had worn their Oriental beards so as to look as much as possible like the saints, and some of them resisted. Churchmen protested and such a clamor was raised that Peter gave ground. Let all mossbacks keep their beards (he ordered), but at the cost of an annual tax and license fee, the license to be attached to the beard.

Peter attacked not only hair but clothing. Russians had always worn the long robes and cloaks of the Orient. Peter ordered them to throw off these hoary garments and get themselves measured for a modern suit of clothes, such as the Germans wore. Tailors and barbers were posted at city gates with orders to raid hair and robes, and at Peter's feasts buffoons were employed to seize cloaked and hairy guests and give them a shave and measure them for breeches and waistcoats, while shaven guests looked on and roared and puffed imported tobacco, condemned by the Russian church, into the victims' faces.

From beards and robes Peter leaped upon the calendar. The Russian year began in September, when grain was sown. The Czar ordered that it must conform to the European way. The new Russian calendar therefore began with January 1, 1700.

The eighteenth century opened with a Russia made new by force. Behind the wrinkling forehead and grimacing face of Peter grandiose ideas were fermenting. By the loose and somewhat mangy scruff of its neck, Peter had taken hold of the Russian Bear, and despite its longing to get back into the cave of custom, its whimperings for the safe refuge of mediævalism, he was pulling, dragging, kicking, booting, its half dormant carcass out into the open; out into the whirling circle of competing European states.

## VIII

Above the cat's whiskers that so often trembled during Peter's convulsions of rage, or laughter, or epilepsy, lay a thick brain-case that housed an astute mind. His visit in western Europe had convinced him of what he had already absorbed from his Scotch and Swiss and German advisers: that a feudal world was being converted into a mercantile one, and that to be rich and have power, one must not stop with owning land but must control the trade-routes that lay across the seas.

He searched a map. There was the Black Sea, but he was not yet navally strong enough to wrench it from the Turks. The Mediterranean, into which the Black Sea led, was controlled by Turkey at one end and Spain at the other. The Atlantic was being fought for by England and France. But at his northern doorstep lay the Baltic. There he might do something. A single movement in that direction, however, would hurl Russia into the face of Sweden, which, owning Esthonia, Livonia, Ingria, and Karelia, controlled the Baltic's southern and eastern shores. Sweden's army, so long in the pay of Louis XIV, was dangerous, but its new commander was only a boy, Charles XII. He would not mature for five years. By that time his army would be wiped out or exhausted.

Joined by Poland and Denmark, with whom he agreed
to divide the spoils, Peter, at the opening of the eighteenth
century, declared war on Sweden. His declaration was over
the protests and against the advice of England, Holland,
and France, which feared their Baltic trade would be dam-
aged.

So began the Great Northern War. It lasted twenty-one
years. In its middle stages it was contemporary with the
War of the Spanish Succession. These were the first two
of the twenty wars which in the course of the eighteenth
century spread fire across the face of Europe.

## IX

Peter went on pulling and hauling at the body of Russia. It may be surmised that on his trip to the west he had
heard of Louis XIV and his grandiose building operations
at Versailles. He, Peter, could build, too; he would show
them. At the mouth of the Neva he already had a little
window on the Baltic; he would take that window and
multiply it.

Among the marshy islands here was the spot where
Alexander Nevsky, afterwards sainted, had beaten the
Swedes in 1541. On one of the islands, Enisari, Peter had
built a little town of wooden huts, called Peterburkh, to
house the workmen who were hammering a navy into
being. After beating Charles XII at Poltava, Peter, his chest
filled out, felt a craving for yet greater exploits. He had
shown Europeans he could make war; now he would
show them he could build cities and palaces. In 1703 he

issued orders: *Let this dirty Russian village be a European city; let no one pause until it is a shining metropolis; let the work begin at once.*

A mob of artisans and serfs duly converted Peterburkh into Sankt Peterburkh, the new capital of Russia. There was no time to wait for tools. Men who had no spade dug dirt with their hands. Piles were driven into the bleak mud while the drivers shivered with cold and fever. Prisoners of war filled sacks with sand; critics of the Czar's new program were sentenced to dig ditches. Recalcitrants and loafers were hanged at street crossings. With difficulty Peter watched the progress of the war. He began to despise Moscow and its slow Oriental habits.[5] On spare days he rushed to the new town, already being called by its German name of Petersburg, and beamed at its rise in severe, classical lines. Although the ground was frozen half of each year, he called it a "paradise" and wrote to friends about "this heavenly place." If men were slow at wharf or workshop, he plunged in and showed them how to do the thing. As often as projects were completed he sent for his dwarfs and clowns and gave feasts at which all hands got drunk.

Slowly the new *burg* raised itself out of the swamps. Peter gave it not only administrative buildings, offices, factories, and forts but academies and colleges. He forcibly brought in the arts and sciences, and after Louis XIV's death imported architects and artists who had been left jobless at Versailles. At last a city was there — looming,

---

[5]In Russia calculations were done with the help of the abacus, a device of Oriental origin which is still in use.

rectangular, long-avenued, regular. Peter took up his quarters there, making it indubitably Peter's burg,[6] and insisted on his nobles leaving Moscow and coming to the new city where, he warned them, they must be modern.

In less than fifty years St. Petersburg was old enough to have a working-class quarter and a strike. The latter occurred in the textile industry, a monopoly of which was in the middle of the century given to two Englishmen, Cosens and Chamberlain. Peter, however, did what he could to keep the trade in Russian products in his own hands; "the Tsar," said his subjects, "is the first merchant in the dominions," and so active was he in business affairs that economists date the rise of industrial capitalism in Russia from the reign of Peter the Great.[7]

## X

Through all this new building and this breaking of old moulds, the Northern War went on. It ended in a triumph for Peter, who won upon the Baltic a foothold from which Russian commerce might expand and grow great. The war ended in dismay for England and France, who were, without reference to any other power, deciding how the world might be divided between them. Peter, exultingly naming himself "Emperor of all the Russias," accepted in 1721 the Peace of Nystad; but to keep his new armies, grown so unexpectedly difficult, in form, he made war on

[6]It was named for St. Peter the apostle. It was renamed Petrograd in 1914 and Leningrad in 1924.
[7]See Alexinsky, *Russia and Europe,* Miall tr., N. Y., 1917.

Persia and took from it several rich provinces on the Caspian Sea, with the object of controlling the silk trade.

The war with Persia, coming so soon after that with Sweden, was characteristic of Peter's policy. In which direction should Russia push herself: west, toward Europe; or east, toward Asia? He was never able definitely to decide. Nor did his successors do better. It has been the fate of Russia, ever since Peter's day, to be the center of these opposing pulls.

## XI

The new forms of life that the hasty Peter, dazzled by a Europe still under the influence of Louis XIV, tried to impose upon Russia, old, hairy, and timid, were numerous. He tried to regulate everything from the structure of the orthodox church to the tariff in soldiers' brothels, and all reforms were to be accomplished instantly.

To wait, to be patient—those were words which caused Peter to burst with rage or to dissolve in tears. So accustomed was he to abject and instant obedience that he once ordered a bear, which had failed to convert itself as ordered into a dancing master, to be whipped just short of death. But not all the ideas he tried to impose upon his subjects were merely whimsical. Many of them were based upon sound sense and cunning observation. (Peter, it was said, copied everything but invented nothing.) But he could not wait for them to take root at the bottom, to evolve and to grow into and permeate an organic whole; he tried to force them upon his people from above. So that his reforms sometimes remained mere plasters applied to a huge, mutely resisting body, which clung to its mediæ-valism even while it whimpered under Peter's lash.

In his haste to modernize Russia and to force it to be more European and less Asiatic, Peter was acting as the unconscious agent of that practical-minded middle class which everywhere was trying, like a chick pipping its shell, to force its head upward through the crust of a hoary feudalism — a movement which in Russia had as its spear-head the strong, active, and organized merchants of the cities.

On his first visit to western Europe Peter was impressed with the wealth and consequent leisure which had made possible a vigorous growth in the sciences and arts. He wished a similar wealth to flow through Russia. From this stream could be dipped greater revenues for a crown al-ways hampered by necessity for economy and even stingi-ness. Hence his determination to foster commerce and his interest in building ships and seaports and in the control of trade-routes. Hence the collision with Sweden, which under the militarist Charles XII lost control of the Baltic and became a second-class power.

But Peter was not satisfied merely to humble Sweden. He also wanted for himself the subsidy paid to the Swed-ish army by France. Hadn't he an army as good as any in north Europe? Couldn't he maintain the balance of power as well as any one? A faulty taxation system was not bring-ing him the revenue due to a conqueror and dictator. The more he thought of the fat French sum annually paid to Sweden, the more avaricious he became. Through envoys he made several overtures to France, but the manners of his emissaries were uncouth, their methods coarse, and they got nowhere. At length, bursting with impatience, in 1717 Peter himself went to Paris and made it known that he and his army were ready to be put on the French payroll. But he succeeded only in shocking the refined Parisians with his drinking, his eating, his belching, and his soiled gloveless hands; besides, Dubois, the French foreign minister, was already deep in negotiations with England. The upshot was that Peter was deceived and delayed until he was compelled to take himself off, defeated, and Russia sank back into its mediæval inertia.

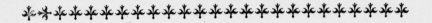

## CHAPTER SEVEN

## DISILLUSIONS

### I

FRANCE WAS then living under the regency of Philip, Duke of Orleans. The Regent was the nephew of Louis XIV and the husband of one of his illegitimate daughters. He had a certain ability, but except for his reputation as an experimenter in chemistry and in various vices, history would scarcely remember him had he not, in the year that Peter the Great visited Paris, imprisoned Voltaire in the Bastille. The charge was that the young lawyer had libelled the Regent in one of the impudent satires for which duchesses were already praising him, although he was scarcely twenty-five years old.

That sentence to the Bastille was the beginning of Voltaire's fame. His stay there was only for eleven months, and since the Regent, being a light man of the world, did not take the lucubrations of young literary men too seriously, these months were a detention rather than an imprisonment. Nevertheless they made the young lawyer a martyr and so much sympathy was, upon his release, poured upon the prisoner that success for his play *Œdipe* was assured, and so was the friendship of other men of letters, particularly Bolingbroke, the Englishman who had been forced to exchange his post of secretary of state under Queen Anne for an exile's farm in France.

It was not like Voltaire long to remain out of trouble, and in 1726 he got into a difficulty with Rohan, an aristocrat, who, to show his contempt for the bourgeois author, had him beaten by lackeys. The victim not only could obtain no redress, but got into the Bastille a second time. To escape it he offered to take himself out of France. His offer was cheerfully accepted and Voltaire went to England for the first time. It was the England of George I.

## II

After Queen Anne's death the Whig mercantile class, fearing a possible return to power of a Catholic oligarchy, had hastily seated on the English throne George Louis, the Protestant and German Elector of Hanover, calling him George I.[1]

George was as heavy as roast beef *mit Kartoffeln* and had the same graces. He could not speak English and never troubled himself to learn it. He was always homesick for his little province in Germany, was bored with England and the English, and asked only to be let alone with his eating, his drinking, and his mistresses.[2] England was glad to give him these privileges. In the streets minstrels still sang nostalgic songs that remembered the gay Stuarts, but a practical ruling class wanted no more of the Stuarts'

[1]George I was the son of Sophia, niece of Charles I of England, by Ernest Augustus, first Elector of Hanover, who belonged to the house of Guelph or Welf.

[2]He brought with him from Germany Fräulein Schulemberg and Frau Kilmansegge, whom he made respectively Duchess of Kendal and Countess of Darlington.

foolishness, their easy selling out to France, and their romantic capering about. "The King was in future," remarks McCarthy, "to be a business King, and not a King of sentiments and romance."[3] Dead was "Merrie England." The commercial classes wanted no more of it. It would cost too much.

## III

Voltaire's letters permit us to see this England under a German king as it appeared to a sharp-eyed Frenchman at the beginning of the second quarter of the eighteenth century. Voltaire landed on the banks of the Thames in the spring when England was mayfresh and maygreen. He first noticed the double rows of merchant vessels lining the river and then the comely young people at a race-course. He particularly noticed the neatness and vivacity of young girls dressed in calicoes who were about to take part in a foot-race for which the prize was a chemise floating from the top of a pole.

He supposed that these active young people belonged to the aristocracy; he was enchanted. He was disillusioned when he met actual specimens of the *beau monde* and found them stiff and cold. Even at the Court, because an east wind was blowing, "gloom and wretchedness possessed everything." A coffee-house which he visited, in the hope of finding light and gaiety like that shed in the writings of Addison and Steele, he found "dirty, ill-furnished, ill-served, and ill-lighted." In the midst of his first glow he had written to a friend, "I know that in England the arts are all honoured and rewarded, and that, though there

[3]*The Four Georges.*

are differences in rank, the only other difference between men is that of merit. England is a country where thought is noble and free, unrestrained by any slavish fear."

Such were the beliefs of a man who had grown up under the semi-Oriental absolutism of Louis XIV and the petty persecution of the Regent, his nephew. In his enthusiasm he sent to King George a copy of his *Œdipe,* together with a fulsome ode in which the heavy-eyed German was advised:

"It is not at all to the King, it is to the sage,
"It is to the hero, that I send it."

George I was willing to believe he, George I, was a sage and hero, and rewarded the compliment with a watch. He later received Voltaire at the Court of St. James's. But further disillusion awaited the trustful Frenchman. Britons might be free and noble, but in literature and the dramatic arts their choice was not always distinguished, and one day Voltaire felt compelled to write to an Englishman: "The taste of your politest countrymen in point of tragedy differs not much in point of tragedy from the taste of a mob at a beer-garden."

At one time lauding Shakespeare, he later regarded the bard as "a clown." He thought the poet Thomson might "have reformed the English theatre which the clown Shakespeare gave birth to and ruined." The bleakness of life in the northern island made him mourn for the gaieties of his own land. He contrasted the grim English method of gathering "their inferior, insipid apples" with the sight of French boys and girls making a festival of the grape-gathering season. English society of the Queen Anne-George I period he could not admire. He said of Congreve's plays: "The language everywhere is that of honorable people, though the actions are the actions of knaves; and this proves that Congreve knew well the people he had to deal with, and that he lived in what is called good society."

And yet on reading Swift and regarding his directness and the vein of his style, he was moved to exclaim:

"How I love the English daring! How I love people who say what they think! We only half live if we dare only half think."

Voltaire was continually reproaching Frenchmen for their intellectual inertia; and comparing France, to its disadvantage, with England as it enjoyed the freedom indifferently granted it by the heavy Hanoverians. He failed to perceive that the English middle class could expand and grew strong and agile only because it had freed itself of royalty's shackles by its uprising against James II in 1688, while the French middle class, half throttled by Louis XIV and half ignored by the regent Philip, had as yet scarcely dared to be born. Measured by the intellectual freedom won, England at the end of the first quarter of the eighteenth century was well in advance of France, but in taste and sensibility the island was far behind; and so Voltaire, while moved to admiration by one thing, was likely to be revolted by another.[4]

---

[4]"Shakespeare," Voltaire told the English traveller Sherlock, "had an amazing genius, but no taste; he has spoiled the taste of the nation." In the same conversation he extolled Sir Isaac Newton as "the greatest genius that ever existed; if all the geniuses of the universe assembled he should lead the band."

Voltaire's vacillation was a symptom of the uncertainty of the period. Although a quarter of its life had passed, the eighteenth century did not yet know what it believed. No philosophy, no faith, had yet crystallized. To give to his age, and to the middle class to which he belonged, a creed, was Voltaire's diligent endeavor. But if he could not at first formulate a creed, he could at least offer slogans. "Remember," he said, later in the century, to Benjamin Franklin's son, "God and liberty."

## IV

It is significant that Voltaire's host in England was not a nobleman, but a merchant, Everard Falkener, who had made money in the cloth and silk trade in the Levant. He had at Wandsworth, not far from London and near the Thames, a luxurious house filled with books and objects of art. Here he was able to give the nervous Frenchman luxury and quiet in exchange for his vivacious company and for conversation on the classics and on the antiquities he had collected. Under George I, Falkener was appointed ambassador at Constantinople and then became secretary to George II's son, the Duke of Cumberland. Eventually he was knighted and made postmaster-general.

Falkener was a representative of that urban trading class which was gradually crowding the Tory nobility and land-owning gentry from the places of power. He candidly rejoiced in his own success in a letter to Voltaire in which he wrote of himself as "enjoying perfect health and in possession of everything that makes life agreeable; without love, without avarice, without ambition, and without envy; and so long as all that lasts I shall boldly call myself a very happy man."[5] In short, Voltaire's host agreed with Pope that "whatever is, is right."

To Falkener was dedicated one of Voltaire's published plays, an act which the Frenchman well knew would cause astonishment in his own country, where the merchant had not yet risen to the place of power and esteem accorded his brother in England, but was regarded as a lowly figure unfit to associate with persons of birth and position.

"It is a pleasure to me," wrote Voltaire to Falkener, "to be able to let my country know the regard paid by England to her merchants, the esteem which England has for a profession which makes the greatness of the State, and the distinction with which some of your class represent their country in Parliament and sit among the legislators of the land." On the same theme he later wrote: "In France . . . the merchant hears his profession so disdainfully spoken of that he is foolish enough to blush for it. Yet I do not know which is the more useful to the State, a well-powdered lord who knows to a moment the hour at which the king rises and at which he goes to bed, and who gives himself grand airs while he is really playing the part of a slave in a minister's ante-chamber, or a merchant who is enriching his country, who gives from his office orders for Surat and for Cairo, and who contributes to the happiness of the world."

It was thus that Voltaire, while he denounced kings and those who served them, strove to exalt that class, composed

[5]Ballantyne, *Voltaire's Visit to England,* London, 1898.

of merchandising and professional men, to which he himself belonged, and whose voice he was. To regard a noble
hanging around a king's bedroom as no better than a
slave, while seeing a trader as an enricher of his country
—here was a sign of changed times, here indeed was evidence of new ideas.

## V

Although in Voltaire's own country the merchant was
lower in social esteem, the banker was higher than in England. Louis XIV had made attentions to financiers fashionable, and then John Law, the Scotch-born banker, promised the Regent of France he would raise his annual revenue to £300,000,000 and give him 30,000,000 tax-paying
subjects; the Regent was quite willing to see in him a
benefactor and deliverer, and, over the objections of merchants and the suspicions of statesmen, gave him authority
to open a private bank in Paris in 1716.

Law perceived that commerce was taking charge of civilization; but that where Britain was riding the commercial
wave toward even greater power, France's commerce was
being choked and its middle class stunted by the antiquated
laws and customs left over from mediævalism and Louis
XIV's absolutism. "What is needed," he proclaimed, "is
credit."

The Bank of England was already several years old and
the Bank of Amsterdam was well established, but France
had no state bank and its politicians would permit none.
However, when Law's private bank was opened under

government sanction, it became virtually a state bank, and although the Duke of Orleans remained Regent, it was Law who rapidly became the invisible ruler of France. Louis XIV had ruined the trading class by repeatedly meddling with the coinage, but Law immediately stabilized commerce by paying off bills in coins of a fixed weight and value. Thereafter the business of the country soon passed into Law's control by virtue of his ability to manipulate the purchasing power of its coinage.

Science, as the practical-minded bourgeois evolved, was replacing superstition in men's minds, but Law was the first man to install science in the financial realm. Even as a gambler wandering among European capitals, he had not depended on luck but had mathematically worked out the laws of chance and had calculated the value of all combinations of cards. Mathematics he also applied to his banking, and as French commerce, stagnant in the last years of Louis XIV, began to have confidence in him and so to revive, the middle class took courage and began to expand. The commercial prosperity that came back to France later in the century may be attributed to the foundations laid by Law, and the renewal of vitality in the bourgeoisie is also to be ascribed in a degree to this gambling Scotchman. It was from the economic blood-stream clarified by Law, too, that French traders drew the strength that enabled them to engage in a death-struggle with England for the control of the Americas, of the seas, and of the New World's supplies and markets.

In Law's intellectual equipment, however, there was one weak spot: he had no clear understanding of the difference

MARIA THERESA

*Mother of Marie Antoinette and an energetic enemy of Frederick the Great.*
*From an engraving after the painting by Martin de Meitens*

FURNITURE OF THE LOUIS XV PERIOD

*Curves and S-shapes replaced the straight lines chiefly favored by Louis XIV and the ornamentation was thick, whimsical, and frivolous*

between wealth and money; and he easily confused price with value. This is not strange, in view of the fact that, for more than 200 years afterwards, bankers and laymen in both the Old and the New Worlds went on groping through the same confusions. For a time, however, all went well with Law, his bank was converted into a state institution, and he became the pet of the great and powerful. Then, misled either by his gambling instincts or his muddy economics, he began to promote trading companies.

He purposed to make France, he said, the strongest commercial nation in the world. His trading companies were to develop foreign markets, discover new lands, mine gold and rare metals, found colonies, and get astride the great sea-routes stretching between Europe and the Indies (meaning Spanish-America) on the one hand, and Europe and North America on the other.

His first step was to obtain for his Company of the West a twenty-five-year monopoly of the trade between France and that province in America which lay on both sides of the river Mississippi, from source to mouth, and which had been named for Louis XIV. He then induced the monarchy to transfer to this company, popularly called the Mississippi Company, the Oriental holdings of the older but ineffective Company of the East Indies and of its still weaker sister, the Company of China. He thus formed a consolidated organization which had vast powers, concessions, and franchises, even the privilege of coining money. It sailed the oceans, controlled empires in both hemispheres, and drew tribute from America, Africa, and Asia. It was too large to be longer called a company; it became known as the *Système*. And it no longer confined its operations to foreign fields, but carried out vast operations at home, even to the extent of deals with the government for funding the national debt and farming the entire taxes of the country.

As one grandiose transaction was piled upon another, the imagination of the public caught fire. And Law, who was a gifted publicist, kept it fed with accounts of new sailings to Louisiana, of new settlements beyond the Mississippi, of new imports of furs and tobacco and Indian chiefs and curious things from the Americas and the Indies. It became a fad to own shares in the Mississippi Company, and then it became a fever. The price of the stock, which at first hung low, rose rapidly. Then in spurts it shot upward and danced in the zenith like a gyrating apparition. Investors first lost their heads and then threw in everything else. Noble and bourgeois and fish-peddler, dizzy with dreams of profit, clapped each other on the shoulder in a new democracy and praised Law from whom all blessings flowed.

In his most fanciful publicity and even in his giddiest promises, Law was not a gross deceiver. Wealth, incalculable wealth, indeed lay in Louisiana; for history eventually justified all Law's dreams. And colonies were indeed founded in the Mississippi country which drew billions from soil and river and forest, all the way from Canada to the Gulf.

The colonists, officers and agents of the government in Louisiana, were, although they bore seigneurial names, not of noble birth. The French nobility, cooped up in Louis

XIV's ante-chambers, no longer had the energy, hardiness, or taste for distant and racking enterprises. Iberville (who fixed the fort which blossomed into New Orleans at a crescent in the bank of the Mississippi a few miles below the lake named for Pontchartrain, Louis XIV's marine minister) and his younger brother Bienville, "father of Louisiana," were the sons of Charles Le Moyne, a Canadian trader who was the son of an innkeeper at Dieppe in Normandy. Charles Le Moyne, having amassed a noble fortune, considered himself entitled to give his energetic sons, one a buccaneer, and the other a forest-runner, noble names; and since money was become the powerfulest of powers, there was none to gainsay him.

In 1718 Law's agents shipped from France the first cargo of colonists and supplies to Bienville, who with them expanded the fort left by Iberville into a village of huts, seed of a new civilization. He and they thought it only right to name the settlement in honor of the Regent of France, the frivolous, the dissolute, the unstable but clever Duke of Orleans, who had been trying very hard, in his way, to liquidate the knotted tangle left behind by his uncle, Louis XIV.

More settlements followed, and men to occupy them; for Law's advertisements had filled them with a yearning to break from Europe's crusted strata and in America to find gold and free portions of that land which Law was careful to call "estates." Men indeed were plentiful and credulous.

But there could be no civilization, no *foyers,* no future, without women. These men were pioneers, but they were also Frenchmen, and they could not imagine—they would not imagine—a life without women.

*Send us then,* they said, *women; send us money and supplies, but also women; we will, if necessary, do without money and supplies, but women we must have.*

History often and often relates how certain men, willingly and even eagerly, have deserted home and habits to journey into remote lands, there to hew, and to have fevers, and to risk and to found, and above all to enjoy rudeness; but it has yet to record how women have done likewise. It may be doubted if history will ever have such a record while wildernesses contain crawling things, and queer noises, and prowling forms, and no hot water. To women Nature's first commandment is: *Thou shalt not pioneer.*

In France the word went forth, plenty of word; but no woman. After the warrings and strivings of Louis XIV's time, the women of France were exulting in peace and imported silks and better shops and Regency gaieties and returning prosperity. The women of France had reason; they suspected the realities behind the romantic dreams of their dazzled men; they had no wish to exchange feather-beds and Regency furniture for bare huts on the yellow, Indian-plied Mississippi; life had appointed them to be keepers and conservators, not hewers and slayers. Again and again the word went forth, but the women budged not.

*Well, then,* said the word, *if they will not go, drag them.* England, in its search for men to man its ships, had accustomed the world to press-gangs, but now for the first time in history—and in *douce France,* of all places—the press-gang was applied to women. Government and Law were now the same thing, and officered squads, weaponed with steel, combed the streets of French cities for women and girls who could wive the Louisianians. The weight of Law and the law fell, of course, on those least able to bear it: on the unattached, on the shelterless, the frail; but hardest on the weakest of all but the most firmly attached to the cities, the women ironically called *filles de joie*. Their weakness was no bar to roughness. At La Rochelle, a herded group of girls, driven to scratching and, no doubt, to language shrill and unrefined, was fired upon. Six were killed and others pierced with bullets.

Since a bonus was paid for every woman accepted for shipment to Louisiana, searches were made through every place of refuge, even through hospitals and reformatories. A girl who was so unfortunate as to fall into the hands of a woman-hunting squad got little time to protest; she could do her explaining in Louisiana. For from there the voice of authority came with increasing urgency.

"Send me wives for my Canadians," wrote Bienville to his government. "They are running in the woods after Indian girls."

"With wives," wrote his brother, Iberville, "I will anchor *coureurs des bois* into sturdy colonists."

In such haste the innocent were only by a degree less liable to be seized than the brazen, and it was out of such a situation that the story of Manon Lescaut arose — Manon and her lover, des Grieux — which, whether in prose or operatic form, still has the power to draw the sympathetic tear. And who can say it is baseless, seeing that a Chevalier

des Grieux was indeed recorded among the arrivals in
New Orleans in 1718 and that relics of Manon are still
sold in the shops there?[6] In the opera, *Manon,* we still hear
the weeping of terrorized women, the hoarse voice of authority, the wail against commerce, and the protest of the
Old World against the New.

## VI

By the end of 1719 Law and his Mississippi Company
were dominating the imaginations of all Europe. Speculators hurried to Paris from all lands to deal in shares that
paid 4000 per cent. The word *millionaire* was at this time
added to the world's vocabulary; it was invented in France
to apply especially to those persons who used the Mississippi Company as a springboard to leap into fortunes.
Everybody bought shares not for the yield, but for the rise.

As is usual in such situations, the first shudders in this
inverted pyramid were felt at the bottom. The price of
bread and other provisions rose until the masses could no
longer buy enough to eat. The circulation of money began
to slacken and share-buyers in alarm began to sell. Hoarders began to save silver and gold. Law and the government
tried to right the quaking structure by legal statutes.
Hoarders of precious metals were attacked by edict, and
at length the payment of debts in gold or silver was for-
bidden. In an effort to maintain the colonization of Louisiana, decrees were issued permitting the seizure of vagrants
and unemployed persons for transportation to New Orleans.

[6]King, *New Orleans, the Place and the People,* N. Y., 1875.

A revulsion of feeling against Law and all his schemes ensued, and when price-fixing and reduction in the value of bank bills were followed by the halving of the face value of all paper money, the people suddenly realized that they had been dealing in myths and fictions, and panic was born. The royal bank hastily resumed specie payment, but too late to quiet the storm. In a mob that gathered at the bank, sixteen persons were suffocated. Four bodies were taken to the Palais Royal, the residence of the Duke of Orleans, and there exposed, and the body of one victim, a woman, was held up to the windows of the infant Louis XV at the Louvre.

Law escaped to Brussels where his friends said he received an invitation from Peter the Great, who had uses for such an ingenious financier, to come to Russia. But Law went on to Venice where he lived on a small pension from the regency. He died there, obscure if not penniless, in 1729.

## VII

Law's collapse sent a quake throughout the civilized world. From the shock France's colonial empire in America never recovered, and even thereafter the French people remained averse to emigration and suspicious of colonial schemes. The French peasant hid his few francs deeper than ever in his woollen stocking and kept them there. To this day the banking system in France remains relatively undeveloped, especially in the provinces, and although it is from France that we get the word *cheque* for a money order on a bank, that canny country still carries out most of its transactions with coin of the realm and not with engraved paper slips.

The regency government liquidated Law's débâcle by calling in all shares and bills and arbitrarily reducing their value and the interest paid upon them. The fortunes made in speculation by the new nabobs and millionaires were levied upon by the government, which acted on the theory that persons not belonging to the upper classes had no right to great riches.

From these assessments, however, the nobility was exempted. No person of rank was named in the list of those subject to fine. Thus to their established privileges of exemption from ordinary taxation the nobility was now able to add exemption from levies on the profits of speculation. Those minor speculators who did not flee the country, or use political influence to avoid assessment, paid up in silence. This silence was ominous. It meant that the middle classes, in which most of the speculation had occurred, had a new grudge against the royal and noble classes. And this grudge was increased when it was whispered among them that a large share of their paid assessments would never reach the State treasury but would go to support the regent duke's mistresses, of which he kept an ample supply.

So did France have its first experience with the complexities introduced into life by banking, credit, the manipulation of currency, and the marriage of government to commerce. If it failed to understand the difference between money and wealth, it only made the mistakes subsequently committed, and re-committed, elsewhere in the civilized world. In fact, at the very time that the Mississippi Bubble in France was rising on the heated air, another bubble, similarly inflated, was being engendered in England which then was very foreign and far away.

## VIII

In England, as in France, the stream of wealth flowing from the New World and from the Orient had begun to go to the national head. From newly opened channels of trade flowed not only wealth but money, and gradually there dawned upon the commercial class a notion of what it might do with this instrument. With money it could not only control governments, but society. With money it could bring the aristocracy to terms; nay more, with money a middle-class man might penetrate the aristocracy itself. Thus there was born into the middle-class mind the idea of *equality,* an idea that never left it for the reminder of the eighteenth century.

While French traders were dreaming of sudden riches from the golden sands of Mississippi, English investors had pitched their gilded dreams in a vague but promising quarter known as the South Seas. They, like their French brethren, were ready to be rich quick, despite Swift's reminder that:

> *A guinea will not pass*
> *At market for a farthing more,*
> *Shown through a multiplying glass,*
> *Than what it always did before.*

Early in the century the South Seas Company had been founded by the pious Harley, Queen Anne's prime minister, to trade with South America and the islands of the

Pacific Ocean. For ten years it did a quiet business, and then in the reign of George I, while the French were dancing to Law's tunes, it suddenly saw an opportunity for what has ever since been the summum bonum of all good brokerage companies—a vast profit through the use of other people's money. The government, after Queen Anne's and other wars, was deep in debt, and Harley's company offered to take this debt over in exchange for a trade monopoly in the South Seas. Roused suddenly, the Bank of England made a competing offer, but the South Seas Company had the stronger political connections and were prompter with their bribes, and so strengthened their political and financial leverage with social pressure applied through selected women accomplices, including the king's mistresses, that they easily won.

The negotiations and the oral bandying about of vast sums of money excited the taste-buds of the public palate, and soon the English middle and upper classes were spinning about the South Sea maypole in a vertigo like that across the channel. In six months South Sea shares rose from 125 to 1000. The prospective profits were so enormous that a brood of lesser schemes hatched themselves overnight, all backed by companies willing to sell shares to investors craving riches, power, luxury, and equality with the great. Dreams of quick profit penetrated the public's imagination like a virus. There were attempts to launch enterprises for providing standardized funerals, for trading in hair, for making snuff of Virginia tobacco, for founding madder plantations, and for extracting silver from lead.

The South Sea magnates, avid for a monopoly of all

SALESMANSHIP IN A BOUDOIR

*An illustration of merchandising methods under Louis XV. From an engraving
entitled "What does the abbé say of it?" by de Launay*

*From a photograph in the Otto Bettmann Collection*

JEAN JACQUES ROUSSEAU

VOLTAIRE, BY HOUDON

DENIS DIDEROT

PETER THE GREAT

profits, made the mistake of trying to suppress these minor blue-sky companies. Investigations followed, political pumps began to draw up the bilge-water, and South Sea shares, thrown over by a timid investing class, fell with thuds that awakened the kingdom. In response to a general outcry, the House of Commons named a committee to look into the affairs of the company. Its discoveries caused further falls in stocks. It found that the company's books were full of false and misleading entries, that important leaves were missing, and that some books had been hidden or destroyed. It found that ministers of State and other respectable figures had been parties to or had protected the company's operations, and that its intrigues had reached even into the Court, involving the King's two German-made mistresses, now known as "The Giraffe" and "The Elephant." Even the Prince of Wales was revealed as the winner in stock manipulations.

Such episodes are familiar now, and subsequent repeated "probes" have made such disclosures commonplaces; but the early eighteenth century was not accustomed to the substitution of engraved paper for tangible wealth, or to the manipulative operations made possible by the introduction of the credit system; the English mind had been trained to revere personages, and it was shocked to discover that titled people had been acting like common rogues. There was a loud demand for punishment, and it may have been only a coincidence that this punishment fell most heavily upon those members of the ministry who had belonged to the inferior classes.

Postmaster-General Craggs was a barber, a member of

that class whose rise had signalled the English ruling class that it must henceforth divide power with the people from lower down. He was a self-made man possessed of all the middle-class virtues of thrift, hard work, and ambition, added to which was an ability to make himself useful to the highly placed. It was disclosed that he had received large blocks of South Sea stock for which he had not been charged a penny; while his son, James Craggs, secretary of State, was revealed as acting as agent for the company in procuring, for a consideration, the Duchess of Kendal and the Countess of Darlington as stock-salesmen at the royal court.

The younger Craggs died suddenly and mysteriously on the very day that he was accused in the House of Commons. His father poisoned himself a few days later. Lord Stanhope, Minister of State, enraged by insinuations against a stock-dabbling relative, burst a blood vessel and died. John Aislabic, chancellor of the exchequer, pronounced guilty of the "most notorious, dangerous, and infamous corruption," was imprisoned. Lord Sunderland, commissioner of the treasury, although revealed as having had £50,000 in South Sea stock placed to his account, escaped, but soon died; of heart-failure, it was said. Estates of the company's directors were confiscated, and these directors were barred from all future public or parliamentary offices.

The wreck of the South Seas Company caused less damage than the collapse of the Mississippi Company in France and its effects were confined to narrower limits. Commercial faith and enterprise soon revived upon the river of trade flowing in from the Americas and the Orient. English merchant families became steadily richer and bolder; they built better houses and filled them with graceful luxuries and comforts; they laid out expensive gardens[7] where nature was tamed and ordered; their patronage became valuable to scientists and artists and writers; Addison did well by teaching them refinements and social graces, while Pope[8] did even better by supplying them with verses of a marvellously exact and ordered form.

Gradually, as wealth and leisure and luxury, so long regarded as the peculiar privileges of noble families, became diffused among traders, ship-owners, importers, office-holders, artisans, and professional men,[9] the philosophy of a way of life began to shape itself into an ideology. It advocated reason, order, decorum. It constructed a temple, with a hard and geometrical façade within, in which altars were erected to regularity and common sense. Between these altars reposed a high chair in Queen Anne style. In it sat the middle class itself, enthroned.

[7]Rare tulips for garden borders were so much sought for that a good collection of bulbs cost £1000. One of the most expensive gardens in England was that of the merchant John Evelyn, which Peter the Great and his fellow rompers trampled down.

[8]Hitherto poets had been relegated to garrets and to the largesse of powerful men to whom they obsequiously dedicated their works. But Pope was able to build himself a villa on the Thames.

[9]By 1715 hackney carriages had become so numerous in London that they were limited by law to 800.

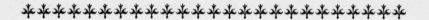

## CHAPTER EIGHT

## PLIGHT OF GOVERNORS

### I

THE RUPTURE of the South Sea dream brought poverty and debt into the lives of many English gentlemen with a taste for speculation or a weakness for gambling. The promptest way to recoup a fortune, provided one had the right political connections, was to procure an appointment in America; and the crown sent out not a few men as governors of colonies who had no qualifications save a desire to fill their pockets as quickly as possible.

Thus when Governor Burrington was about to be recalled from North Carolina, the Duke of Kent urged upon the Duke of Newcastle the appointment of his friend Christian Cole on the ground that "his misfortune has been to have lost in the South Seas . . . which makes him desirous to leave his own country and to go abroad and would be very happy to have your Grace's favor and protection for this employment, which I hear is but £500 a year salary."

Such posts were deemed so desirable that there was much dealing and trading to get them; and it is not strange that so many colonies found themselves saddled with thorough rascals acting as vicars of King George. On the other hand, many English governors were able and fair-minded men. Most of these were no better and no worse than other men of their class and upbringing. They were eighteenth-century gentlemen wearing lace on their cuffs to symbolize the fact that they did no work with their hands. Their habits inclined them toward reason rather than emotion, toward conversation rather than action, and toward a good-natured tolerance rather than an angry condemnation of things. Their views had been molded to a degree by reading Addison and Steele; they preferred to talk about science rather than theology; and they had as a background the comforts of the drawing-room and the ease of the London coffee-house.[1]

Such men on landing in America found themselves compelled to live in small, semi-frontier towns whose streets were deep in provincial mud and in houses where comfort, not to say luxury, was either new or scarcely known. They had to deal with assemblies often made up of farmers re-

---

[1]Robert Hunter came to New York as royal governor in 1710 with encomiums bestowed upon him in No. 69 of *The Tatler,* to which he had sometimes contributed. He was well past middle age, but Cadwallader Colden, the Philadelphia surgeon whom Hunter called to New York as surveyor-general, wrote of him as "an exceedingly well shaped and well proportioned man." Hunter was fond of learning and literature, and drew around him men of similar tastes, whom he delighted with his gifts as a story-teller. He wrote good verses and while in New York was joint author of a play, *Androborus, the Man Eater,* in which the assembly's antics were ridiculed. He had been an intimate friend of Doctor Arbuthnot, physician to Queen Anne, and a soldier under William III. He was present when Marlborough beat Louis XIV's armies at Blenheim and again at Ramillies. In politics he was a Whig. In New York he succeeded Lord Cornbury whose financial manipulations caused his recall. See Osgood, *American Colonies in the 18th Century.*

sentful of crown taxes, of merchants who could not pay their English creditors, and of small-town lawyers anxious to make an impression with their oratory. Such bodies were always hostile or suspicious, and the tension between governors and assemblymen was kept tight by the fact that the latter held the string to the governor's salary, while the demands of mercantilism compelled the governor to labor not for the welfare of the colony but for the interests of English shippers and landlords.

The colonial governor was the direct agent and officer of the crown, and as such he was supposed to be enforcer of the orders of the king and the laws of parliament; while maintaining the English monopoly of trade and navigation and keeping up a pressure for the payment of American debts to English business men. At virtually every point governors and colonists were in inescapable opposition.[2] The more conscientious a governor was as king's officer, the greater the friction with colonial assemblies. The consequence was that most royal governors lived a life filled with harassments; not strange that some of them committed suicide, while others prayed for a berth in the genial West Indies.

But even if exasperation had not been created between governor and assemblies by opposed interests, it would probably have been aroused by class bias. Of the 300 governing officers sent from England between 1624 and 1783, about a fourth belonged to titled families; forty-eight had attended college at Oxford or Cambridge or elsewhere, and

[2]"I have to steer," wrote Governor Belcher of New Jersey, "between Scylla and Charybdis; to please the king's ministers at home and a touchy people here; to luff for one and bear away for another." — Osgood, *op. cit.*

many of them had been admitted to legal or cultural institutions; while most of the colonial representatives with whom they wrangled over salaries and expense accounts had a background of nothing save hard, gritty work in the field, woods, counting-houses, or bare wood-walled offices. Governor Hunter thought the New York assembly was made up of "inferior men," and Governor Dinwoodie found Virginia burgesses "obstinate and self-opinionated."

Royal governors could not help hating such men. At the same time, they feared them. The governors showed their fear by their repeated temporizings and concessions, and the governments at home showed it by instructions to governors to avoid show-downs, lest the government lose face. Even in the early years of the eighteenth century it must have been evident to the keener royal governors that the future belonged to these energetic and obstinate colonists, some of whom had only recently risen into the embryo American middle class out of indentured servitude, debtors' prisons, or landless poverty.

## II

The history of the gentleman in America has been since the earliest times a sad one. Even in the first and feeblest beginnings there was no place for him. Deprived of the prop of towns and of urban society, he was not even valued as an ornament. In America rude Nature looked at him, and he instantly shrivelled. "The eighteenth day," reads the record of the Jamestown settlement in 1607, "there died Robert Pennington, and John Martine, Gentlemen." Nearly half of the original Virginia colonists were so described,

and after watching them starve, suffer, and finally drop
their once-wigged heads in exhaustion or death, John
Smith in disgust sent this beseeching message home:

> *I entreat you rather send but 30 carpenters, husbandmen, gar-
> deners, fishermen, blacksmiths, masons, and diggers up of trees'
> roots, well provided, than a thousand such as we have.*

And in Louisiana Diron d'Artaguiette, inspector-general for John Law's Western Company in 1722, prayed:

> *That the company should send into this colony Frenchmen
> who have a thorough knowledge of indigo, tobacco, and silk,
> and also vine-dressers, wheelwrights, shoemakers, tool-makers,
> carpenters, cabinet-makers, coopers, and other workmen.*[3]

He also recommended "sending a great force of Negroes,
to the number of about 4000 to 5000."

In short, early America, facing realities and compelled
to begin with the very foundations of life, could use only
the producers of wealth. The consumers of it would have
to wait until there was a handsome surplus.

## III

Thus failed the attempt bodily to transplant Old World
institutions, such as a nobility and a gentry, to America.
The debris of European feudalism were not wanted and
could not be assimilated. The gentleman and lady, old
style, would have had no function in a frontier society and
so could not have survived.[4]

[3]Mereness, *Travels in the American Colonies.*

[4]T. J. Wertenbaker writes that but few men of high social rank in England established families in Virginia and that the larger part of the aristocracy of the colony came directly from merchant ancestors. See *Patrician and
Plebeian in Virginia,* pp. 2–3.

The advantage to the embryonic American middle class in being thus relieved of the pressure and fixity of European social strata was enormous. With land cheap and a host of privileges free, the common man, even though he might have begun life as a convict or indentured servant, quickly rose into the propertied and even into the ruling class. From a small freehold he passed easily to ownership of a farm and then of an estate, or into possession of a trading or shipping business, or into one of the professions. Soon he was a burgess or assemblyman defying royal governors and resisting taxes and quit-rents.

## IV

The first quarter of the eighteenth century found the English colonies in America crystallized into three geographical divisions along the Atlantic seaboard. Below the Potomac River was an agricultural economy taking its color from a nascent plantation system. At the other extreme was New England, which, owing to its rocky land but abundant harbors and plentiful streams, had taken to trade, shipping, and small manufacturing. Between the Potomac and Long Island Sound were the middle colonies whose interests lay both in trade and in farming.

These straggling colonies had five towns of some consequence — Boston, Newport, New York, Philadelphia, and Charleston. In them grew up small circles of merchant and shipping families which in time formed a colonial aristocracy. Having some leisure and a margin of income, it patronized the arts, imported luxuries from abroad, and cultivated a social life. In every activity its models were almost wholly English. To England it looked not only for its governmental patterns but even for styles in architecture and furniture. In every way members of this inchoate aristocracy strove to build up along the Atlantic seaboard miniature eighteenth-century Londons flavored with small admixtures from the Versailles of Louis XIV and the Paris of the regent Duke of Orleans.[5] Members of this class were never so complimented as when some traveller from abroad complimented them on their refinement, and the foreign visitor soon learned that it delighted his hosts to hear it said, "Why, this is just like England."[6]

Outside any of these five towns, however, and within a half mile of the outskirts, the character of the colonial population, the very atmosphere itself, changed. Here was found the freeholder, living in a log-cabin or boarded house without refinements and with few comforts; planted on his little farming homestead of fifty acres, which he had perhaps enlarged by frugal saving and canny purchases; proud of being a property owner where a few years before he had been an immigrant with scarcely a handkerchief

[5]Late in the eighteenth century Lord Fairfax of Virginia had a suit of brown colored silk, one of velvet, one of blue cloth, one of drab cloth, a green damask laced waistcoat, a gold tissue waistcoat, a brown laced coat, a green silk waistcoat, a pair of black velvet breeches, and a pair of scarlet plush breeches. — Wertenbaker, *op. cit.,* pp. 124–125.

[6]"All contemporaneous writers, in describing the character of the Virginia middle class in the eighteenth century, agree that their pride and independence were extraordinary. Smythe says, 'They are generous, friendly, and hospitable in the extreme; but mixed with such an appearance of rudeness, ferocity, and haughtiness, which is, in fact, only a want of polish, occasioned by their deficiencies in education and in knowledge of mankind, as well as their general intercourse with slaves.'" — Wertenbaker, *op. cit.,* p. 213.

in his pockets; jealously independent and fiercely resentful of quit-rents and other taxes due to crowns or to lordly proprietors; and nervously eager to get ahead, to win more acres, and to enlarge himself in property, power, and importance.

Everywhere there was a craving for equality, a thirst to be level with the highest; but of democracy there was scarcely a trace. Indeed, the Fundamental Constitutions drawn up in 1669 by the philosopher John Locke for the Province of Carolina, which the Lords Proprietors were trying to enforce, were as late as the early years of the eighteenth century expressly mentioned as for one purpose, "that we may avoid erecting a numerous democracy;" and most of the colonies conceded votes and seats in assemblies only to property-owners. The artisans and workmen of towns not only had no franchise, unless they could prove a property qualification, but were not considered as entitled to it; while the black slaves, who increased rapidly after England had wrenched the Asiento slave-carrying trade from France and Spain, were of course regarded only as useful animals.

But between and often below these social strata was a fifth class which had never been able to own land or had lost it, and which could not even be sure of the precarious livelihood of town artisans or of the coarse but plentiful food given to slaves. Unable to earn wages on the land because of the competition of slave labor, and forced out of towns by the superior skill of trained artisans, they had to perch where they could. In the course of years they lost hope and finally energy. They became an American class of untouchables. The Marquis de Chastellux, who visited America in the third quarter of the eighteenth century, found that by this time they had sunk to the condition described in this picture:

It was there that for the first time since my crossing the seas I saw poor people. Indeed, among these rich plantations, where the Negro alone is unhappy, are often found wretched cabins inhabited by whites whose wan faces and ragged clothes proclaim their poverty.[7]

[7]*Voyages dans l'Amérique Septentrionale.*

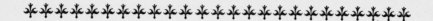

## CHAPTER NINE

# DEATH OF CERTAINTY

## I

JUST AFTER the opening of the eighteenth century Europe found itself in bondage to England's colonies in America. The thing that had forged the chain was tobacco.[1] The light, mild weed from tidewater Virginia and Maryland was, from Spain to Russia, preferred to all others. The constantly widening demand enriched American planters and put new wealth in the hands of English traders and commission men, for England's Navigation Acts compelled all American shipments to go through England.

For the first ten years of the eighteenth century the production of this wealth in America and its flow across the Atlantic enriched the commercial classes and enabled new refinements and luxuries to be added to social life. In America the more important settlers began to wear broadcloth coats, and in London was created that ease and well-being which impressed Voltaire on his first visit across the channel.

[1] Attorney-General Seymour of Virginia snorted at the establishment of William and Mary College, which was founded not only to inculcate learning but to save souls. "Souls?" he cried. "Damn your souls. Make tobacco." — Wertenbaker, *Planters of Colonial Virginia,* p. 136.

But in binding Europe to itself with tobacco, colonial America put itself also in bondage. It linked itself to the world-market, and so became dependent on the market's whims and accidents. Such swaggering creatures as Louis XIV of France, Charles of Sweden, and Peter of Russia might have seemed to have no relation to American tobacco or to the little seaboard colonies that produced it. Yet the moment that Louis XIV forced a Bourbon monarch upon Spain and Charles XII of Sweden ferried his peasant soldiers across the Baltic to attack Peter's moujiks, the foundations of the world-market in tobacco began to crack and subsequently all but collapsed. Europe's rulers, giving themselves up to a feudal delight in fighting, needed all available money and ships for war; exports were stopped or crippled; and the distant markets of Spain, Scandinavia, and Russia were cut off entirely.

The effect on colonial lives in middle and southern America was withering. Yeomen who had just begun to taste prosperity were ruined. Farmers existing upon a narrow margin lost their lands. Town artisans could no longer find work. The ranks of the poor-whites received large accessions. Even the importation of slaves, who were taking the place of the indentured white servant and the hired man, was suddenly checked, and serious doubts were entertained as to the value of slavery as an institution.

This depression, which lasted some eight years, drove hard-pressed and disillusioned men out of Virginia, vast and fertile though it was, into territories where land was cheaper and free of planter-control and of competition with slaves. It was one of the agencies which caused sinewy and independent men to desert Virginia for other areas, and to begin the great movement of emigration from the east to the virgin lands of the west. This surge continued by rises and falls throughout the eighteenth century. It peopled Ohio, Tennessee, and Kentucky, caught up in the tide the early Daniel Boones and Davey Crocketts, and brought the axe and rifle-bearing Saxon to the banks of the Mississippi, where he found himself confronted with angry and suspicious Frenchmen, behind whom stood suspicious Indians.

## II

The westward-roaming hunter was succeeded by the trader, settler, and land-speculator. The English trader was in search of furs; and so was the French one, for in Europe clothing and ornaments of rich fur had become the proof and symbol of prosperity, and the middle and upper classes had set up an insatiate demand for fur of every kind. Both English and French companies wished to monopolize the fur trade, and competition introduced sharp-dealing, trickery, and finally fighting and fire-water. Liquor was one of the instruments used by both sides to induce the Indian to yield furs and loyalty, and soon the red man found himself subjected to three pressures. The trader poisoned and incited him with liquor; the settler pushed him away from sites desirable for homesteads; and the land-speculator showed an early determination to drive him out of all desirable areas east of the Mississippi.

The French tried to hold the Indian's trade and loyalty

with a mixture of liquor and religion, added to liberal doses of social equality. The English wasted no time wooing the Indian. If he failed to heed their desires, they shot him. They next shot the French. The latter, inadequately supported from home, could not hold the line of the Mississippi against an enemy ever reinforced by new men and money from England. Louis XIV's policies were still potent in France. But as preserved in America they were fatal. They lost a continent.

The first quarter of the eighteenth century saw England's supremacy rivetted in virtually every sphere. France, so long the leader of Europe, had been compelled, with Louis XIV broken and dead, to yield first place on both sides of the Atlantic to Albion. And England's resistless advance was led no longer by its knights and noblemen but by its middle class of traders, merchants, shippers, and by manufacturers governed and directed by monarchs and statesmen with middle-class instincts and tastes—well fed, unvitiated, and not too much invested with sensitivity or sensibility. It was armed with the new weapon of finance and it calculated everything in terms of cash. "Every man has his price" became a popular saying.[2]

Not only England's ideals but her ideas began to be studied and copied by other nations. Voltaire, Le Sage, Montesquieu and other French visitors carried back with them from England a host of novel and exciting notions, and these notions spread from France over the Continent.

---

[2]This adage is often attributed to Robert Walpole, the cynical Whig Prime Minister. But there is reason to believe that he actually said, referring to Parliament: "All those men have their price."

In politics the doctrines of John Locke, son of a small land-owner and lawyer, were respectfully studied — particularly that government was a mutual contract and a moral trust; that no faith was to be placed in the masses, which "put passion in the place of reason;" and that the mind was a blank sheet on which experience writes. In religion, deism, which taught that the universe was ruled by a common-sensical God with manners like an English gentleman's, replaced ritual and reliance on saints. In science new concepts were introduced by a study of Newton's writings; the world as seen by Copernicus and Kepler had been a geometrical one; Newton introduced a sculptural universe made up of masses acted upon by enormous forces.

The new conception was dazzling. Active minds seized it, and mounting it, rode out into space on exhilarating journeys. Among the foreigners who discovered Newton none was more delighted than Voltaire. He went back to the Continent and converting himself into an evangelist for the new freedom, went about preaching the gospel of Saint Newton to all who would listen, and to plenty who would not. He made his lady companion, Mme. de Châtelet, read Newton and encouraged her to translate the *Principia* into French. He mounted a bust of Newton in his library and burned intellectual incense there. He wrote copious letters and talked Newton and English science without end. The world was to be saved through knowledge. The path to knowledge lay through the pleasant fields of reason. The guide was philosophy, which Voltaire construed to be synonymous with philosophizing.

## III

The propaganda spread by evangelizing Frenchmen made its way across the Rhine, where dwelt a young man who, wearied of German boorishness and Prussian military drills, had found a secret refuge in French literature and French philosophy. In his aversion from the incessant stamp of soldiers' boots about him, he did not realize that this drilling and trampling was Germany's reply to Louis XIV's military amusements, during which the French king had permitted his soldiers to do as they pleased among a helpless and disunited people east of the Rhine. The German young man was Prince Frederick, the soft and idealistic son of the hard-boiled Frederick William, who was king of Prussia and grandson of George I of England.

In 1738 the young Frederick, then twenty-four years old, wrote an admiring letter to Voltaire, who was forty-two, asking for his notice and friendship. Voltaire wrote back amiably and flatteringly. Thus was the pavement laid for the transfer of the new French ideas—and through France, modern English ideas—eastward across the Rhine.

## IV

These new ideas were here and there being shaped to a focus, and this focus was already assuming a spiral, revolving shape. In the suction thus created, in the winds thus raised, men were becoming bewildered. The young German prince's letters to Voltaire were appeals for guidance. The world of certainties presided over by Louis XIV and other absolutists had vanished within a few years. Common men as well as princes craved now to know what to believe, how to behave, and what to do. The intellectuals of Europe answered that salvation was to be had through reason, guiding a rational conduct which should observe the natural order of things. Even in the forms of religion there were to be order and rationality.

In 1729 William Law, son of a grocer who had the means to send his son to Cambridge, perceiving that religion had become mere convention or ornament, had published his *Serious Call to a Devout and Holy Life* in which he declared that salvation could be had "so far as you reduce your desires to such things as *nature and reason require;* so far as you regulate all the emotions of your heart by the strict rules of religion." Law outlined the character of a good man as follows: "He is to believe that it is the effect of God's great wisdom and goodness, that the world itself was formed at such a particular time, and in such a manner. That the general order of nature, the whole frame of things, is contrived and formed in the best manner. He is to believe that God's providence over states and kingdoms, times and seasons, is all for the best."

That whatever is, is right, as Pope said, and that whatever occurs is all for the best, as William Law proclaimed, were two tenets that shaped the whole of the eighteenth century's workaday philosophy, culminating at last in the *laissez-faire* or let-things-alone doctrines proclaimed, as the century expired, by Adam Smith. It was Law, too, who in these terms enunciated the growing and comforting belief that the fearful Trinity of God, Son, and Holy Ghost might now be replaced by a milder duality consisting of God and Providence; God being the temperamental and choleric deity of the pastoral Jews who was subject to the more benign superintendency of an over-ruling Providence.

One of William Law's pupils—until they quarrelled about the place of mysticism in religious life—was John Wesley, the hard-headed young Oxford Fellow[3] who while at the University had discovered the existence of the working classes and had visited them in their homes, workhouses, and jails. In 1738, the very year that Frederick-not-yet-the-Great opened his correspondence with Voltaire, Wesley, then thirty-four years old, returned from Georgia, newest of the American colonies, where he had gone to convert the Indians. ("But who," he asked in his Journal, "shall convert me?")

## V

Wesley had not understood the colonists of Georgia, or they him. His devotion to Church of England ritualism and to the stricter ecclesiastical formulas made him appear to be stiff-necked and lacking in adaptability; and he did both the Georgia settlers and himself a service when he returned to England.

Back in London, he attended one evening a religious meeting in Aldersgate Street and on hearing Luther's praise of faith, as given in his preface to Romans, felt his heart "strangely warmed." He then went to the Continent and

[3]"During the eighteenth century our two universities, famous despite their faults, were always open to the poor scholar who was ready to subscribe, not to boat clubs or cricket clubs, but to the Thirty-nine Articles. Three archbishops of Canterbury during the eighteenth century were the sons of small tradesmen."—Augustine Birrell, *Heart of John Wesley's Journal.*

spent some time among the Moravians at Marienborn and Herrnhut, feeling himself much "comforted and strengthened by the conversation of this lovely people."

In the spring of 1739 Wesley was persuaded to come to Bristol and attend an open-air meeting led by George Whitefield, the evangelist who had also been lately in America and who had been a member of Wesley's circle at Oxford. Whitefield's service in the fields interested Wesley and also shocked him.

"I could scarcely reconcile myself at first," he afterwards wrote, "to this *strange way* of preaching in the fields, having been all my life, till very lately, so tenacious of every point relating to decency and order, that I should have thought the saving of souls almost a sin, if it had not been done in a church."

Wesley was convinced that Whitefield's way was the right one, and that since the people would not come to the church, the church should be carried to the people. He at once began to preach in the open air, and began to witness those phenomena which at first were as bewildering to himself as to observers.

At one meeting certain persons "cried out aloud with the utmost vehemence, even as in the agonies of death." Two other persons were "seized with strong pain, and constrained to roar for the disquietness of their heart." Another "called upon God as out of the belly of hell." A woman "broke out into strong cries and tears . . . great drops of sweat ran down her face, and all her bones shook." A scoffer, on reading a sermon by Wesley, "changed color, fell off his chair, and began screaming terribly, and beating himself against the ground." One and another and another were "struck to the earth . . . as it were, in strong convulsions." Other seizures were characterized by bursts of wild laughter, which were more than once disconcerting both to Wesley and his brother Charles. In nearly every case, however, the most formidable convulsions were followed by evidences of peace and even joy. Wesley looked on and marvelled. He could only ascribe the calm that followed the most violent fits to "the gift of the Holy Ghost."

Wesley was now certain of what his future course was to be. "I look upon all the world as my parish," he wrote to his brother Charles in June, 1737. "I am . . . to declare unto all that are willing to hear the glad tidings of salvation."

So was founded Methodism, whose mission was "to reform the nation, particularly the Church; to spread scriptural holiness over the land." So began a ministry which lasted for fifty-five years. During this period Wesley went up and down in England, Scotland, and Wales, sometimes travelling 8000 miles a year, chiefly on horseback, and preaching thousands of sermons annually. Everywhere the masses received him sometimes with respect, occasionally with sticks and stones, but oftenest with convulsions. Everywhere he gave the people a powerful emotional catharsis, for which they were grateful and after which they were at ease.

Wesley himself, however, was no emotionalist. His mind remained a good eighteenth-century mind up to his last sermon in 1790 — practical, objective, and sane, except for

JOHN WESLEY

*The Oxford graduate who became a missionary to the common people and the founder of Methodism*

*From prints in the Metropolitan Museum of Art*

ROBERT WALPOLE

*He did not say, "Every man has his price," but he acted as if he believed it*

MADAME POMPADOUR

*Her hands ruled a kingdom and her hairdressing set a style.*
*From a pastel by La Tour*

a rooted belief in devils, witches, ghosts, and other apparitions. His language had no whit of the hysteria-producing eloquence of Whitefield, but was simple, sinewy, and direct. It was all the more powerful because it was stripped of ornamental rhetoric. His method was to begin with a detailed picture of an eternity in hellfire. When he had his congregation cold with fear and dread and conviction of sin, he suddenly changed his tone and message. What had been threat and invective was now compassion, love, and mercy. Who would not be washed in the blood of the Lamb? Who would not run to the loving arms of The Bridegroom?

The snapping of the tension created by fear of punishment, and the sudden release into a pictured heaven where all harsh memories were blotted out, produced powerful and sometimes shattering emotional reactions. Persons with undeveloped, atrophied, or ill-balanced emotions fell in a swoon or abandoned themselves to public ecstasies.

The effects on women were particularly marked, so much as occasionally to frighten Wesley. Again and again his Journal records his being summoned to one whom "the enemy had begun to tear"; "she screamed out as in the pangs of death"; "a young woman came to us at Islington in such an agony as I have seldom seen"; "the thousand distortions of her whole body showed how the dogs of hell were gnawing her heart. . . ."

Wesley's own Journal is the best record of his action and thought. It is a faithful reflection of the eighteenth-century English mind—full of credulity and a certain willingness to believe in wonders, but held in check by an obdurate canniness and a gift for objective observation which later led to a cultivation of the sciences. "O what want of common sense!" is an exclamation testifying to Wesley's frequent discovery of human weaknesses and stupidities. His concern for souls did not interfere with a scientific speculation upon the objects that came under his eye. He was capable of pausing between sermons to study the tea tree and to observe the difference between green and bohea tea; and to learn that in Ireland "the grand fashionable medicine for twenty diseases" was mercury sublimate, which had replaced blistering. "Why is it not an halter, or a pistol?" he wrote. "They would cure a little more speedily."

Upon his seventy-second birthday he observed with satisfaction that his bodily powers had abated but little, and that his vision and nerves had improved in thirty years. He thought his robustness was due to (1) his rising at four every morning; (2) his preaching at five; (3) his average travel rate of 4500 miles yearly.

When in 1746 Benjamin Franklin began in America his electrical experiments Wesley eagerly read all the reports prepared by Peter Collinson in England, and six years before the Royal Society recognized the value of Franklin's discoveries, Wesley was exclaiming in his Journal for 1753: "What an amazing scene is here opened for after-ages to improve upon."

Wesley found England full of receptive ears. Frowned upon by the churches, he preached in open spaces and soon had audiences of 5000, then 10,000, and at length 20,000. It was the common people who heard him gladly. Wesley wrote in 1739: "I have not found such love, no, not in

England; nor so child-like, artless, teachable a temper, as He hath given to this people."

To the working classes of England it was a new thing to find that religion had anything to say to them. The Reformation had come but had left them untouched; Luther's teachings, they may have instinctively felt, were designed only for the middle classes. As for Catholicism, that had long ago ceased to offer the working classes anything that was not in origin mediæval or feudal. The Church of England, set up by Henry VIII, had become a conventional arm of the government. Robert Walpole had filled it with politics and corruption. Calvinism had not relaxed its belief that only the elect—those having education and property—were worthy of the clergy's attention. But Wesley's teachings and methods were democratic. In his diary for April 24, 1739, he wrote that in the course of a sermon he "was insensibly led, without any previous design, to declare strongly and explicitly that God willeth all men to be thus saved."

England's working people were at first astonished and then edified to hear from Wesley that there was a heaven willing to love them—all of them. They came out of their holes, their mines, dram-shops, and beds of straw, to hear him. And at Wesley's proclamation that salvation was not the property of the upper classes but had been provided by the blood of a democratic Lamb, they often, in Wesley's words, "sunk to the earth: they dropped on every side as thunderstruck."

Whereas in England Wesleyan Methodism seemed to take most effect, at first, at least, in towns and urban com-

munities, it seemed to be equally gripping when transferred to the rural communities of colonial America. Whitefield's Methodist sermons gathered American yeomen and
backwoodsmen into enormous camp-meetings, while even
in the towns his eloquence swept thousands into emotional
fervors and sent hundreds into wild storms of weeping or
into convulsive ecstasies. In America Methodism broke up
the frontiersman's isolation, gathered him and his followers
into assemblies knit by a bond of interest, and gave the
small proprietor a perception of his political power which
later evolved into Jeffersonianism; while in England it
perfected the work begun by Cromwell and insured that
British customs and policies should henceforth be shaped
by Non-Conformism heated and pointed by Evangelic-
alism.

## VI

While all this was going on in England and America,
the continent of Europe was otherwise occupied. For example, Voltaire and young Frederick of Prussia were carrying on the correspondence which was to last for forty years.
Frederick, in soliciting the Frenchman's friendship, began
by making scornful references to "the vapor of gran-
deur."

This was a new note from a princely flute in Europe,
and Voltaire in reply revealed his gratification. He begged
the young Prussian to detest "persecution and superstition," and to avoid the quarrels of learned men and of
theologians; the peaceful pursuit of truth would bring
artists and philosophers flocking to Frederick's feet; he

would welcome a sight of Frederick's *Treatise on God, the Soul, and the World;* he congratulated the prince, already being called "the Solomon of the North," that he had been spiritually nourished by Newton, Leibnitz, Bayle, and Locke.

When Frederick wrote again it was from Rheinsberg, where he had been permitted to retire after he had tried to run away from his father, who had persistently tried to ram down his son's throat a bolus composed of parental tyranny and military discipline. But in two years Frederick William was dead and in 1740 Frederick was able to write that as king of Prussia he had already enlarged his army, founded an academy, imported four philosophers, and established a new college for commerce and manufacturers.

This last item of information was significant. It signified that through commerce and manufactures Frederick had already determined to make Prussia, which had been one of the most insignificant of the separate and quarrelling German states, formidable; and out of commerce and manufactures to foster the growth of a middle class, of a stratum of burghers who would be in energy equal, and in discipline superior, to the burgesses of England and the bourgeoisie of France.

Before the year was out Frederick was writing from military camps in Silesia. His father, Frederick William, had, after all, got his way: he had converted a timid and idealistic young introvert into a hard-fibered man of action; out of a youth who had been satisfied to play the flute and read French verses, he had forged a cynic and militarist who was to push and shove his way among the serried nations of Europe until he had established Prussia in the midst of them.

## VII

As the wealth from the Americas continued to cross the Atlantic and to fill the rusty arteries of Europe with new elixirs, each of the stronger nations struggled for a position that would give it the chief benefits. To be competed for there was not only a golden flow from the New World but a rising one from the Orient. Competition created fear and suspicion. Fear and suspicion created rage, and rage found vent in war.

Ever since the signing of the Asiento agreement in the reign of Queen Anne, English merchants and ship-captains had tried to evade Spanish restrictions on trade by an organized system of smuggling. Its base was in the West Indies. In 1738 one of these smuggling captains, by name Jenkins, got caught by the Spaniards and went home with only one ear. Interested persons worked up a crusade, and in order to avenge Britain's honor and Jenkins's ear, and at the same time to force Spain to lighten its restrictions, they induced Robert Walpole to declare war. Europe saw no peace again for ten years, for the War of Jenkins's Ear merged into the War of the Austrian Succession.

Under cover of the smoke and the noise of the trampling, Frederick II, by virtue of that strange duality of character introduced by mercantilism, moved, even while he exchanged idealistic sentiments with Voltaire, to do what he had been trained to do by his father. In 1740 Maria Theresa came to the throne of Austria, and Frederick, deeming her to be weak and poorly advised, marched his grenadiers over the border and seized the Austrian province of Silesia. He pretended that some agreement had been vaguely broken; otherwise his action was unblushing. The Prussian invasion set a whirlpool in motion, and the other nations were sucked in.

At once the old rivalry between England and France was awakened. England's dream was to control the world's seas and so to command the world's commerce. France's dream was to win back the power that had made Louis XIV lord over Europe. Great Britain went to Maria Theresa's rescue with cannon and cash, and brought Holland, Sardinia, and Saxony into an alliance against France, Spain, and Bavaria. When in 1742 the French threatened Vienna, the English put armies in the field and drove them out. In 1744 the French countered with an invasion of Bohemia and tried to divert the English with an expedition to their coast in favor of Charles Edward, the Young Pretender, son of James, the Old Pretender. In 1745 the English attacked the French for the first time on their American colonial flank. This was at Louisburg, Cape Breton. In 1746 Bonnie Prince Charlie and his feudal and anachronistic force of Scottish Highlanders were beaten by a middle-class English army at Culloden. There followed the expulsion or flight of Charles's followers, with feudal ideas unimpaired, to Ireland and then to America. In the same year Madras in India was taken by the French from the English, who had taken it from the Dutch, who had taken it from the Portuguese.

As the war gradually became old and tiresome, Euro-

peans perceived they were merely getting shot in what was
at bottom a war for mercantile supremacy between England and France; and these two nations, finding they were
unable to confine the war to Europe, prepared to extend it
east and west, to India and to America. And it was evident to a few observers, as the first half of the century
closed, that the second half would see events far vaster and
more intense; that nations were being racked and strained,
and that some must topple and make a pile on which others
would climb higher; and that kings and aristocrats would
be pressed to hold their ground against merchants, lawyers, and bankers.

## VIII

An observer looking down from a height upon the intrigues, wars, and alarms of the last decade of the eighteenth century's first half would doubtless have shaken his
head over this evidence of human weakness and human
malignity, and ascribed all the world's wickedness to the
depravity of human nature. But in England there lived
a canny individual named Joshua Gee, a merchant, who
had no doubt what the struggle and the fighting were
about. Near the middle of the century Gee published at
Glasgow sundry observations and notes on *The Trade and
Navigation of Great Britain Considered,* designed to prove
that "the surest way for a nation to increase in riches is to
prevent the importation of such foreign commodities as
may be raised at home" and that Britain was "capable of
raising within itself, and its colonies, materials for employ-

ing all our poor in those manufactures, which we now import from such of our neighbors who refuse the admission of ours." Gee's "surest way" was the way of Colbert under Louis XIV—in short, mercantilism.

Regarding England's wars with the Spaniards, Gee had this explanation: "Formerly we received a great balance from them in bullion; but since the house of Bourbon has filled the Spanish throne, and introduced French stuffs and French fashions, it is presumed the balance is but very small in our favor."

Regarding trade with Italy, Gee wrote: "Formerly we received a considerable balance from them; but the French now supplying them with very great quantities of woollen manufactures, and also having got part of the Newfoundland trade from us . . . it is thought the balance now against us is considerable."

As to Germany Gee wrote: "Germany takes from England broadcloth, druggets, long-ells, serges, and several sorts of stuffs, tobacco, sugar, ginger, East-India goods, tin, lead. . . . England takes from them prodigious quantities of linen, linen-yarn, kid skins, tin plates, and a great many other commodities. . . . Since the high duty upon French linens, the Emperor, and other princes of Germany, have gained that manufacture, which has greatly enriched them." Gee concluded with a complaint that the German States had reduced or prohibited the importation of English woollens, "which gives them a very great balance upon us." With Holland and Portugal alone was there a trade balance in favor of Britain.

Finally, Gee observed, "France, above all other nations, is the worst for England to trade with." He complained of the enormous quantities of French wines, and brandies, linens, and silks smuggled into England from Lands-End even to the Downs. "This," he exclaimed, "must drain us of our gold and silver." He recalled how Louis XIV "would wear nothing but what was the manufacture of France," and how Colbert had fostered the making of fabrics that would please the fashionables of England, contriving to make silk, once confined to women's wear, the mode for men's coats, waistcoats, and breeches. Everywhere the French, as Gee pointed out, labored to make the world wear French clothes and follow French fashions. "The same methods," he remarked bitterly, "they take with the Indians, which lie on the back of our settlements, from the river Mississippi to the river Canada, and so down to Cape Breton."

Gee found further fault with the French for subsidizing their sugar plantations in the West Indies to such a degree that Britain's control of the sugar trade in Europe, which it had taken away from the Portuguese, was threatened. He urged that Britain "not only vye with the French in foreign markets, but, if possible, to beat them out, as we formerly did the Portuguese." He discovered that even in woollens the French had "supplemented us in foreign markets and undersold us."

Gee's conclusions were that as the French in their commerce had shown no scruples, but had used every means possible to further the interests of their traders, Britain must be prepared to do likewise; and he particularly counselled that England make more use of its colonies in America, encourage them to forward a wider variety of useful products and raw materials, restrict their exporting and shipping operations, prevent their developing manufactures, and if defection should be raised by turbulent spirited men, to "place standing forces among them to keep them in order."

Already in 1732 the Royal Commissioners for Trade and Plantations had reported to the House of Commons on the state of America "with respect to any laws made, manufactures set up, and trade carried on there, navigation, and manufactures of this kingdom." In the words of McCarthy:[1] "The inquiry was set on foot in order to find out whether the colonists were presuming to manufacture for themselves any goods which they ought by right to buy from English makers, and to recommend steps by which such audacious enterprises might be rebuked and prevented." In short, the new but not yet firmly established manufacturers of England did not propose to permit the growth of a rival class in America. England purposed to keep its colonies on the Atlantic seaboard peopled exclusively by farmers, traders, fishermen, miners, trappers, and axe-men.

The European and American peoples of the middle of the eighteenth century were permitted to believe that the wars of the period resulted from questions of dynasty, from the ambition of princes, from diplomatic intrigues, or even

[1] *History of the Four Georges*, I, 408.

from the personal whims of royal personages. But somewhere in official bureaus sat the clerks, accountants, and statisticians who knew that the drilling and trampling were due to questions of wool, iron, and wine, of hemp and potash, of sugar and tar.

## *INTERLUDE*

WE HAVE reached the end of the first half of the eighteenth century. It is time for a pause, for a backward look, and review.

It has taken fifty years for the century to gather itself together and to find its path and direction. Whither is it to go?

It does not yet precisely know. So far it has been satisfied to be rid of the Louis XIV's, the English Stuarts, and the German Frederick Williams. With these repressors out of the way, it has been able to proceed to the *accouchement* which has given birth to the great middle classes, known in France as the bourgeoisie, in Germany as burghers, and in England and America as burgesses. All these words are from one root meaning "a town." These bourgeoisie, burghers, and burgesses are townmen — traders, merchants, bankers, lawyers — who must be near to such urban centers as markets, counting-houses, and law-courts. On the land they would die. The land — except for small country estates which symbolize their new position and power — they willingly leave to the aristocracy, which, sucked in by great capitals and forced to revolve around monarchs, is losing its fiber.

These new-born middle classes, although still reverent toward royalty and the nobility, have reacted against virtually the whole ideology under which their fathers were brought up. They believe in bills of exchange, not castles. They go to church but trust in a mariner's compass and dry powder more than they do in Providence. They are utilitarian and cautious. A thing is what it appears to be. They talk of the future, not the past. They are suspicious of emotion, mysticism, and supernaturalism. They are skeptical, rationalistic, and avid for that knowledge which will increase their power. They bow to authority but revere the reason of the individual when dealing with a particular case. With such absolutes as those set up by Louis XIV they are finished. They contend that even truth itself is not absolute, but relative.

In France the rationalistic and skeptical regent, the Duke of Orleans, has been succeeded by Louis XV, who, provided his amusements are not interfered with, is content to permit his merchants to get rich.[1] In England George II, who is bored with politics, permits Robert Walpole to turn the government over to the great owners of land. In Germany Frederick the Great pushes his country forward aggressively and cynically, finding formidable obstacles only in the women whom he bawls at as "the three whores" — Maria Theresa of Austria, the French Madame de Pompadour, and Elizabeth of Russia.

[1]Voltaire: "One who should see the memoirs of the first years of Louis XV would remark nothing in our nation but its effeminacy, an extreme avidity for wealth, and too much indifference to everything besides."

Whereas during the first fifty years leadership in ideas and intellectual inventiveness have belonged to England, at the middle of the century the torch of enlightenment is taken over by France. No sooner are the repressions of Louis XIV removed than France, its appetite sharpened by long starvation, draws its chair up to the banquet table which has already been garnished by a freer England and begins eagerly to taste the dishes. In science it looks up to Newton, in political philosophy to Locke and Bolingbroke and Shaftesbury, in history to Hume, in fictional literature to Richardson. The indifference with which Louis XV regards the activities of his subjects is favorable to French letters. With a happy zeal the writers of France plunge into this ocean of opportunity. They would inform the world, teach it, and finally mold it.

The next forty years are starred with great names— Montesquieu, Buffon, Diderot, Rousseau, Condorcet, Turgot, Condillac, Holbach, d'Alembert, Helvétius; with Voltaire, who believed himself old and hypochondriac, rising to even more sparkling performances than before.

It is significant that so much occurs just at the middle turn of the century. In 1749 Montesquieu publishes his *Spirit of the Laws* and Buffon his great natural history. In 1751 Denis Diderot publishes the first volume of the *Encyclopédie*. It was the same year in which Clive for England and Dupleix for France meet in the death struggle for the body of India. And it is only three years later that the young George Washington, a major in the British colonial forces of America, is beaten at Fort Duquesne in one of those English efforts, not yet fully organized, to drive the French out of America. The French are still a very hardy people. And at the moment they are the most thought-taking in Europe.

# PART TWO

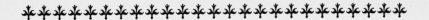

## CHAPTER ONE

## ANOTHER BOURBON

### I

WHEN Czar Peter of Russia was last in France, he asked to see the infant Louis XV, son of Louis XIV's grandson, the Duke of Burgundy, and of Marie Adelaide, the former princess of Savoy. Meeting the child, frail, large-eyed and wanly smiling, at a door, Peter picked him up in his gorilla arms and kissed him with a hairy kiss. Peter went away laughing, well pleased that once more he had been able to shock the stiffish French courtiers with a demonstration of honest human feeling.

About the boy-king there was indeed something winning. He was so amiable and artless that he was called the Well Beloved; and courtiers, nurses, and tutors combined to spoil him and make him self-centered, erratic, and morbidly selfish. One day Louis, who like all the Bourbons was fond of guns and hunting and was easily bored, called to him his chief pet of the moment, a small hind. As the animal responded, Louis shot it. Wounded but trusting, the animal crept forward to his young master's feet. Louis then shot it again until it was dead. Calling attendants to remove the body, Louis lolled back in the boredom that in his later years renewed itself like a chronic malady.

But the very ennui with which Louis gazed upon the doings of his ministers and subjects gave his people a certain freedom of behavior and opinion. This, although sometimes curtailed, was, in comparison with the strangling regulations of his great-grandfather, of wide latitude, and a burgeoning class of intellectuals eagerly availed themselves of it.

One of them was Denis Diderot, the son of a provincial cutler. After a lifetime of hackwork and literary vagabondage, Diderot began to put his more serious ideas down in writing and then into print. They were not original with him; they were the property of his time and associates. They were to this effect: that the chief end of man is to work and to know; that ideas are born out of the employment of the five senses; and that revelations are to be looked for in the natural world, not the supernatural. These notions got him into prison; from which he emerged self-dedicated to a supreme purpose — to compile and publish an encyclopedia which should digest and summarize all existing knowledge. Thus was the work begun by Pierre Bayle in his little Dutch attic taken up and carried on in the land from which he had been exiled. The first volume appeared in 1751. In 1759 Louis XV suppressed Diderot's encyclopedia. It rebounded, so to say, and in so doing, it helped to sweep the Bourbon kings from their thrones. The way of it is now to be told.

## II

In the middle ages knowledge was an ornament. In the eighteenth century the middle classes seized it and sharpened it into a weapon. One of the sharpeners was Diderot. The germ of his encyclopedia was no doubt taken from Bayle's one-man dictionary. But the chief spur and model came from England, where in 1728 Ephraim Chambers had published his Cyclopedia, using a system of references by which parts were connected with wholes, so that there was created what was called a "commonwealth of learning." Diderot saw the value of this system and when a French translation was published in Paris in 1745, he resolved to adopt it. If in writing this encyclopedia, he could have assistants and collaborators, they would be welcome; but if they did not come, he would write it himself. It was not wholly a labor of love or one undertaken for altruistic purposes.

"I had arrived in Paris," he afterwards wrote. "I was about to don the fur gown and to settle among the doctors in the Sorbonne. I meet on the way a woman of angelic beauty. . . . We marry, four children are born to us, and there am I, compelled to forsake mathematics, of which I was fond; Homer and Virgil, whom I always carried about in my pocket; the theatre, for which I had some inclination; glad enough to undertake the *Encyclopédie*, to which I shall have sacrificed twenty-five years of my life."

Diderot's was the first voice raised since Bacon's time in behalf of a study of useful, and not merely ornamental, things. Thus was he responsive to the demand of the middle classes for more utilitarian, and less purely speculative, science. He praised Colbert as "the man who peopled France with engravers, painters, sculptors, and artists of every kind, who snatched from the English the secret of the stocking-loom, who took the velvets from the Genoese, the looking-glasses from the Venetians," thus doing "hardly less for the State than the man who beat its enemies and took their strongholds by storm." This comparison of an industrialist with a general, this elevation of the business man to the level of the military man, was a new concept.

### III

While Diderot, intent and enthusiastic, was busy with his encyclopedia, through which the empire of learning might be extended, another Frenchman was harboring visions of an empire of another character.

Under Louis XIV, Colbert had founded the French East India Company primarily to import from the Orient those spices and condiments which an expanding prosperity had brought to the table of the mercantile families. Although occasionally suffering severe losses, it had in good years made profits of 30, 40, and even 50 per cent, and had widened its activities until it was dealing in many commodities of luxury and owned strong trading centers, chief of which was Pondicherry in India. Troubled by sharp competition from the English and by irregularities in management and operation, the Company sent out Joseph François Dupleix, armed with the royal appointment of Louis XV, to be governor-general. Dupleix was forty-five

years old, vain, energetic, meticulous, and permeated by
that love of money which Voltaire declared was the chief
characteristic of Frenchmen under Louis XV. And he had
a wife who loved it even more.

As soon as Dupleix had established himself in India in
1742, he set about the achievement of certain desires and
ambitions which had inflamed him ever since a practical
father had converted him from a student of books into an
aggressive young mercantilist with some military and moral
training.

Dupleix's visions went far beyond the routine ideas of
the ordinary company official. He dreamed not only of
maintaining the dividends of his company and of strength-
ening it against English competition, but of laying in the
Orient the foundations of a French empire. Of this empire
he meant to be the monarch; and this would be the easier
because he was responsible only to distant employers and
to a negligent king. Incidentally he intended to feather
well his own nest, for he loved power and position as well
as money; so that one day he might return to *la douce
France* as a rich and successful bourgeois, powdered, silken-
vested, escorted by lackeys, and bowed to in court and
street.

To the furtherance of these ends he addressed a consuming zeal. Concealing his distaste, he suborned and flattered
native sovereigns and leaders into joining hands with the
French. Detesting the cast-offs sent to him as soldiers and
the incompetents supplied to him as clerks and petty officials, he drilled and organized and molded them into
fairly effective bodies. When he was not directing and su-

pervising, and pocketing any stray sums that his opportunities and position brought floating into his orbit, he
wrote letters. He wrote to the Company long advices, reports, and explanations. He wrote to associated military
and naval commanders. He wrote to aides and subordinates
—urging, counselling, criticizing, and occasionally praising. He wrote until his hands wearied and then he dictated until he was hoarse. He watched details until he was
exhausted and lived only on his nerves, harassed and trem-
bling. At first his continuous pressure on men and events
brought results; his successes, military and commercial,
enabled him to regard virtually all Southern India as a
French preserve. And then his path was crossed by Robert
Clive.

Clive was the erratic son of an English provincial lawyer. He had come out to India as a clerk for the English
East India Company. Soon tiring of commercial tedium,
he obtained a transfer to the Company's military division.
Aggressiveness and a restless energy brought him to the
top. Repeated victories were giving the French a reputation
for invincibility, but Clive beat them easily. The French,
owing to poor support from their own company at home
and to their thirst for individual glory, lacked effectiveness, and Clive's daring and his better disciplined troops
overcame them in three campaigns that placed England,
in the eyes of native princes, at the head of affairs in India.

Dupleix's eager but neurotic energy failed to halt the
decline of French influence, and eventually he was recalled
to France where he spent his last years in poverty and bit-
terness of spirit. He left behind a memoir in which he ex-

plained his philosophy of imperialism. Referring to the secure position of the Dutch merchants in India, he wrote: "It was war which won them their revenues. . . . We too can acquire ours only by war."

## IV

The career of Clive, Dupleix's successful rival, was much more spectacular. His military and political feats were well advertised, and soon he was Lord Clive and the most feared Englishman in India. But about the time that he should have been able to enjoy the fruits of his labors, he was made the target of formidable accusations. He was charged with looting, trickery, corruption, and even forgery. It was shown that at the age of thirty-five he had been able to return to England with a personal fortune of £300,000 and a yearly income (from quit-rents paid by Indian natives) of £27,000. He was accused of looting the treasury of Bengal, after the capture of its capital, Murshidabad, where he had found a store of money, plate, and gems worth a million and a half sterling. From this glittering heap he had taken £160,000 for distribution among the English conquerors. He did not deny it; he was "astonished," as he said afterwards, "at his own moderation."

It was further charged that the affairs of the Company in India were riddled by graft, both civil and military; that under him English merchants had won a monopoly of the internal as well as the export trade, and that thousands of native merchants and tradesmen had been pauperized. The attacks on Clive were led chiefly by Colonel

Johnny Burgoyne, who as a general subsequently was beaten by American colonial forces at Saratoga.

Clive had agile friends and powerful political connections. They encouraged him to reply. Clive admitted that certain deeds, such as the forging of an admiral's name to a treaty and the acceptance of large gifts from Indian rulers, appeared peculiar, but declared he had acted only from necessity. He pointed out that in 1765 he had obtained the grant of the provinces of Bengal, Behar, and Orissa for the East India Company, which made it ruler over 30,-000,000 people; and that he had abolished abuses and caused many reforms. His demeanor indicated a proud but hurt dignity.

Burgoyne continued his attacks and made them more stinging. He at length virtually accused Clive of making personal "acquisitions" which really belonged to the State. Clive's poise, maintained with difficulty, gave way. He made the mistake of losing his temper and in his replies he accused the Company directors of incompetence and stinginess. Clive had the further misfortune of being defended by Alexander Wedderburn, a thick-witted and tactless solicitor-general, who later, in 1773, made mortal enemies for England in America by a rancorous attack on the colonial envoy, Benjamin Franklin. Clive's temper had been fretted by ill health and nerves kept too long taut. He suffered constant pain from gall-stones and to allay it took opium. Storms of criticism burst on him, and his replies, once measured and dignified, became shrieking. Travel failed to restore his hold on his intellect and in 1774, just after his forty-ninth birthday, he killed himself, not before, however, he had virtually destroyed the nascent French empire in India and had substituted for it an English one.

This was the beginning of what the world afterwards called Imperialism, an institution and a doctrine which often destroyed its agents as well as its victims.

## V

The zeal exhibited by Dupleix in one sphere was matched by Diderot in another, and while monarchs, ministers, and generals racked a world with plots and campaigns, Diderot was running about Paris streets, laboring on the foundations of what was to be a new empire of knowledge and virtue. In gathering material for his encyclopedia he did not rely upon libraries alone, but invaded what to the intelligentsia of the period had been a remote and unknown sphere — the workshop. With his own eyes he studied processes, and with his own hands he tested those mechanical devices which with teeth and wheel and gear were shaking the decaying pillars of an old and outworn society.

He was ready to publish his first volume at the middle of the century (1751). Five years previously a fellow countryman, Jacques de Vaucanson, had introduced a device of hooks and wires which so improved the operation of the old hand-loom used in weaving fabrics that ever since it has been called the Jacquard loom. Diderot went into the shops and back-rooms where this and other machines were in motion. He sat in the operator's seat and worked them. He came out dazzled, impressed, and enthusiastic, and went back to his lodgings filled with a new conception as to what his encyclopedia must do—if it could not always explain why things happen, it could at least show how things are done, to the end that every man might know comprehensively and work effectively.

For twenty years he toiled like a nervous but happy ant, surviving suppressions, trickery, desertion, fraud, and poverty, until at last he had not only published an encyclopedia but created the Encyclopedists, that group of Frenchmen who believed that men had only to obey Encyclopedist doctrines in order to be rational, happy, and free. They were also called the *Philosophes,* a term not to be taken as an equivalent of "philosophers," a word that has taken on a restricted meaning, but in its derivative sense signifying lovers of wisdom. They were the founders and leaders of the Enlightenment, that period which regarded feudalism and medievalism as unhappy nightmares and itself as the apex and culmination of the process of intelligence.

Some of them were, like Diderot, poor men happy in the possession of a dressing-gown, a lodging, and a little leisure. Others were men of income and position like Helvétius and Holbach. Few of them were systematic thinkers or logical writers, but together they wrought an intellectual platform on which the middle classes of the world could stand. They guided the thinking and shaped the ideas of two hemispheres. Their teachings flowed far over the borders of France and beyond their own century, and influenced Frederick the Great in Germany, Catherine II in Russia, Joseph II in Austria, Adam Smith, Priestley, and Burke in England, Benjamin Franklin and Thomas Jeffer-

son in America, and finally the Revolutionists and Napoleon Bonaparte in their own land.

Seldom has any circle of men intent upon the diffusion
of knowledge had so good a time. If persecuted they found
friends with power, even in court and close to the throne.
In salons they were favored guests and in palaces they made
the literary man the social equal of the noble. In the second
half of the eighteenth century the world of ideas was entirely theirs. Their father was Pierre Bayle and their ma-
ternal uncle was Montesquieu.

## VI

While still a young man Montesquieu, provincial official
and owner of a comfortable property, published his *Persian
Letters,* a series of satires on the inconsistent manners and
customs of the time—inconsistent because they were in
part still feudal and in part incompletely responsive to new
modes of life. Resting on the attention thus acquired, Montesquieu published other works, and gave himself to the
compilation of *The Spirit of the Laws,* a work containing
the fruit of reading and reflection, of consultation with
traders and explorers, and of notes made on travel in England and the Continent. When the manuscript was completed he called in a circle of learned and worldly-wise
men, and read it aloud. They advised against its publica-
tion; it might stir up the government and offend the
church. So Montesquieu published it in 1748.

*L'Esprit des Lois,* to give it its French title, has been
called the greatest book of the eighteenth century. This is

extravagant. It is the work of a literary, not a logical, mind. It is scattered, desultory; it worships property; it backs and fills; it is in parts formless; but in other parts it is solid and suggestive. Its merit is that it is a synthetic and sympathetic account of the groping attempts of men, ancient and modern, primitive and sophisticated, to establish earthly legality. It offered a philosophy of jurisprudence; it laid the foundation for economics and sociology—for the rise of the social sciences in the twentieth century. It dealt not with man as a metaphysical abstraction, but with men as they live in societies. It discovered men as social beings. In that respect it established a new date in the history of men in their relations to one another.

Montesquieu's brain as an organizing agency was not great, but its perceptiveness was acute. He perceived, for example, the basis for the problem of the difference between wealth, riches, and money—a problem that troubled men at the middle of the eighteenth century just as it troubles them today. He saw wealth as residing not in possessions, but in labor. He said: "*A man is not poor because he has nothing, but because he does not work.*" Had he lived a century later, he might have written it: "because he does not—or cannot—work."

He anticipated Hume when that Scotsman said: "Everything in the world is purchased by labour, and our passions are the only causes of labour"; and again when Hume taught that wealth is increased through "conjunction of forces" (co-operation?); that efficiency is increased by "partition of employment" (division of labor?); and that security is obtained by "mutual succour." And that Montesquieu's book gave ideas and stimuli to that other Scot, Adam Smith, when he wrote *The Wealth of Nations,* so long the economic bible of the Anglo-Saxon peoples, is certain.[1]

## VII

If Bayle and Montesquieu paved the road by which the Philosophes might march into the center of events, the Philosophes in turn laid down a pavement for a smaller and looser but intenser group known at the time as the Economists and later as the Physiocrats. It was they who introduced into common speech the phrase *Laisser faire, laisser passer*—a phrase summing up a doctrine that was to govern the world's thinking for almost two centuries. This phrase was a declaration of independence pronounced in behalf of the trader, that active being who was subtly taking power away from the kings. It said to governments and all other interferers: "Let things be. Let the checks and bars be taken away from that which has become the chief end of man—to buy and to sell."

Immediately Physiocracy was an uprising against the vexatious duties and regulations, inherited by Louis XV from Louis XIV, that burdened the free passage of goods, especially grains, from province to province and from na-

---

[1]There is no evidence that Montesquieu was influenced by his Italian contemporary, Giovanni B. Vico (1668–1744), or that he ever read Vico's *Principles of a New Science,* published in 1725, which was also a study of laws and their origins. Vico taught that law in its beginnings is unconscious and instinctive and ends in abstraction and formula. The history of ideas, he wrote, begins with a poetic wisdom and ends in conscious philosophy. The history of men and events, he said, passes through three phases: (1) divine, (2) heroic, (3) human.

tion to nation. It was a demand for the freedom of trade that was making England richer and more powerful than France and making the dream of a recovered French hegemony over the Continent ever remoter from realization.

Physiocracy was also a protest against the rise of an urban plutocracy. It was a revolt of country against town. It taught that the products of the land were of primary importance and should receive the first consideration of governments. It elevated the peasant and farmer above the town mechanic, and gave agriculture a place above trade and industry. It regarded men who owned and farmed the land as the only "class productive"; the men of all other occupations belonged to the "class sterile." It was one of the first movements to recognize that class divisions exist in society, and that class ambitions and interests frequently clash.

Again, it was a reaction against the Colbertism that had governed France in the early days of the century. It was at the same time an effort to carry on the teachings begun by Vauban and Boisguillebert under Louis XIV; like them it advanced the wiping out of numerous and complicated taxes and the establishment of an *impôt unique* — a single tax on land. Although the Physiocrats never attained a political influence equal to that of the Philosophes, they made an impression whose effects were carried across the Atlantic, becoming visible later in the writings of Thomas Paine, Thomas Jefferson, and Henry George.

Notwithstanding their emphasis on the supremacy of land and agriculture, Physiocracy's chief advocates were not men who soiled their hands with dirt. Among them were

Quesnay, who was physician to the king's mistress, and Turgot, intendant of the province of Limousin. It was Turgot whose financial measures made the last stand for Louis XVI in a vain attempt to fend off the Revolution.

No expert eyes were needed, however, to see the wretched condition to which the agricultural regions had been brought by burdensome taxation, by the exactions of landlords, and by the upbuilding of the towns at the expense of the countryside. In the years 1739 and 1747 bad harvests reduced certain provinces to actual famine. From Touraine d'Argenson wrote: "During this last year the general distress throughout the kingdom has grown to unprecedented dimensions. People are dying like flies from poverty and eating grass." He mentioned three risings by peasants unable to feed their children. From Auvergne the preacher Massillon wrote to Cardinal Fleury: "The people of our countryside are living in dreadful misery, and have neither beds nor furniture. For half the year most of them lack even the barley or oat bread which is their only food, and which they have to withhold from themselves and from their children in order to pay the taxes."

The most hated of the taxes that stripped the peasantry was the *taille* or land tax. The collectors of it were so hated that they went about in bands. If payment was not made, they were authorized to break open doors and seize furniture. To escape their system of espionage and the consequent assessments, the peasants concealed all evidence of wealth and even of comfort. Rousseau in his *Confessions* relates that on a journey to Lyons he stopped at a farmer's house to buy food. The owner said he had only skim milk and barley bread, but on being convinced that his visitor was not a disguised tax-collector, he produced a wheaten loaf, a ham, eggs, and a bottle of wine.

"With shaking limbs," writes Rousseau, "he told me he had to hide his wine on account of the subsidies and his bread on account of the *taille,* and that he would be a lost man if any one began to doubt that he was not dying of hunger."

The subsidy tax was officially if ironically called the *aide,* and was applied to the consumption of all wine above an amount allowed for personal use. It kept the collectors constantly measuring wine barrels and watching the consumption at public celebrations and even at mass.

A third bitterly hated tax was the *gabelle* or salt tax. Salt was a royal monopoly and if revenues were to grow, sales must be encouraged, even if force was necessary. Hence a peasant was supposed to take so much salt for his table, so much for his cooking, and so much for his hams. If he fell short, he was liable to fines and confiscations. As Voltaire explained it, "a man who has so many pigs should use so much salt for pickling them, and if they die he must still take the same amount, or else he is fined and his furniture sold." Official exactions had the effect usual in such situations—they put a premium on smuggling. The profits in illegal salt were so great that men abandoned farming for smuggling. To suppress this traffic an enormous body of police, spies, and inspectors was created. The consequence was a hatred of all law and an increase in crime, oppression, and corruption.

A principal source of oppression was the Court of Woods

and Forests which forbade the peasant to kill or catch hares, game birds, or fish, even though they might be found on his own land and might be damaging his crops.

A fifth tax, levied on certain provinces, was the smoke tax. Dues were collected on fires, whether for heating a house or for other purposes. Rural inhabitants were thus driven to live without heat all the year round, and in winter to sleep and eat among their cattle in order to keep from freezing.

After the middle of the century conditions improved throughout France and from prosperity grew fat towns filled with the solid houses of merchants and professional men. This prosperity, however, touched the countryside but rarely, while official exactions continued in one form or another. So that eventually when in 1789 the townsmen rose against kings and nobles, the peasants joined them and in their rage did not always discriminate between useful men and parasites. If Louis XVI was guillotined, so was Condorcet the philosopher, and if Robespierre was carried down in the blood-stream, so was Lavoisier the chemist.

## VIII

A perception of these inequalities and injustices which, although accepted under Louis XIV, seemed monstrous under Louis XV, made France, at the mid-century, intellectually restless and speculative. Why, as J. J. Rousseau expressed it, was man, although born free, everywhere in chains?

There arose everywhere an enormous interest in gov-

ernments, in the sciences, in economic fabrics, in social relations. Everything was examined, everything searched,
everything analyzed. Surely to this welter of chains, locks,
bars, and traps a key could be found—a master key that
would open all doors, reveal all passages. The way to rev-
elation was through discussion, debate, talk. Conversation,
invented as a pastime, became an art and then a passion.

For conversation to be born, to develop, to have form—
in short, to become opinion—it must have a center, a
home, a *foyer*. So arose the Salon.

The French salon was the birthplace of public opinion.
That was a new thing in the world. Previously there had
been only the notions of kings and the prejudices of nobles.
The salon was new evidence of bourgeois power. It persuaded the aristocrats to come forth and be polite to the
men of letters. And the men of letters were all from the
middle class.

The Philosophes and Physiocrats, like other groups, had
their salons where their presence and wit were especially
welcome. The Encyclopedists were particularly favored at
the salon of the Dowager Duchess of Aiguillon. The broth-
ers Goucourt[2] have left us a description of this formidable
lady. She was not externally attractive, being too massive
of body and heavy in manner; "she lacked taste as well as
grace"; but she was capable of astonishing and subjugat-
ing her guests by the vigor and range of her conversation,
while her ideas and traits communicated an impression of
great personal power.

A salon that served as a center for the opposition and the

[2]*La Femme au Dix-Huitième Siècle.*

clerical party was maintained by the Princess of Robecq. Her innocent face, described as "sweet and serene," her large blue eyes under black eyebrows, her blond hair, gave no hint of the animosity with which she hated the mild Diderot and his fellow Encyclopedists. Stricken with a fatal disease at the age of thirty-six, her last act was to stage a play satirizing the Philosophes and all their works, and she prayed daily and successfully that she might live to see it acted.

Turgot and other Physiocrats were made particularly welcome at the salon of Mme. d'Anville. She had a passion for the good. "Her heart was open to all utopias, her spirit to all illusory systems."[3] Belonging to a noble family, she knew how to pull the right strings at court, and Voltaire was once glad to appeal to her to get him a safe-conduct for one of his journeys.

The salon that the Academicians and literary men loved most to frequent was that of Julie de Lespinasse, who, coming to Paris from a provincial refuge without the advantages of a good name, of money, or of good looks, first subdued d'Alembert, chief of the Encyclopedists and secretary of the French Academy, by her charm and generosity, and then brought Turgot, Condorcet, Chastellux, St. Pierre, La Harpe, and many other writers into a circle of which she was the center for twelve years. She had won this circle away from her former companion, the older Mme. du Deffand, who had been hostess to many celebrities.

The most famous and hospitable salon of its time was

[3]*Idem.*

that of Mme. Geoffrin, whose social triumphs were deemed all the more astonishing since she was the daughter of a valet and the wife of a glass manufacturer—a bourgeois who although possessed of great riches had nothing to recommend him beyond a mild and affable stupidity.

No foreign celebrity, whether a practitioner of politics or of the arts, was permitted to pass through Paris without attending one of Mme. Geoffrin's intimate and expensive little dinners. Her prestige was unsurpassed. And yet she resembled in no way the traditional conception of what a great salonière should be like. She was small, homely, and old-maidish. Her manner was quiet and gentle rather than vivacious. She could read, but she wrote with difficulty and could never learn to spell. With a prim little cap upon her head, a ribbon knotted under her pointed little chin, and muslin ruffles around her neck, she made one think of some worthy man's mouse-like and self-effacing maiden aunt—serene, wise, and neat. She remained respectable, and, in a day when voluptuousness was a cult, she upheld all the moralities. She suffered neither from the romantic impulsiveness which made Julie de Lespinasse's life a kind of fever nor from the boredom which constantly afflicted Mme. du Deffand. In her corner all was orderly and all was interesting.

Her salon drew all the notabilities—Montesquieu, Voltaire, Diderot, Marmontel, Grimm, Holbach, d'Alembert, Morellet, Algarotti; and when Stanislas Augustus Poniatowski came to Paris, it was there that he found a hospitality so warming that he called himself Mme. Geoffrin's son and when he became king of Poland, she left Paris

AN EVENING AT THE SALON OF MADAME GEOFFRIN

*It was the most famous and popular in Paris. The hostess is seated in the center.*
*From an aquatint by Débucourt*

IMPORTER OF FRENCH CULTURE

*The empress Catherine II of Russia. From a painting by Lampi,*
*engraved by Walser*

for the first and only time in order that she might visit him. She was then sixty-five and a widow. Preparations for the journey occupied her more than a year and her progress across Europe was like that of royalty. At Vienna she received warm attentions from Maria Theresa and was introduced to Marie Antoinette, then twelve years old, whom she found "beautiful."

At Warsaw she found that she was no longer comfortable or at ease in Poniatowski's presence. She returned to Paris not to leave it again and when at the age of seventy-six paralysis seized her frail frame, she resigned herself to death with tranquillity. Her last words were characteristically sententious and thoughtful. When she overheard a discussion of the means by which the government might make the masses happy, she roused herself to say: "Add to them the need of procuring a few pleasures."

She had thoughtfully provided not a few pensioners not only with the means of procuring a few pleasures, but of existing. Mlle. de Lespinasse maintained her salon by dint of Mme. Geoffrin's life-pension. Morellet and other writers received from her a regular allowance. Only on Sundays did she refuse to receive guests. That was a day reserved for the sacred office of doing up money in little bags and gifts in little parcels which were the next day distributed to persons whose names appeared on her private lists.

One other woman of the middle class was mistress of a salon which in Paris was a center of power. This was Mme. d'Épinay, who at nineteen had been married to one de la Live, who on succeeding his father as a farmer of taxes changed his name to d'Épinay. His friends knew him as a liar, petty tyrant, and philanderer and were not astonished when he presently made it known to his bride that he meant to amuse himself as he liked and that she might, for all he cared, do likewise.

She took him at his word and found what pastime she could in lovers, literature, and amateur theatricals. One night she was presented to the author of a play in which her group was interested. He was Jean Jacques Rousseau, then thirty-seven years old and described "as poor as Job and with wit and vanity enough for four."

Soon afterward she obtained a legal separation and a large allowance from d'Épinay, and with this new freedom and money she established a circle that included Rousseau, Diderot, d'Alembert, Holbach, Melchior Grimm, and other Encyclopedists. Grimm she accepted as a lover, but was fascinated enough with Rousseau to bestow upon him the little house known as the Hermitage in the forest of Montmorency near Paris. Rousseau took the house, but because he could not bear the obligation that went with it, he quarrelled with her and talked of her scandalously.

From this time on Rousseau never had any luck or any peace. As for the Épinay, she went on being serene, hospitable, generous, and gay until she was fifty-eight years old and white-haired, when she quietly died of cancer. She had gifts as a writer, and her *Conversations d'Émilie,* designed to promote the education of a grand-daughter, was crowned by the Academy, while her *Memoirs* are still treasured for the lights they throw upon the times.

For example, she is relating how her friend, Mlle. d'Ette, advised her to replace her wandering husband with a lover

—"a man of thirty, a man of discretion; a man who is able to advise, to guide you, and who has enough affection for you to think only of making you happy." Mme. d'Épinay demurs and is doubtful, and her adviser returns to the charge with an observation that no doubt adequately sums up the viewpoint of Paris salon society in the latter half of the eighteenth century.

*"It is only a woman's inconsistency in her tastes," says Mlle. d'Ette (whose face, wrote Diderot, was like a large bowl of milk on which rose leaves have been thrown), "or an evil choice, or the publicity she gives to it, that can injure her reputation. The choice is the essential thing."*

Mme. d'Épinay sketches for us this portrait of herself when she was about thirty:

I am not pretty, and yet I am not plain. I am small, thin, a very good figure. I have a young look, without freshness, with a dignified, gentle, animated, witty and interesting air. My imagination is tranquil. My mind is slow, correct, thoughtful, and inconsequent. I have vivacity, courage, constancy, exaltation, and excessive timidity.

I am true without being frank.[4] Timidity has often made me appear dissembling and false; but I have always had the courage to confess my weakness in order to destroy the suspicion of a vice I did not possess.

I have enough shrewdness to attain my end and to remove obstacles; but I have not enough to see through others' plans.

I was born tender and susceptible, constant and not coquettish.

I love solitude and the simple and retired life; I have, however, almost always led a life contrary to my taste. . . .

Poor health, keen and repeated griefs, have turned my character, which is naturally very cheerful, to seriousness.

Did she read herself correctly? Diderot saw her as not

[4]Sainte-Beuve (*Causeries du Lundi,* April–July, 1850) says she got this remark from Rousseau, who had made it to her.

quite so simple and naïve as all that. In fact, in a letter to his friend Sophie Voland he said:

Mme. d'Épinay's portrait is finished; she is portrayed with her bosom half exposed, a few locks scattered over her bosom and shoulders, the others held by a blue ribbon encircling her brow, her mouth half open; she breathes and her eyes are full of languor.

Rousseau could find no charm in her, while Voltaire saw her as "truly a philosopher." She was "an eagle in a gauze cage."

## IX

The salons of Paris were kept open until the Revolution fell in upon them and crushed them. The salon created opinion; sharpened it, gave it form and substance; the outside world seized upon it and made it public opinion — a thing that has since held nations together when laws have been futile or corrupt. The creation of public opinion in France was the joint work of men and women, meeting in the salons. The salon permitted ideas to enter society and flow freely in and out. Any one could have ideas, women no less than men. When to the discussion of ideas were added other human needs — food, warmth, courtesy, consideration, social communication, gregariousness — the salon began to have solid feet even though its head might remain airy.

The salon drew women out of the boudoir, out of the pantry, away from the backstairs, and brought them into the world of thought and action. This world had been exclusively male; gross, obstinate, and thick. Women added to it lightness, ease, form. The sexes, when meeting in groups on the same plane, have a civilizing influence on each other; men left to their own society become brutal; women left to their own society become petty; each sex improves in the presence of the other; this was the discovery of the salon.

The influence of the salon was felt throughout France. It was one of the agencies that fostered a respect for intelligence. Even today there is no people who have a higher regard for intelligence—for intellect married to intuition, and for logic joined to wisdom—than the French. It was perhaps of the salon stage of French civilization that Talleyrand was thinking when he said that "only those who lived in Europe before the French Revolution have really experienced the sweetness of living."

But the salon had its weakness. It was wholly Parisian, and so urban and artificial. It produced a fine fermentation of ideas in Paris, but it left the provinces dumb and inert. It provided a field in which a new crop of intellectuals might operate, and it encouraged the rise of a literature in which the ritual and gossip of courts gave place to science, speculation, and objective observation; but its comforts and gayeties, its wines and dinners, were paid for out of a wealth created in fields and workshops by a people who not only never shared in these luxuries, but lived in a social fabric rotting from within. It was a French official who wrote that there were peasants who ate meat "not three times a year," and another who reported: "Some of these wretches who are cotton-spinners are so destitute that they have nothing with which to clothe themselves."

Still, there were compensations. The road to Versailles was always open, and any one who had the strength could walk it, and curious if not always well-fed crowds gathered every Sunday to see the king dine in public. They "greatly admired his skill," we are told in the memoirs of Mme. Campan, "in removing the top of his egg with one back-handed stroke of his fork."

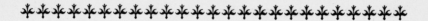

## CHAPTER TWO

## DARK SEA

### I

IN THE French salon of the eighteenth century woman discovered herself. In the salon she became person and personage. In the salon she found a world in which the feminine intelligence could marry the masculine one and produce another intelligence.

From the other side of Europe, on the border where the western mind did battle with the eastern one, a woman looked upon the Paris salon with envy. She could not take Russia to Paris, but she could bring portions of Paris to Russia and with these grafts and stones build something to be admired.

Peter I, worn out with exertions and violences, was dead, leaving behind in his new capital on the Neva a little island of European forms surrounded by a dark Asiatic sea. Intrigues had brought to the throne his second daughter, Elizabeth Petrovna. She was her father's own child—tall, lustful, czar-like, with a figure like a man's—one of the trio of European feminine meddlers whom Frederick the Great called "the three whores." Repeated and wide-rang-

167

ing amours having produced no issue, she saw that the throne would descend to her nephew, the Grand Duke Peter, a half wit. To check Peter's furtive pursuit of waiting-maids and to keep him watched and amused, she married him in 1745 to Sophia Augusta, a healthy German girl, daughter of the Prince of Anhalt Zerbst, a Prussian Lutheran.

At the ceremony Sophia's name was changed to Catherine Alexienna.

Elizabeth frequently had the young couple locked in their bedroom while she went off to amuse herself; she was fond of balls and drinking parties at the military barracks. While Catherine lay ill, as she often did of feminine complaints, Peter amused himself with his dogs—he kept a kennel hidden in an alcove behind the bed,—with his puppets and military dolls, and occasionally went off to drill and to bawl at live soldiers. Catherine passed the hours reading Pierre Bayle's dictionary. She had found the fourth volume tossed away in the palace and she unearthed others which she read in a quiet absorption, while outside her door intrigues crept up and down the stairs, petty despotisms kept watch from corners, and lunacies roamed through the corridors.

## II

What wonder that Pierre Bayle is called the intellectual father of the eighteenth century? His books, composed in his solitary Dutch attic, took to themselves feet and through Europe walked into the libraries of kings, the boudoirs of princesses, and the garrets of philosophers and scribes. His ideas insinuated themselves into the cracks of minds that had been long indurated, while his clarity and roguishness delighted the young. Superstition he undermined with ironic wit. Ignorance he heaped with contempt. He made the young intellectuals of Europe skeptical, tolerant, hospitable to letters, and avid for learning. His conquest of Catherine was as complete as that of Frederick the Great. She spent two years reading his dictionary and got through a volume every six months. She prided herself on her intellect, and fancied that it looked well in a tailored coat of masculine cut.

"I was a *true gentleman*," she said in her memoirs, "one whose cast of mind was more male than female; and yet I was anything but masculine, for joined to the mind and character of a man, I possessed the charms of a very agreeable woman.'"

It pleased her to think that in this hermaphroditic composition the predominant element was male.

"I don't know whether it is custom or inclination," she wrote, "but somehow I can never carry on conversation except with men."

And one day when Diderot, fetched from France, was arguing with her in her palace and used an expression he feared might not be suitable for an empress's ears, she waved the consideration aside.

"*Allons*," she said, "*entre hommes tout est permis*"—"between men everything is allowed."

Starting with Pierre Bayle she made further excursions into French literature and philosophy. She read Montaigne, Scarron, Rabelais, Molière, and Corneille. Montesquieu's *Spirit of the Laws* she called the breviary of kings. When she came to power she sent presents to Voltaire and corresponded eagerly with him and Mme. Geoffrin. In the hope of establishing a circle of wit and learning revolving about herself as center, she tried to induce d'Alembert of Paris and Beccaria of Florence to move to St. Petersburg. But neither came. With Diderot she was successful. When he had placed his Paris library on sale, she had ordered it to be bought in her name, and then directed him to keep it as her librarian, with a subsidy to live on.

Diderot came to her in 1773 and remained for five months. On certain afternoons he conversed with her from three to five. "I listened more than I talked," she said. Discoursing vehemently, he would gradually draw his chair up to her knees. In his excitement he would pound them until they were blue, compelling her to place before her a table on which he could vent his punctuation. He lectured her on political and economic reforms, urging changes, improvements, until her head ached and her cannier instincts rebelled.

"Monsieur Diderot," she said to him at length, "you work only on paper, which endures all things; it opposes no obstacle either to your imagination or to your pen. But I, poor empress as I am, work on the human skin, which is irritable and ticklish to a very different degree."

Therefore politics was dropped, and the conversation concerned itself only with letters.[1]

[1] In a plan for a Government University in Russia, which he drew up at Catherine's request, Diderot recommended courses in which practical or technological instruction would have first place, while languages and literature would come last. The plan failed to interest Catherine.

## III

Catherine came to power in 1762, just after the Empress Elizabeth's death. Perceiving that her childish husband, who had become Peter III, had offended the army and nobles by his pro-German leanings and the clergy by feebly enforced reforms, she resolved to carry out a determination that had been in her mind all through the infinity of boredom and indignities she had suffered under him as grand duke and under Elizabeth as empress: it was a determination to survive it all, to beat it all down, and eventually to become mistress of Russia. She knew that she was abler, better read, better educated, and more stable in mind, nerves, and temperament than any of those persons around her.

Her lover of the period, Gregory Orloff, having assured her that the army commanders would support her, she, one July night, drew on military boots, cut down to an attractive feminine size; mounted a white horse; put an oak leaf in her hat; and at the head of 15,000 men proclaimed a palace revolution. Peter, rabbit-souled and hysterical, made no opposition and Catherine had him locked up and sent Alexis Orloff, brother of Gregory, to visit him. Peter failed to survive this visit. Catherine's subsequent proclamation announced that he had come to his end "by the means of a bloody accident in his hinder parts, commonly called piles" joined to "a most violent, griping cholick"; but cynical Europe whispered that the cholick was of a species named Orloff. The men of letters whom she had flattered and subsidized now came to her rescue and shielded her from public opinion with a protecting mantle of words.

"I am quite aware," said Voltaire, "that she is reproached with some bagatelles in the matter of her husband, but these are family affairs with which I cannot possibly think of meddling."

## IV

Though Catherine made so much of writers and philosophers, she gave them only half her respect. Her supreme hero was Louis XIV of France. To hear him criticized she could not bear, and even his minor sins she defended energetically. So she set about becoming La Grande Monarque of St. Petersburg. She established academies and colleges on a vast scale, but half the buildings were not completed, and the other half housed only a few pupils, rattling around like very small pills in a very large box. She imported teachers and artists from France; she encouraged noble families to import clothing and furniture from Paris; she set up a French theatre in her bleak capital and rounded up audiences for it with horse-patrols. She invented and bestowed honors and decorations without end. She imported the American commander, John Paul Jones, to reorganize and lead her navy. Her reward was that flattery from Voltaire which he knew how to lay upon sovereigns with a butter-paddle. He called her the Semiramis of the North and a star in the firmament surpassing Andromeda, Perseus, and Calliste.

"Louis XIV was less magnificent than your majesty," he wrote. "He rewarded merit in foreign countries, but other people pointed it out to him, whereas you, Madame, go in search of it and find it for yourself."

But all these cultural institutions were bestowed upon a nobility and gentry consisting chiefly of great landowners and the courtiers and merchants of cities. For the shaggy farmers of the countryside and the workingmen of the towns Catherine had nothing, scarcely even a thought. When the peasants revolted she was amazed and offended, and punished them with soldiers. Although she made her nobles so French that they were foreigners to their own people, and although in the pursuit of westernized culture she wrote stories, plays, histories, and even a treatise on Blackstone, her heart was not deep in these things any more than it was in her amorous exploits.

Amour, like culture, was for her only a pastime and diversion, and neither was permitted to interfere seriously with what had been her tenaciously held aim ever since she had been married to a ducal moron—to make herself supreme, like Louis XIV, over a supreme empire. Her notion of fostering the growth of this empire was to encourage the development of a strong trading and shipping class which should do for her *ménage,* as she called her empire and its government, what had been done for England under Queen Elizabeth and for France under Colbert. To this end she enthusiastically promoted the expansion of Russia westward through the partition of Poland and southward by an attempt to drive the Turks away from the Black Sea.

## V

Having been subordinated and suppressed for eighteen years, she reveled in doing what she pleased. "O Freedom," she wrote, "the soul of all things: without thee there is no life." But when the miners and other serfs of the land rebelled, she decided that freedom was too precious to be scattered around, and she wrote to Vyazemsky, who had quelled the revolt with cannon: "The Russian empire is so vast that any other form of government than that of an autocratic emperor would be detrimental, for every other form fulfills itself more slowly and embodies passions which dissipate its strength."

Again she wrote: "I love uncivilized countries," but when revolution wrecked the old regime in France, she drew back; this was an uncivilization not in the catalog of the quaint and picturesque, and she wrote around to her fellow monarchs: "I advise all powers to adopt the Greek faith in order to protect themselves from this criminal, anarchistic, devilish epidemic." She ordered all Russians living in infected France to come home, and those imported Frenchmen who wished to remain in Russia she compelled to swear oaths of adherence to the institution of royalty. She imprisoned editors and critics, stamped out the Freemasons as being too sympathetic to the ideas of liberalism, and when after the Revolution the powers began to sign treaties with a kingless France, she wrote: "To sign treaties with the murderers of kings is deliberately to encourage fresh murders."

In short, Catherine, like other amateur philosophers of

the eighteenth century, admired freedom as an abstraction and as an idea to be tossed like a silver balloon from hand to hand in salons and drawing rooms; but the moment it got out into the streets she resumed the armor of an empress and summoned her soldiers; she became the reincarnation of Peter I and caught up the lash.

And yet as she aged she was becoming, in person, more gentle and womanish. She threw herself down on the floor and played with children like a hoyden. Where her envoys expected diplomatic instructions she wrote them that her grandchild was the seventh wonder of the world. She quaked with terror when her former lover, Gregory Orloff, came around grumbling and sulking, and she tried to put him off with promises and presents. She purred when the one-eyed Potemkin, her latest lover but one, called her his little golden pheasant.

At the age of sixty-five she took a new lover, Platon Zuboff, forty years younger than herself, and though he had never been in a battle, she appointed him inspector-general of all the Russian armies and made this "little black boy," as she called him, an imperial pooh-bah with thirteen offices. She took huge and hairy young soldiers and made ogling and smirking fancy-men of them until they had learned all the airs and manners and flatteries of female prostitutes dependent on a man not only for bread but for position and luxury. Indeed, she introduced to Europe the gigolo or pleasure-man, proving that what are called masculine qualities and feminine characteristics are creations of code and circumstance. Until she was old, corpulent, and shapeless she tried to live a life founded on random sensation, only to have it make her its prey and victim. The mode of government she established had neither form nor solidity; it was a patchwork composed of whim joined to love of novelty. Her western ideas were imposed on Russia from above; they never penetrated below the surface and so were never built into an organic structure.

She was a typical eighteenth-century figure in her belief that discussion was creation, that there was something within institutions and systems that would gradually make them better, and that freedom, though always adorable, had for the present better be confined to those persons who knew how to behave in drawing rooms.

## CHAPTER THREE

## *BOUDOIR RULE*

### I

IT WAS Catherine's great merit that although she took so many lovers that a military squadron might have been formed of them, she permitted none of them to interfere with the operations of the State or the policies of government. With mistresses, however, her contemporary, Louis XV of France, had no such strength. The ladies of Louis's languid choice were tempted to snatch up the reins of government as often as his bored hands dropped them. The consequences were that while in Russia Catherine's selections aroused only shrugs and grins, Louis's loves created laughter edged with a corroding cynicism.

Louis XV began his line of mistresses with four sisters, taken in succession, all belonging to the house of Nesle. They were the Countess of Nailly; Mlle. de Nesle, who became the Marquise of Vintimille; the Duchess of Lauragnais; and the widow of Marquis de la Tournelle, to whom he gave the title of Duchess of Chateauroux.

Then came the reign of La Pompadour, who had been christened Jeanne Antoinette Poisson. She was the daughter of an equerry to the Duke of Orleans, and gossip said he had once been a butcher. She was surrendered to Louis with ill-grace by her husband, Le Normand d'Etoiles, a director of public works. He was a man of some pride and when he was introduced to strangers, as he sometimes was, as Monsieur Pompadour, he concealed his rage with difficulty.

Under Louis XV the selection of royal mistresses became a state matter. Louis XIV had chosen his own, but Louis XV showed no more interest or initiative in these matters than in any other, and the Pompadour became his mistress only as the result of a conspiracy that required huge exertions. Her mother was an energetic and ambitious woman. Perceiving that under a fixed aristocratic regime, a bourgeois woman could not aim directly at luxury and power but could attain them through only the most finished sexual arts, Mme. Poisson began from the first to groom her daughter to please men so as to be able to influence and rule them. When after years of humiliation and sacrifice she succeeded in placing her daughter in the hands of France's king, the social sensation was felt in the farthest corners of Europe. Never before had a middle-class woman won so public a success. Indeed, Pompadour's rise from the floor of society to Louis XV's bed was a triumph for the bourgeoisie no less momentous than that already won in commercial spheres, and it was seen that the merchant of sex could dream of reaching heights not second to the merchant of wool or gold.

Louis XV's example made sexual liaisons a fad. What had been begun as an effort to amuse and distract a man suffering from a pathological form of boredom became a fashion which the classes immediately below royalty hastened to copy. To hold up one's head in advanced society one had to have a mistress or lover. These unacknowledged unions brought on no end of inconvenience. The letters left behind by the pitiful Julie de Lespinasse, who had the misfortune to be living with one man while she was in love with another, and before she had rid herself of a third lover who was dying, reveal the very frenzies of torture. The effort to idealize and to build a permanency upon what subsequently proved to be only a momentary attraction was destructive to the more sensitive souls, while those less sensitive were compelled to become completely callous in order to escape wreckage.

## II

As soon as the slender blonde Jeanne Poisson had been installed as the royal mistress with the title of the Marquise de Pompadour, she began to exercise an executive ability that was greatly superior to the king's. She was practical where Louis was languorous, ambitious where he was indifferent, and he was perfectly willing that she wield a power for which he had no talents. There is no proof for the eighteenth-century belief that she was a born meddler; she took the power because it gravitated upon her. Cardinal Fleury, long the king's chief agent, was dead, and since there were no strong male hands to pick up the reins, they fell into feminine ones.

And so Jeanne Poisson, the butcher's daughter, became the director of government. She made decisions and appointments, shaped policies, and gave orders in the king's name. She did no more damage than a male favorite might have done. She made mistakes, but she was also responsible for positive achievements. She had an instinctive sympathy with the Philosophes and Encyclopedists, and it was to her that the middle-class men of literature, science, and philosophy resorted when they wished favors and protection. She encouraged the arts, in which her taste and sense of design were distinctly superior to the somewhat stodgy standards of Louis XIV; and her delight in "objects of art" produced a flood of trinkets in enamelled ware, gold, silver, leather, wood, and textiles for which France has been famous ever since.

She founded the manufacture of Sevres china and her interest in such things produced visible improvement in architecture and furniture-designing, especially after she had obtained the appointment of her brother, the Marquise de Maneguiz, as director-general of buildings, gardens, arts, and manufactures. Not only was the external but the internal designing of buildings improved; and comforts such as pipe-heating were installed that banished the afflicting chill, ghastly draughts, and repellent odors common in Louis XIV's palaces. She kept the king amused and interested and she did nothing to mar the dignity of Marie Lescynska, the Polish princess who was Louis's pious wife.

But the Pompadour was extravagant. Having been used to the economies of a bourgeois household, when she suddenly found the treasures of royalty open to her, she lost her head. It must be said that the evidence is that she spent no great sum on any one enterprise and that most of her extravagances, such as buildings, fêtes, routs, and other diversions intended to keep the king interested, were relatively harmless; but such conspicuous consumption made the taxpayers, already burdened by the debts accumulated in Louis XIV's time, murmur that if Louis XV was to continue to be the Well Beloved they should not be called on to pay the cost of the affections bestowed upon him. They muttered the more throatily because the regime was doing nothing to foster that commerce which they contended was the spring of all revenue. Even in the face of criticisms, the Pompadour failed to abate her whimsical expenditures; that is, they appeared whimsical to the sullen taxpayer, although they were logical enough when it is considered that it was the Pompadour's assigned task, at all cost, to keep the king occupied and diverted.

Having prepared an effective information service, she was aware that, despite the pessimism of the merchandising classes, a new wealth was steadily rising throughout the kingdom, and that since Louis XIV had established the doctrine that all wealth belonged to the king, she no doubt believed she was justified in dipping into it deeply.

This new wealth had several sources. In part it was due to the few years of peace that followed the treaty of Aix-la-Chapelle, which gave the country an opportunity to resume its labors undistracted by military drainings; and in part to the construction of a new road system that made possible improved communications and exchange of products between province and province. Roads were built under the administration of Philibert Orry, controller of finance, who pleased the commercial classes by abolishing some of the worst imposts and spurring up the provincial intendants to pay closer attention to their duties. Orry, despite his beneficial labors, failed to please Mme. Pompadour. He was stingy with the State's money; he wanted to spend certain funds on roads when she wanted grants for entertainments; besides, his manners were gruff. When at length he was accused of taking bribes and failed to defend himself, Mme. Pompadour seized her opportunity and procured his dismissal. It broke Orry; he crept off and died within two years.

Orry was succeeded by Machault d'Arnouville, who strove to establish some kind of regularity and uniformity in a chaotic taxation system,[1] but he too fell out of Mme. Pompadour's favor and died in the prison to which she had him consigned.

The middle classes would have been willing to ignore the king's lack of interest in governing, the defeats of his armies in battle, and the whims and extravagances of his mistresses; even the Pompadour had her defenders due to her interest in the philosophers, her resistance to the clergy, especially the Jesuits, and her occasional bursts of lavish giving to the poor; but they could not forgive Louis XV for his failure to take the shackles off commerce and for his maintenance of a complicated and wasteful system of taxes, imposts, tithes, and rates. His weak egotism lost for Louis the respect of the bourgeois classes, but it was his tax system that brought upon him their hatred. His courtiers criticized him for having chosen a mistress from the lower

---

[1] In 1745 the ordinary revenues were lower than the expenses by about 100 millions: Lavisse, *Histoire de France*. III, p. 230.

middle class, and the politicians and military men condemned him for deterioration in the army and decay in the navy. And this deterioration, this decay, were occurring at the very time when it was recognized that France must soon fight England for the possession of world-colonies and world-markets.

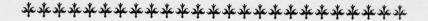

## CHAPTER FOUR

# WORLD EXPLOSION

### I

Six years after the middle of the century Europe exploded into the Seven Years' War. It was the first world war. It was waged in both the new and the old worlds, and it made navies for the first time more important than armies. It began as a coalition that included Austria, France, Russia, Sweden, and Saxony against Prussia in the hope of destroying the rapidly expanding power of Frederick the Great. Europe had been watching him and had become frightened.

The chief inciter was Maria Theresa of Austria, who believed it to be her mission to maintain Austria as the head of the Teutonic system which once had been called the Holy Roman Empire. Maria was the mother of five sons and eleven daughters. When not enduring pregancies and suckling babies,[1] she was sending out her ministers to obtain allies in her indefatigable determination to win back Silesia, which Frederick had cynically taken from her in the War of the Austrian Succession. Maria's efforts won

---

[1] "All my realms were the field of battle," she once wrote, "and I knew not where I could be brought to bed in peace."

much sympathy, also generous subsidies. She was at one time on the payroll both of England and of France, the governments of which were willing to help maintain her court and her armies as long as she could hold Frederick in check.

Maria did indeed succeed for a time in fending off the furious German plunges; for the common people of Austria had become accustomed to supporting her in her struggles with the nobles and landed aristocracy; they found her yoke just a trifle lighter than the feudal burdens which were preventing them, like the other middle and lower classes of Europe, from striking out for freedom of trade and of knowledge.

When England, however, went over to the side of Frederick, matters took a new turn and soon it became apparent that the war was resolving itself into a struggle between France and England for supremacy on the sea and control of the world colonies and markets.

The English determination to get rid of France as chief competitor was solidified by the elder William Pitt. On him was bestowed the significant title of The Great Commoner. Pitt was the first of the politicians of the Old World to lay down a policy of avowed imperialism on a grand scale. He had both the money and the power with which to carry out his program. Having been given £10,000 by the will of Sarah, the Duchess of Marlborough, he had entered politics as a young man. Soon he found himself carrying out the work begun by Robert Walpole.

Walpole had made himself political leader of a merchant state which aimed at peace and prosperity at any price. He maintained a government permeated by bribery and corruption, which were merely indications that one class was trying to buy power over the heads of another. Walpole, as a Whig, kept the merchants, shippers, and bankers satisfied by his aggressive efforts in behalf of British trade and kept the masses quiet under the rule of a squirearchy and landed gentry.

Much of the common lands, long set aside for the grazing and wood-cutting of the peasants, had already been taken over under enclosure acts by private hands. Smallholders and yeomen, no longer able to get a living from the soil, were driven into the towns. The ensuing overcrowding fostered the growth of slums, and with the slum came its brother, crime. The larger capital invested in land made possible the use of improved tools, and steel plows and harrows began to replace the wooden implements of feudal times.[2] These steel-shod tools were forged in small furnaces fed by charcoal. The charcoal was obtained by cutting down the forests. The ensuing scarcity of lumber and of naval stores forced England to depend more than ever upon her American colonies for timber and for the tar, pitch, and turpentine necessary to her enlarged shipbuilding program. William Pitt, who as a commoner was responsive to the needs of merchant and shipbuilder, saw the necessity not only of keeping present colonies but of obtaining new ones. Hence his policy of destroying France's power both in the new and old worlds, in America, India, and at sea.

[2]A seed drill was developed in England by William Tull as early as 1721, while almost simultaneously in France Réaumur was discovering new processes that revolutionized metallurgy.

## II

In 1745 England had dealt France a double blow by taking Louisburg, which commanded the vast fishing grounds off Nova Scotia, and by smashing Bonnie Prince Charlie, financed by French money, at Culloden.

These blows were merely preliminary, however, to those she rained upon France in America when the Seven Years' War opened in 1756. The French, led by Governor-General Montcalm in Canada, had begun to build southward a line of forts—Ticonderoga, Niagara, and Duquesne, intending to keep their communications open with the Mississippi country and to pen up the English on the narrow strip of land along the Atlantic seaboard. They feared the English hunger for land, the English aggressiveness in trading. Momentarily they won successes. They won at Duquesne when the English were led by the young George Washington and again when led by the older Braddock.

And then the English fleets began to intercept French ships. It was the prelude to an inevitable end; Louis XV and his ministers, fascinated like Louis XIV with grandiose exploits on land, had failed to perceive that the world had become a commercial one and that the greatest prizes would go no longer to land-power but to sea-power. The French navy of war and merchant vessels received small attention from a careless court; the great ports built by Vauban were neglected; the officers, drawn from the aristocratic class, fancied intrigue more than efficiency.

The French in Canada, moreover, were far from united. Montcalm could not agree with de Vaudreuil, the viceroy.

Their quarrel, when taken to Louis XV, was settled to the satisfaction of neither. Montcalm, realizing that nothing further could be expected from Versailles, made his dispositions and prepared to die.

Louisburg was again taken, this time by General Jeffrey Amherst, who had been recalled from the German front. Amherst was to march on Ticonderoga and afterward join forces with General Prideaux and assist General James Wolfe against Quebec. They failed to effect the junction and Wolfe, one of the youngest and most aggressive of the new Pitt-named commanders, was left to attack Quebec alone. In his battle with the French on the heights of Abraham, Wolfe was killed and Montcalm was mortally wounded. The French, abandoned by Louis XV, became discouraged and in 1757 the viceroy surrendered to Amherst at Montreal.

In 1761 France, frightened by her inability to halt England, induced Bourbon-ruled Spain to join her. The only consequence was new colonial booty for Pitt's imperial bag. The English added new conquests year after year, including Havana and Manila. By 1763 France had no ships able to take the sea, and thus prevented from supplying her armies, she joined Spain in signing a humiliating peace.

England's booty in colonies, markets, ports and islands was enormous. France's surrender of her Canadian and Indian possessions made Great Britain the strongest imperial power, established her as first among merchant states, and left her in control of the world's sea-lanes.

## III

On the Continent Prussia did scarcely less well for itself. With its little population of 5,000,000 under Frederick II, it stood off and at length prevailed over a coalition of nations numbering a hundred million. Frederick's victories at Prague, Rossbach, Leuthen, Zorndorf, and Torgau, some of them won upon the forlornest of hopes and with but a handful of money and men, showed European onlookers that Frederick could lead armies as well as write French verses and play the flute. It was the Seven Years' War that introduced upon the Continent an armed and united Germany to replace a weakened Austria as the spearhead of a new Teutonic empire. If this had been made possible only through English subsidies to Frederick, it served to show that the payrolls for kings and captains had been moved from Versailles to London. England was now the timekeeper and paymaster of Europe.

For Prussia's rise while France decayed there were easily perceived reasons. Louis XV ignored trade and despised the trader; royal taxes and restrictions everywhere interfered with commerce. But Frederick II was sagacious enough to see that his little country, to survive the jostling of stronger neighbors, must be converted from a mediæval principality into a modern merchant state.

To this end he put into effect, as completely as Prussia's position allowed, the system laid down by Colbert under Louis XIV. Foremost in his program was the fostering of agricultural production. The only genuine wealth, he said, was "whatever the earth produced." Therefore he viewed farming as "the foremost of the arts, without which there would exist no merchants, no kings, no poets, no philosophers."

But meantime he gave chief attention to the promotion of trade and manufactures. He had surveys made to show the population of his cities, what goods they produced and needed, and what factories they could support.

"It is not sufficient to know the cities," he said, "but one must also care for them."

As fast as possible he set up industries subsidized and controlled by the State. He especially encouraged the fabrication of wool, linen, and silk. He also established porcelain, metal, leather, and other industries making objects of luxury. It is easy to see here that he had his eye on France and England and was resolved not only to be independent of them but to compete with them.

Commerce and industry — without these, he said, it was not possible to support an army, and without an army it was impossible to hew out a place for Prussia among the competing European powers. And so the State organized everything, regulated everything, interfered in everything, imposing on Frederick as the State's first servant multitudinous duties that sometimes burdened his energetic frame.

"You write to me of wax candles," he once wrote plaintively to a friend, "and here people talk to me about herrings. Indeed I might become a merchant toward the end of my life. I consider the whole matter, *mon cher*. I regulate the mintage and other things of greater importance for the State; bread and meat belong thereto, yet herrings,

FREDERICK THE GREAT AS WARRIOR

*A portrait painted in the Prussian king's youth by Antoine Pesne and hung in the castle at Potsdam*

FREDERICK THE GREAT IN HIS OLD AGE

*An engraving by Daniel Chodowiecki showing the monarch surrounded by his generals and by the male atmosphere that he then affected*

boots, and wax candles will be arranged separately after the main matter will be settled. Adieu, *mon cher,* I have counted all day long; I am tired."

At moments he nursed dreams of hurling all his burdens aside and retiring to a secluded place where he might at leisure read French literature (when he had built his play-house in the woods he gave it the French name of Sans Souci—"without care"), write verses (with him unusually bad), and argue with imported philosophers like Maupertuis, d'Alembert, and Voltaire. Yet even of French philosophers he tired; after bringing Voltaire to Berlin he quarrelled with him and subsequently treated him more as if he had been a mistress than a master. Once when a courtier spoke to Frederick of a beautiful day, he said there was but one beautiful day—that on which one dies. But such gloomy fits seldom enclosed him long, and in his occasional threats to "get away from it all," he was posing a little; for he had tasted power, and persons having that are like Benjamin Franklin's office-holders—few die and none resign.

Frederick consolidated his power by conciliating all parties and dispensing favors to all classes. He pleased the peasantry by relieving them of the most oppressive feudal burdens and tolls; he mollified the nobility by reserving for them the high offices and commands; he delighted all classes by making taxes low and uniform; but his most conspicuous achievement was his creation of a middle class—a thing not before seen in the mediævally inclined German States. By removing restrictions on commerce, and by

State aid to the merchants and manufacturers, he cemented his kingdom upon a base of solid burghers, who in the face of all criticism of his erratic and sometimes unjustifiable acts were ever ready to give him a *Lebe hoch*.

## IV

Frederick did more for his burghers than to free for them the channels of buying and selling that had been choked by feudal obstructions. Calling himself an "attorney for the poor," he reformed the Prussian legal system by simplifying and then codifying it so as to rid it of "confusing Roman laws" in favor of "German laws based on natural reason and the country's constitution." In this he agreed with Montesquieu's dictum that legislation should be in accord with the character of the people.

His reform of taxation was one of Frederick's hugest efforts. His gospel was: "Taxes must neither apply to the laborer, nor to the soldier, nor to the poor, but only to the wealthy and rich." Unfortunately Frederick's love for everything French induced him to install the French system of tax collection. This was done in accordance with information given him by Helvétius, the Paris philosophe and farmer-general, who once visited Potsdam and spent several weeks conversing with Frederick on financial topics. But in Prussia the French method of laying and collecting duties and excises never gave satisfaction, and among Frederick's experiments it was one of his worst failures.

The army he reformed by requiring of it a mobility and aggressiveness new in Europe, but he had no patience with military snobbery or pedantry. When a general praised a young hussar officer to him as a genuine patrician, Frederick wrote him:

So much I would like to tell you that his father was not a nobleman but a forester, and also a paramour of the old duchess of Mecklenburg-Strelitz, so you may know his whole generation.

As for the private soldier, Frederick's opinion was that which the world later called typically Prussian: "He must fear his officers more than the dangers to which one exposes him."

Finally, Frederick filled Prussia with schools. He made the schoolmaster second only in importance to the army officer and merchandizing burgher.

## V

"Man's plan it is," Frederick once wrote d'Alembert, "to aid his neighbors in every respect; that is the nucleus of all morals."

Yet all these reforms, all these labors, for his subjects, failed to make him beloved. His people learned to have a fondness for him; they called him, in his mastiff-like old age, old *Fritz;* but they could not love him. They were not permitted to.

Frederick was never able to overcome a habitual mistrust toward the human race; and the human race replied with a like mistrust toward him. It is a penalty that accompanies the rationalizing intellect, which surrounds itself with sentinels and outposts. It cannot lower its guard; it permits nothing to approach without an examination of baggage for concealed motives; and so its abode is cold and often lonely.

Frederick was particularly apt to ruffle the bristles on his back in the presence of women. His two exceptions were his mother and his sister Sophia of Bayreuth. What his prejudices were due to, we do not know. There is evidence that in his youth he did not object to occasional routs, and, in a period when it was as fashionable to have mistresses as a three-cornered hat, he had his share. And then he closed that book and established a cult of maleness. He preached an austere life for his soldiers, growled at their marryings, and when in the field permitted his officers to eat on nothing grander than tin. Occasionally, however, he sighed over the consequences of a self-imposed aloofness and of his incurable misanthropy.

"I dine alone," he once wrote. "I spend my life in reading and writing, and I do not sup. When one is sad, it becomes at last too burdensome to hide one's grief continually. . . . Nothing solaces me but the vigorous application required in steady and continuous labor."

Since he expected to discover something base in every human being, it is not surprising that he often found it. He found it even in his adored Voltaire.

## VI

"Realized Voltairism," wrote Carlyle. "Is that not pretty much the net historical product of the eighteenth century?

"Voltaire was the spiritual complement of Frederick. What little of lasting their poor century produced lies mainly in these two. A very somnambulating century. But what little it *did,* we must call Frederick, but what little it *thought,* Voltaire."

## VII

The mid-century found Voltaire living in retirement at Cirey with the Marquise du Châtelet, the translator of Newton, as companion. There are people who can do one thing supremely well, but they fancy their real forte lies elsewhere. It was so with Voltaire. As a writer he was Europe's most eminent figure. But he fancied that his real talents lay in diplomacy, with a little speculative gambling as a branch activity. Backed by Mme. Pompadour he tried his hand at court intrigue, but succeeded only in offending Louis XV, and at once found it desirable to take himself out of the way.

With his Emilie at Cirey he was comfortable. They used to receive visitors in a stately fashion; she sitting under the piled head-dress of the period, ornamented and jewelled, with black face-patches near her large red mouth, as if to offset her reputation for intellectual interests with extra femininity in appearance; he standing thin-legged with high red-reeled shoes on his feet after the manner of Louis XIV, a laced hat under his arm, and a satin court-coat on —for he was by now a rich man and could not resist showing it.

In accordance with the social requirements of the period, the Marquise, although having one man as a husband, and another as domestic companion, had taken a third as lover. It was all an arrangement to which no one could object.

Unfortunately nature disliked it and intervened; the Marquise, although no longer young, one day found herself with child. Voltaire, although not the author of this new drama, accepted the situation and nursed her faithfully. He wrote to Frederick, who had beset him with invitations to come to Potsdam, that he must delay his visit.

"Madame du Châtelet," he said, "is not yet delivered; it gives her more trouble to produce a child than a book."

Frederick could be blunt about such matters. He replied:

"Since Madame du Châtelet writes books, I do not think she will produce her child in a moment of distraction. Tell her to hurry, for I wish to see you."

The Marquise did not survive the birth of her child. Voltaire, smiling valiantly, departed for Frederick's court.

## VIII

The idealized friendship that had thriven upon correspondence could not survive the intimacy of daily contact. After close examination German and Frenchman daily learned to like each other a little less. Frederick had at a distance been enchanted with the Voltaire-mind; it had everything that he himself lacked — the gaiety that "made his spirit laugh," lightness, luminosity, precision of expression. But Frederick found he could not admire the Voltaire-person; it seemed to him vacillating, hypochondriac, prone to duplicity and intrigue, and permeated with a simian malice. As a practical man who had won his way to a certain integration, he could not avoid slightly despising this Proteus from France who was all ideals and no action.

On the other hand, Voltaire was disillusioned to find in Frederick a man who had stripped himself of ideals and who was anchored to no central belief in anything. Voltaire was a libertarian and a liberal, believed in progress, had faith in the ability of men to improve themselves, and was willing to fight for his ideals. He was disappointed to find that Frederick was at all times willing to fight for an abstraction called a Nation but not so often for an abstraction called Justice. He resented his host's occasional tendencies to be more monarch than man. Once when at a dinner party he observed Frederick stiffen at a bit of levity, he called out:

"Attention, gentlemen, the King of Prussia has come in."

At length Frederick discovered that Voltaire was carrying on a little secret diplomacy and was speculating in Saxon notes. There was a row, Voltaire fled, and Frederick had him arrested at Frankfort. Voltaire wrote him beseechingly and Frederick replied:

I was glad to receive you in my house; I esteemed your wit, your talents, your knowledge, and I thought a man of your age weary of skirmishing with authors and of exposing himself to disturbances, came here to take refuge in a quiet port. . . . You went to the Russian ambassador and talked of matters which did not concern you. . . . You interfered in Madame de Bentinck's affairs. . . . Now you have the basest affair imaginable with a Jew. . . . I maintained order in my household until your arrival. . . .

There was a long break in the correspondence, but eventually it was resumed, for Frederick was lonely and Voltaire was secretly proud of his connection with the Prussian court. They exchanged letters regularly until both were old men.

It was Frederick who survived. He no longer had any close companions except two dogs, who slept with him. Every day he wore his old blue campaign coat with red facings. He spilled snuff on it and ate with dirty fingernails. He became at last as shrivelled as the Frenchman he so long admired. When his body was put in its grave it was as light as a little child's.

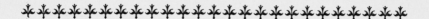

## CHAPTER FIVE

## *LACKEY'S BLOW*

### I

A WAR lasting as long as seven years cannot fail somewhere to cause dislocations, and the social body of France emerged from this struggle with England, and with Frederick the Great, not only emaciated but made anemic through the prolonged piping of blood and money into the veins of an aging Austria. Argenson, Louis XV's minister, looked upon it all with foreboding.

*"Cela pourrait,"* he wrote in his dairy, *"aller à la revolution*—"That could lead to revolution."[1]

It was probably the first appearance of that formidable word on any paper written by a minister. Argenson had reason to be gloomy. In the winter of 1757, the second year of the Seven Years' War, famine (Louis XV and a circle of speculators had cornered the grain crop and were selling it at high prices), joined to weeks of harsh weather, had caused so much sullenness that the king no longer dared to visit Paris.

In the town of Arras, north of Paris, there lived at this time a lackey named Damiens. He was twenty-two years

---

[1]Michelet, *Histoire de France*, XVI, 540.

old and was so dark of visage and black of hair that he was often taken for a Spaniard. His hawklike head, set upon a long, thin body, and his deep-set eyes were features so conspicuous as to attract notice. His father had belonged to a family of good farmers living near Arras, had tried several occupations, only to become at last a prison porter. The father so often beat his son, who was one of ten children, that the lad was taken in charge out of pity by an uncle, who tried to make him first a hairdresser, and then a locksmith. The boy Damiens, however, seemed unable to endure any systematic instruction and finally chose to become the servant of an army officer. He changed jobs often, learned to read and write a little, and often quit his employment without collecting the full wages due him. He had none of the usual lackey vices, of which drinking was chief, but when he did take a little wine he often became disputatious. For a time he was a servant at a Jesuit college. Here the fathers tried to induce him to abstain from wine, but Damiens walked out rather than give up his right to have it when he chose.

He then served as a domestic in the homes of several members of the Paris parliament, which for years had been struggling with the court and the nobility. One of Damiens's employers was Beze de Lys, who was a Jansenist-opponent of the high churchmen and also a caustic critic of royalty. Beze was at length sent to a State prison, and after that Damiens often joined the corner and café circles that read the *Gazette de France* aloud and listened to accounts of the efforts of the *parlementaires,* as representatives of mercantile and professional groups, to uphold the interest of the middle class against reactionary kings, clergy-men, and nobles. His love of argument carried Damiens more and more to the side of the *parlementaires,* and his usual austere self-control sometimes gave way to passionate declamations against despotisms.

His next employment was in the house of La Bour-donnaie, ex-governor of French-India and at one time the associate and then the rival of Dupleix. La Bourdonnaie, no less than Dupleix, had been maltreated by his government, which imprisoned him in the Bastille. His chagrin broke his spirit and he died.

Damiens, once more unemployed, made a living by vending petty wares about the streets. He married a woman much older than himself, a cook, and by her had a child, but the marriage was not happy, and although Damiens sent money with some regularity to her for the benefit of the child, he was oftener in the company of a chambermaid whom he had met in service.

Failing as a street vender, Damiens again hired himself out as a lackey. It was in the house of a *dame a la mode,* who while her husband was busy at his job in Versailles, received his chief in her Paris boudoir. This man was a great laugher, and was fond of intimate suppers. Damiens recognized him as Marigny, brother of the Pompadour, the king's mistress. Damiens became sullen and at length so aloof and morose that Henriette, his mistress's maid, took a dislike to him. She amused herself among the other servants by reading their palms and pretending to make prophecies. One day she seized his hand, looked in it, and pushed it away.

"You will be hanged," she said. "I can read it in your hand."

Soon afterward Damiens left this house and in departing turned and threw stones at it. Again jobless, he thought of going to Arras and then of going farther, to some unknown place.

He got a job with a Russian named Michel, a merchant from Peter the Great's capital on the Neva. This man kept his money in a pocketbook, not locked but merely tied with ribbons. Damiens opened it one day and found in it 12,000 gold francs. From this he took 130 louis and bought himself a coat, also a hundred measures of wool which he took to his brother, a weaver.

This brother, learning that the money had been taken without authorization, refused to accept the wool and told his people, who heaped Damiens with reproaches and advised him to escape to Flanders. Damiens went away and tried to kill himself. He opened his veins, he took arsenic, he tried to drown himself, vainly. He went to Flanders, but at once returned to Paris, where he visited his brother, a servant, who received him coldly. To this brother and his wife he said, "I am going to speak to the king."

Walking out into the cold streets, he wandered about. In the rue de Condé he met a painted girl, a daughter of the pavements, and went to her room with her. He sat there, scarcely moving or speaking, until one o'clock in the morning. He left her abruptly and returned to the streets where he hired a public carriage, ordering the driver to take him to Versailles. He reached Versailles at three o'clock in the morning. He paid the driver well and then treated him to two warming drinks, saying to him:

"I am going to the islands . . . to the islands — far off. I will be there in twenty-four hours."

To the woman who fetched the drinks he said he was unwell and asked that she send for a surgeon who would bleed him. She said, "Nice time of day to be bled," and laughed it off.

Listening to the conversation around him, Damiens heard it said that the king was at the Trianon palace. Walking out into a deserted park he met there a wanderer like himself. This man said he was an inventor and had a machine that he wanted to show to the king. The inventor, eager to talk, gave Damiens some of the gossip of Versailles, mentioning among other things that Mme. Pompadour was ill with a cold and that Louis XV would visit her that afternoon at five o'clock.

Just before that hour Damiens, wearing a pair of red breeches and keeping his hat on, appeared before the door of the Trianon. He talked with the guards there and with the postillions of the king's carriage. They, taking him to be a simple person, were being amused by his meaningless remarks when Louis XV suddenly came out, leaning on the arm of the Master of Horse.

Everybody sprang to attention and several persons clustered around the king to make the usual ceremony out of the simple act of entering a carriage. The king was about to step into the vehicle when he turned and exclaimed in a voice indicating surprise rather than fear:

"Somebody has jostled me. That drunkard there struck me with his fist."

Damiens did not move. No one had seen him use his knife, which he had closed and replaced in his pocket. A guard exclaimed, "Who is this man that keeps his hat on in the king's presence?" And he struck Damiens's hat off. Then the king said:

"Is there a pin sticking me?"

He put his hand under his cloak, withdrew it, and stared at it. It was wet with blood.

With a motion toward Damiens, who still had not moved, the king said:

"It was this monsieur."

The guards sprang upon Damiens, hurled him against a pillar, threw him down, and tied him. They took him to their headquarters, took off all his clothes, and dragged him naked before their captain, Ayen, for questioning. Damiens answered boldly:

"Yes, I did it. I did it for God and the people—for religion."

"What do you mean by that?" said Ayen.

"I mean that the people perish. Isn't it true, monsieur, that France is perishing?"

"What is the principle of your religion?" said Ayen.

"My principle," said Damiens, "is the misery that is spread over three-quarters of the kingdom."

Soldiers had searched Damiens's clothes and now brought in the contents—the penknife with which he had struck the king, a pair of small scissors, and twenty-five coins. Seeing the money, a guard said:

*From a photograph in the Otto Bettmann Collection*

PORCELAIN STATUETTE CARICATURING THE MOUNTAINOUS HAIRDRESSING FAVORED
IN FRANCE, ENGLAND, AND GERMANY DURING THE MIDDLE PERIOD OF THE CENTURY

*From a photograph in the Otto Bettmann Collection*

A ROYAL BED IN THE ROCOCO MANNER FAVORED BY LOUIS XV

"Wretch, you got that for striking the blow!"

"I will answer that before my judges," said Damiens.

He told Ayen that he had not wished to kill the king; if he had, he could have done so easily. And he pointed out that in a sleeve of his coat he had carried two more knives, but he had used the penknife only.

"Well, then," said the captain, "since you preserve such fine sentiments, tell us who your accomplices were. The king might pardon you."

"He cannot, and he should not," said Damiens. "I want to die in pain and torment like Jesus."

Word then came from the king's chamber that Louis XV wanted to know if the knife had been poisoned.

"No, on my soul!" said Damiens.

## II

About the king's couch there were hysterical scenes. Louis was certain he was going to die. "A priest, a priest," he cried. Women ran about, weeping. The queen alone was cool.

"Come, sire," she said. "Calm yourself."

The doctors came and examined the wound. It was very light. The indications for recovery were good, they affirmed; more they would not say, for there might be politics even in a king's wound. But among themselves they said:

"If he were not the king, he could be about his business tomorrow."

A priest was found; he was only a servants' chaplain,

but he confessed the king. On his heels came a Jesuit priest from Paris and he confessed the king again. Louis sent for the Dauphin and, looking very pale and weak, made him "lieutenant-general of the kingdom," and said to him: "Govern better than I did."

## III

Damiens now became the center of a political whirlpool around which circled Jesuit and Jansenist, aristocrat and *parlementaire*. Machault, keeper of the fountains, suspected that Damiens had been inspired by the Jesuits, and to make him confess, had the back of his legs burned with hot irons. Damiens remained defiant.

Efforts were made to wring from him the names of conspirators, employers, or accomplices, for the king's agents could not believe Damiens when he insisted he had acted alone. But the prisoner shouted there was none.

For four days Louis XV believed he was going to die. A priest sat by his side, absolving him every moment. Then a delegation of Bretons, coming from a province that had recently been in revolt, called at the palace. They brought a present of a lounging robe and cried aloud that the king could take their property, their very lives—only he must live.

Their message was taken to Louis. He felt better and sat up in bed. Believing himself once more the Well Beloved, he tossed aside all vague notions of reform. In a few days he arose, crossed himself, and resumed his calls at the house of Mme. Pompadour.

Damiens was tried and condemned. In a final effort to make him confess a conspiracy and to give the names of accomplices, he was put to torture. He was placed on a mediæval rack and stretched until he cried out, "Lord, have pity!" On his naked body were thrown burning oil and sulphur and melted lead until he screamed, "O God, more strength." But he would say nothing beyond, "No plot, no accomplices."[2] At last the order was given to saw his joints in two. His thighs were the first to fall. . . . He died at a quarter past six, March 28, 1757.

## IV

Even at a distance it had been perceived that affairs in France were drawing toward a crisis and the friends of that country felt forebodings. In England Philip Dormer Stanhope, Lord Chesterfield, referring, in the course of one of his celebrated letters to his son, to affairs in France wrote:

They grow serious, and, in my opinion, will grow more and more so every day. The king is despised, and I do not wonder at it; but he has brought it about to be hated at the same time, which seldom happens to the same man. His ministers are known to be as disunited as incapable; he has a taste between the church and the parliaments, like the ass in the fable, that starved between two hampers of hay; too much in love with his mistress to part with her, and too much afraid for his soul to enjoy her; jealous of the parliaments who would support his authority; and a devoted bigot to the church that would destroy it.

The people are poor, consequently discontented; those who have religion are divided in their notions of it; which is saying that they hate one another. The clergy never do forgive; much

[2]Michelet, *Histoire de France.*

less will they forgive the parliament; the parliament never will forgive them. . . . In short, all the symptoms which I have ever met with in history, previous to great changes in governments, now exist, and daily increase in France.[3]

In another letter Lord Chesterfield felt even more certain, and wrote:

This I foresee, that before the end of this century the trade of both king and priest will not be half as good a one as it has been.

[3]Letter 57, Bond, *Chesterfield, Letters and Other Pieces*, New York, 1935.

## CHAPTER SIX

# MERCANTILE MORALIST

### I

THE PERCEPTIONS, ideals, and career of Lord Chesterfield are worthy of attention; for as an Englishman whose tastes had been molded by French influences, he was an excellent representative of the middle period of the century. Chesterfield, on one of those Continental visits which were deemed necessary to the education of the sons of the English upper classes, had in Paris enjoyed a round of the salons and had sat in the company of such leaders of the Enlightenment as Voltaire, Fontenelle, and Montesquieu. An incident will indicate what he may have absorbed from them and from the spirit of the times. Noting the ancestor-worship and blood-pride around him, he once placed among the portraits of his own Stanhope ancestors two heads which he labelled *Adam* de Stanhope and *Eve* de Stanhope.[1]

A long career at court, in the army, and in politics enabled Chesterfield, when in his late fifties, to consolidate a certain philosophy of Get-Ahead which he outlined in

[1]Bond, *Chesterfield; Letters and Other Pieces.*

a series of advisory and admonitory letters to his natural son, whose mother was a French lady, Elizabeth du Bouchet. Although Chesterfield brought this lady home and took care of her, she never became his wife. He married Melusina de Schulemberg, Countess of Walsingham, who was the daughter of George I of England by one of those strong and useful mistresses whom the Hanoverian monarch had brought with him from Germany and to whom he had given the title of Duchess of Kendall.

In these letters, long and carefully composed, there is to be found a mirror of the period and an anatomy of its society. In them the piety of the seventeenth century and preceding ages has disappeared and has been replaced by the counsels of a studied system of reasoning proceeding from an intellect schooled by mercantile institutions.

"Every man's reason," his lordship advised, "must be his guide." And then he added: "And I may as well expect that every man should be of my size and complexion so that he should reason just as I do." Here were sounded two of the grace notes of the eighteenth century—reason and tolerance. Here is to be perceived, also, that undercurrent of critical and aloof common sense that shaped the eighteenth-century gentleman's views and conduct.

Dr. Johnson's strictures on the Chesterfieldian doctrines were severe. He said his lordship taught "the morals of a whore, and the manners of a dancing master." The doctor had his grounds. Chesterfield told his son that the chief end of man was to please and to be pleasing; that unless he knew how to be *aimable,* in the French sense, he was no better than a resounding ass, or the tinkling symbol of an inane society. One must please with the whole man. Even trifles were tremendous.

"I insist," he wrote the unfortunate Philip, "that you wash your teeth the first thing every morning with a soft sponge and warm water. . . . The ends of your nails should be small segments of circles."

The emphasis the father laid upon pleasing might have inculcated dissimulation and hypocrisy upon the son; but nature had already protected the latter against such low arts by giving him a thick integument and a head with no little fatty tissue. There is no evidence that he ever paid any attention to the laboriously wrought counsels of his father, to whom he was a disappointment which the parent concealed with his philosophy of *fortiter in re*.

Chesterfield tried diligently to impress upon his son, and godson as well, the necessity not only of observing "the infinite utility of pleasing" but of avoiding ridicule. "There is nothing in all the world," he wrote, "so carefully to be guarded against as ridicule." To this end he counselled a studied course of conduct designed to attract favorable attention and to promote advancement. In his series of injunctions he said many good things, derived from a sharp-eyed study of men and events, but his advice was based chiefly upon respect for the temporary and pompous conventions of society under George II and an almost religious devotion to the canons of conformity. His counsels enjoined probity, honesty, and fair-dealing, but were practically devoid of imagination or human warmth. He even warned his son against laughter. A smile was permissible, but not the spontaneous and inextinguishable laughter of the gods.

His most emphatic warning of all was against women, and it is in Chesterfield's remarks upon them that he drew a portrait of the society in which he lived. "Every man," he wrote, "is to be had one way or another, and every woman almost any way." And again: "Good night to you, whoever you pass it with."

"I never thought a woman," he wrote to Arthur C. Stanhope, "good company for a man tête-a-tête, unless for one purpose, which, I presume, is not yours now."

The best he could say about women was that their companionship was "lenitive," and that because their suffrages established a man's character in the world of fashion "it is necessary to please them"; "but a man of sense only trifles with them, plays with them, humours and flatters them, as he does with a sprightly, favored child"; however, "he neither consults them about, nor trusts them with, serious matters. . . . They have in truth but two passions, vanity and love."

For marriage Chesterfield had small praise. "The only solid and lasting peace," he told his son, "between a man and his wife is doubtless a separation."

Chesterfield's skepticism here may have been due to his own experience in marriage. Before it took place he told a friend that he looked for only two things in a wife, "money and merit," and apparently he got no great amount of either, for his bride was forty and after marriage maintained her own separate establishment. His views, however, about women in general were shaped by the prevalent male opinions of his nation and time, concerning which his sprightly and plain-spoken contemporary, Lady Mary Wortley Montagu, once wrote this complaint:

> There is no part of the world where our sex is treated with so much contempt as in England. I do not complain of men for having engrossed the government: in excluding us from all degrees of power, they preserve us from fatigues, many dangers, and perhaps many crimes. . . . But I think it is the highest injustice to be debarred the entertainment of my closet, and that the same studies which raise the character of a man should hurt that of a woman. We are educated in the grossest ignorance, and no art omitted to stifle our natural reason.

From Chesterfield's letters to his son can be drawn lines and colors sufficient to make a convincing portrait of the well-born young English male of the period's leisure class. This being was often an idler and gamester, a frequenter of taverns and a brawler, a collector of snuff-boxes, ornamented swords and other gauds, with a taste for coarse women and expensive pleasures. (His father flatly warned the son: "I will, by no means, pay for whores, and their never-failing consequences, surgeons.") The young blood of the mid-century was already acquiring that arrogance of manner, insularity of mind, and condescension toward foreigners which on the Continent was making his demeanor synonymous with boorishness, and which was probably the consequence of England's growing commercial supremacy, with accompanying sensations of overwhelming wealth and power.

Chesterfield himself, however, was a product of a reaction against the cynical mercantilism and public corruption of the century's first half, begun under Queen Anne and extended under the Georges. This reaction made him prefer personal integrity, sobriety, and even a certain moral stiffness to the loose codes favored by Queen Caroline, consort and ruler of George II, and by Robert Walpole, manurer and waterer of a new merchant-state. Of Walpole Chesterfield has left a sketch, which, as all biographies do, reveals the writer's traits as well as the subjects.

> Money, not prerogative [his lordship wrote], was the chief engine of his administration, and he employed it with a success which in a manner disgraced humanity.
> He laughed at and ridiculed all notions of public virtue.
> He would frequently ask young fellows, at their first appearance in the world, while their honest hearts were yet untainted, "Well, are you to be an old Roman? a patriot? You will soon come off of that, and grow wiser."
> He was the easy and profuse dupe of women, and in some instances indecently so.
> He was loved by many, but respected by none.

Thus we behold in Chesterfield an eighteenth-century Confucius who believed that the sober virtues and restrained conduct of a high-minded gentlemanliness would be sufficient to counteract the evils engendered in a society governed by the ideals of the trader. It was his fate to see his careful advice go to waste upon his son and then upon his godson, both of whom became the undistinguished products of the potato-like period of the Hanoverian kings.

Chesterfield probably deserved better of his world, even though he raised its resentment by despising it. He had democratic instincts mixed with an aristocratic intellect and he had an acute perception as already noted, of the trend of things. As early as 1751 he wrote to his young friend, Lord Huntingdon:

If our accounts here from Paris are true, the change of the temper and genius of the French people with regard to their government is astonishing. They used to hug their chains and boast their servitude; they now seem to be galled by them and struggling to shake them off. If they have found out (though late) that kings are not part of the Divinity; that they are not exactly the images of God upon earth; that they are neither anointed nor appointed by Him to be the scourges of their fellow creatures; that they have no other rights but those of civic and mutual compact; but that mankind in general have natural and inherent rights which no power on earth can legally deprive them of; if, I say, they have at last discovered these truths, which by the way are not very abstruse ones, their natural vivacity, and their shame of so long having entertained error will probably carry them very far the other way.

*"Civil and mutual compact."*
*"Natural and inherent rights."*

These are some of the words, some of the edged phrases, that split the eighteenth century asunder. They are words and phrases that establish a certain kinship between Lord Chesterfield, the English aristocrat, and J. J. Rousseau, the French lackey.

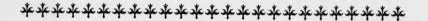

## CHAPTER SEVEN

## REASON'S REBEL

### I

IN 1741 Jean Jacques Rousseau, son of a Geneva clock-maker and dancing master, came to Paris. In his pockets were fifteen louis, the manuscript of a comedy, and a scheme for writing music with numbers.

In music, as well as political and social strata, old fixities were being broken up, and a rebellion against outworn modes was being led by Rameau, greatest French musician of his day, with his proposals for new geometrical forms.

Rousseau, who was twenty-nine years old, was at first uncertain whether he should go on with musical or literary ambitions. His first associations surrounded him with a literary atmosphere and thus was determined his career, for he met such men as Diderot, Fontenelle, Saint-Pierre, and Grimm, and he found that ideas were being shaped by Voltaire, Buffon, and Montesquieu.

Rousseau wished to look up to such men, and in turn be admired by them. But something in them affronted him. He had twice been a servant in rich houses; he had been a runaway and a vagabond; he suffered from ill-health, from recurring neuroses, and from alternating feelings of inferiority and superiority.

He looked at such men, accustomed to the ease of salons, to women with curls draped over their shoulders, and to the society of the fashionable and prosperous, and he could not abide them. In the maturity of their success it seemed to him that such men had become complacent if not smug. He could not resist the impulse to prick them, to outrage them. Of this group, with Diderot alone he had something in common, but at length he quarrelled even with Diderot.

With men he was incapable of keeping the peace. Their indurated self-esteem, their imperception of nuances and subtleties, their bland satisfaction with maleness, constantly rasped nerves which nature and fortune had too lightly covered with the bone and muscle of masculinity.[1]

But with women how different things were! In their presence he was not subjected either to coarseness or to contempt. And above all, they were not indifferent to him. They provided him with houses and retreats, they wrote him letters and sent him money, they sheltered him like mothers and poulticed him like nurses. With their help Rousseau conquered Paris, then France, then Europe— omitting the British Isles, which remained unalterably impervious to foreign ideas.

He rewarded women by writing about them as God-created to please and serve men. But Rousseau was rarely

---

[1]For example, he wrote in his *Confessions:* "Seeing that the sweet and amiable Madame d'Holbach still received me kindly, I bore with the gross vulgarity of her husband as long as it was endurable."

capable of returning aught for good except evil. He could not endure an obligation, real or imagined; it aroused his seven devils of contradiction. He punished those devils by exposing them in his *Confessions,* in which he flagellated himself as a monster to be saved only by the mercy of God, and to be excused only because society had made him what he was.

These women who most assiduously sheltered and protected this Swiss lackey belonged to the upper classes. He was a novelty; he was an ex-footman who could write divinely; he was more than half feminine — they understood him even when he puzzled and shocked them; they confided in him; they put up with his humors and tempers; they soothed him until his eyes shone with admiration and devotion; they tended him as if he were a sick child. Well, was he not one?

But Rousseau was in his secret heart, even while he admired them, afraid of these great ladies. He felt that, in a crisis, he could never cope with their *savoir-faire* and assurance. For instance, there was Mme. de Luxembourg, wife of the great marshal who was an intimate of the king. She made the marshal climb up, puffing and scraping his sword and plumes against the passageways, to Rousseau's Paris lodgings, where he sat among "dirty plates and broken pots," and take him away to the park of Montmorency, in the country, where he was installed in a little white and blue apartment in a small château built for his own use by the painter and architect, Le Brun. Though the house was called "little," it was large enough to contain a ballroom, billiard room, and kitchen. It was the apartment over the kitchen that Rousseau chose (he always loved kitchens: the smell of them, the everydayness of them, the sordidness of them).

"It was in this profound and delicious solitude," he wrote, "amid woods and waters, bathed in the songs of birds of every note and the perfume of orange flowers, that I composed, in one long ecstasy, the fifth book of the *Emile*. . . . I had a heaven on earth, living in all the innocence and enjoying all the pleasures of Paradise."

His heart enlarged and beamed upon Mme. de Luxembourg. He searched his mind for a way to serve her. Knowing that great ladies suffered chiefly from boredom, he offered to read to her from his *Nouvelle Heloise,* with its novel passages. She was enchanted. And so every morning at ten he came to her bedside and read.

Here in La Marechale's boudoir, in the presence of her husband, Rousseau read to her in a voice charged with emotion. By certain passages she was so affected that she would arise and embrace him. She wrote him notes saying, "I love you with all my heart," and at table she made him sit by her side.

"And if any great lord or other made to take his place," he wrote with a pride imperfectly concealed, "she would tell him it was mine, and have him sit somewhere else."

It was a sign of the times, that members of the nobility should have to make room for a plebeian, and that great lords should have to take second place to a writing man who only yesterday had been sitting amongst dirty pots and pans. But despite the honors she lavished upon him, Rousseau, his veins laden with Genevan Calvinism and his instincts as an ex-footman on guard, could never wholly yield to Madame's seductions.

"I was exceedingly afraid of Madame de Luxembourg," he wrote in his journal. "I knew she was lovely. . . ." He had heard of her numerous affairs as the Duchess de Boufflers, he knew her reputation as a wicked one, he feared her stately manners and her satiric tongue. Yet to him she was all melting grace. "I found her charming, charming with a charm that is time-proof. . . . Her flattery is all the more intoxicating from its perfect simplicity."

Whenever a woman was kind to Rousseau he instantly idealized her. He did not wish to touch her; he was content to sit and be bathed in his thoughts of her. The physical woman was nothing; the aura he bestowed upon her was everything. The Marechale almost carried him away; the daily meetings with her gradually transported him to that Neverland which was his natural habitat.

But as every action creates its opposite and as there is a serpent in every Eden, Jean Jacques was not left undisturbed. The disturber was Madame's young daughter-in-law, the Duchess of Montmorency. She sometimes invaded these seances, and as often as the Marechale anointed the Genevan's head with oil, she was moved to do just the opposite. She asked J. J. questions veined with malice. To her mother-in-law's praises she offered acidulous amendments. Into Madame's continuous sweetness she injected doubt and vinegar. She broke up lulling conversations with barbed comments. She railed at Jean Jacques and into his wounds poured the salt of laughter. She eyed him askance, sweeping him with analytical glances, making him sud-

THE SECOND ACT IN THE AMERICAN REBELLION

*Benjamin Franklin negotiates for French help. From a painting*
*by Stanley Arthurs*

HE LOST THE AMERICAN COLONIES

*Idealized portrait of George III by West in the collection of the Historical
Society of Pennsylvania*

denly aware of his shabby clothes, of his muddy shoes, of his inferiority and lowness. She shrivelled and shrank him, cut into his pride, made him wonder if she saw the lackey in him; she wrecked the idyll with the Marechale.[2]

Was she moved by jealousy, by a latent antagonism toward her mother-in-law, or was she herself secretly attracted by Rousseau? We cannot know. Rousseau was often blinded by his engulfing egotism. We only know that she made him doubt himself, and for that Jean Jacques never forgave any one; even a woman.

## II

To protect himself from the aggressiveness of these highborn ladies, to interpose a buffer, to save the capillaries of his sensitive surfaces, Jean Jacques took a servant and seamstress, Thérèse Levasseur, and made her his companion and mistress. Thérèse never read books or entertained theories; she could not even add figures; she was only a healthy vegetable, like a carrot fresh from the ground or a cabbage whose stripped leaves smell fresh. But he liked her — in his own way. He tells us in his *Confessions* that he did not, could not, love her. Yet he was continuously devoted; for her sake he endured her unendurable, commercial-minded mother-in-law; he passed some of his happiest, most tranquil hours with Thérèse. She was the comfort, the quiet, that enabled Jean Jacques to go on with his writing and shake the intellectual world as it had not been shaken before.

[2]It was not resumed due to the departure of the marshal, who was called to Paris to confer with the ministers upon the victory of Wolfe over Montcalm in Canada and the fall of Quebec.

Rousseau ran counter to almost every "movement" of his time. He reversed all the trends of the century. He broke into the temple of all the day's gods and mocked at the high priests. He laid impious hands upon the ark of the salons and threw dirt upon the glittering banners of Science, Progress, Philosophy. He attacked the rule of the great triumvirate: Voltaire, Montesquieu, and Diderot— perhaps from envy, perhaps from the irresistible proddings of his contradicting nature. ("All my conversations with Diderot," he wrote, "tended to make me more satirical and biting than it was in my character to be.") He sickened of the attentions of delicate ladies and resented even their gifts. Of Mme. d'Épinay's loan of his retreat, the Hermitage, he wrote:

One must be poor, without a valet, hate constraint, possess my soul, to guess what it is to live in the house of others. Yet I lived two years in hers, reduced to servitude, while listening to the finest speeches on liberty, served by twenty lackeys, and every morning cleaning my own shoes, burdened by sorry indigestion, and ever sighing for my own porringer.

He heaped loathing upon great cities such as Paris as centers of maleficence. He said that science and art, those two idols of the century, owe their existence to our vices. He said that, as coming from God, everything is good, but in the hands of man is corrupted. He said that society and culture were sources of evil. He rushed upon the great god Property and battered its worshipped head, shouting that "the fruits of the earth belong to all, the earth to none."

"The first man," he wrote, "who, having enclosed some land, thought of saying *this is mine,* and found people simple enough to believe him, was the real founder of civilized society."

His assaults culminated in his ripping open the covers of France's secret cancer — inequality, that thing hated by France's repressed classes. "Inequality," he wrote, "at last becomes permanent and legitimate by the establishment of property and law." Laws, he noticed, are more concerned about property than persons; they aim "to secure order, not virtue."

It was probably his attack on inequality that most endeared him to the masses. He had, says Mallet du Pan, "a hundred times more readers among the middle and lower classes than Voltaire. He alone inoculated the French with the doctrine of the sovereignty of the people, and with its uttermost consequences."

But he was not yet finished. In his *Social Contract* he exclaimed that all government rests upon the consent of the governed. (This doctrine was not original with him; it was first voiced among the Greeks, was echoed in France during the sixteenth century, and had been most lately repeated by Locke, England's philosopher of individualism; but it was Rousseau who dramatized the idea and made it live and move.)

And then at the last he wrote this warning across the face of the world: *"We are approaching a crisis and a century of revolutions."*

### III

In literature Rousseau caused equal overturnings. He evicted the intellect and substituted the heart. He rejected reason and replaced it with feeling. "I felt before I thought," he said. He brought the not-quite-a-gentleman into the novel and the romance, and introduced the ugly and the sordid upon the same plane as the elegant; he destroyed the influence of the drawing room on literature.

He made nature not an analytical collection of facts but a spirit and a pervasion; he made nature so delightful that the French took it into their homes and petted it, and fashionable women got a new thrill by suckling their own babies. His ideas and language got into the American Declaration of Independence and the French Declaration of Rights, and his tones sounded in the voice of Robespierre during the French Revolution. And he did it all not by thinking logically, but by feeling intensely what was already astir in the arteries of Europe.

## IV

In 1766 David Hume, the philosopher and historian, carried off Rousseau to England and tried to get a pension for him from George III. Rousseau was beginning to suffer from the persecution obsession that afflicted his later years, but at first he was purring and grateful. Then his old suspicions, his old hatred of being under obligation, came back upon him and he began to explode nervously. At such times Hume could only pat him on the back, exclaiming:

"What, my dear sir? . . . Eh, my dear sir! . . . What *now,* my dear sir?"

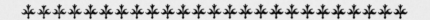

## CHAPTER EIGHT

# THE THIRD GEORGE

### I

IN 1766, when Rousseau came to England, George III had been reigning six years. It had been a year since his first symptoms of insanity had been noticed and three years since the Treaty of Paris had transferred France's power to England. (Those 1760's! So much happened in these ten years that not even the half of it can be recorded. The decade was one of the pivots of the eighteenth century.)

For half the century the Whigs had governed England, and traces of the Whiggish spirit had penetrated almost all Europe. The commercial classes protected by the Whig mantle had gained so much ground at the expense of monarchy that kings had become alarmed and a wave of royal reaction was set in motion. It made itself visible in Catherine II, Frederick the Great, in Maria Theresa, and then in George III.

George's German mother, if the gossips were to be believed, had said to him, "George, be a king," and George began his reign as if he had some such thought in mind. Even the robes prescribed for the peers attending his coronation in 1760 were imperially rich, according to this written order:

The robe to be of Crimson Velvet edged with Miniver pure the Cape furred with Miniver pure powdered with Bars or Rows of Ermine according to their Degree — viz.

| | |
|---|---|
| Barons | four rows. |
| Viscounts | two rows and a half. |
| Earls | three rows. |
| Marquesses | three rows and a half. |
| Dukes | four rows. |

The under Habits of very rich Gold or Silver Brocades, White Silk Stockings and White Kid Shoes with silver buckles.

Swords in Scabbards of Crimson Velvet appendant to a belt of the same, and

Either in full bottomed Peri-Wigs or Wigs without Bags tied behind with a Ribbon curled and flowing down to the small of the back.

Coronets, Silver Gilt, Caps of Crimson Velvet turned up with Ermine, no jewels or precious stones in their Coronets, or counterfeit Pearls, instead of Silver Balls.[1]

Elsewhere in England there was evidence of imperial power and its concomitant display. The governing and commercial classes, grown rich on the wealth flowing in from the Americas and India, had put up vast mansions the architecture of which, now known as Georgian, aimed at a classic elegance owing much to Italian influences derived from Roman solidity softened by a Greek grace. Internally these houses wore the grand manner of Louis XIV. The corridors, the mirrors, the panelling, the molded plaster work, the gilt chandeliers, all remembered Louis XIV and Versailles.

[1] *Correspondence of King George III,* Fortescue ed., Vol. I, p. 5. London, 1927.

And indeed George himself remembered Louis XIV architecturally and otherwise just as his fellow sovereigns Louis XV, Frederick II, Catherine II, and Maria Theresa remembered and, as well as they could, imitated him. Although he was only twenty-two years old when he was crowned, George was already an imposing figure; he carried himself with a pronounced dignity unmarred by any sense of humor, and at the first opportunity he revealed himself as every inch a Tory. "I will have," he said, "no innovations in my time." His eyes were bulbous, his lips and nose protruding, while in his riper years a kind of dewlap extended down his throat in the fashion of a park bull.

But at twenty-two he was almost handsome. And England was very satisfied with him; it liked his solidity and shared his suspicion of the dramatic and the unexpected; it liked his Englishness—he gloried, he said, in the very name of Briton; it liked his kindly way of conversing with farmers and old women; and being already a little tired of the long rule of Whiggery, it was even prepared to like his Toryness.

## II

In a very simple way George set about collecting scattered patches of power into his own hands. His was no quick intellect or agile intelligence, but he had at his command three weapons that needed no finesse in handling: secret funds; appointments to office; and the gracious nod of royalty.

George must have been astonished at the effectiveness of these weapons even when coarsely displayed and bluntly used. The great Pitt, the Whig leader and fabricator of empire, was got rid of by a pension of £3000 a year and a title for his wife and her issue. Bribery, offices, and favors, distributed by agents and deputies in Parliament[2] while George kept his face averted, soon broke the Whig oligarchy and cleared the way for a Tory march over the prostrate body of government. But George, who observed little and read less, was not aware that new forces had arisen which were making monarchs less and less necessary except as ritualistic figures on a decorative tapestry. Government was becoming no longer a royal function but an affair carried on by committees of great merchants and their agents, the politicians, who had their own private committee called the Cabinet; and the mercantile-minded classes wished Parliament and the Cabinet to have the executive as well as the legislative power.

George III's notions were otherwise. He had read a little in Blackstone and he had found the views of that eloquent rationalizer an echo of his own, particularly when Blackstone said:

The King of England is not only the chief, but properly the sole magistrate of the nation, all others acting by commission from and in due subordination to him.

[2]"Seats were bought and sold in the open market at a price which rose to £4000, and we can hardly wonder that a reformer could allege without a chance of denial, 'This House is not a representative of the people of Great Britain. It is the representation of nominal boroughs, of ruined and exterminated towns, of noble families, of wealthy individuals, of foreign potentates.' "— Green, *Short History of the English People.*

## III

George had been brought up under a mixed tutelage that included the offices of two bishops and two earls. One of the latter, Lord Waldegrave, wrote: "I found his Royal Highness uncommonly full of princely prejudices contracted in the nursery, and improved by Bedchamber women and Pages of the Back Stairs."

These princely prejudices imparted to George very serious ideas of what was expected of him as head of an enormously expanding empire. Day after day he sat at his desk compiling lists of his ships and regiments, and writing countless badly spelled notes of advice, adjuration, and admonishment to ministers and to subjects operating in a hundred spheres. All these notes, trivial or not, were meticulously marked with such cryptograms as: "5/m pt. 12," which could be decoded by the knowing into: "five minutes past twelve." He converted himself into a royal clerk and imperial bookkeeper. He spared himself no time for those amusements beloved by his Hanoverian predecessors —loose loves and ladies, but as bachelor passed his leisure hours with his German mother, Augusta of Saxe-Gotha, at her botanic gardens at Kew, and as married man he passed them in the bosom of a family that rapidly resembled that of the old woman who lived in a shoe. (He was the father of fifteen children.) Dutifully he put out of his mind the charms of Lady Sarah Lennox and the sober graces of the Quaker-maid, Hannah Lightfoot, and took as wife and queen the homely but industrious German princess, Charlotte of Mecklenburg.

But at first these self-denying deeds and assiduities brought George little popularity. His strict attention to domesticity and decorum softened the country people toward him and at length they were fondly calling him "Farmer George"; but the townspeople, especially in London, remained his critics and enemies. Crowded into the cities by Enclosure Acts that swept away the common lands and angered by laws that interfered with their food and drink, landless and jobless men rioted against George's ministers and then against George himself. The coal heavers and the sawyers erupted and then the sailors mutinied. George's answer to these uprisings was the deploying of soldiers dressed in red-coats, mitered caps, and white gaiters. The struggle between government and people culminated in the Gordon or No-Popery riots of 1780 when 285 persons were shot down, 59 condemned to death, and 21 executed. George III could easily forgive an offense against his person — he was several times attacked by demented individuals — but toward an offender against the royal dignity or a critic of the royal prerogative, he was implacable with the pitiless rigidity of an organism whose cells were filled with plasma and obstinacy.

"Firmness and resolution," he once wrote, "must now be shown, and no one's friends save but as dare to fly off. This alone can restore order and save this country from anarchy."

Firmness and resolution — those were the Herculean twins upon which George relied to bring him safely out of all troubling situations. A mob was a mob, whether in London or Boston, and if it became unruly, it deserved

GEORGIAN INFLUENCE IN COLONIAL ARCHITECTURE

*Independence Hall at Philadelphia, an example of the simple and refined design favored in the late eighteenth century*

GEORGIAN ARCHITECTURE IN AMERICA

*Rotunda of library at the University of Virginia designed by Thomas Jefferson after the Palladian principles laid down by Palladio, an Italian architect much admired in England. He drew both from Greek and Roman elements*

to be shot into. He had no patience with ministers who argued that a rabble in America deserved treatment different from that given to a rabble in England.

"What? What?" he said to them, using his favorite twin exclamations, varied occasionally by "Hay? Hay?" And to show them what his opinions were as to his rights and duties he went to his desk in 1766 and wrote this memorandum:

Feb. 3. That the King's Majesty by and with the advice and consent of the Lords spiritual and Temporal and Commons of Great Britain in Parliament Assembl'd had, hath, of Right ought to have full power and authority to make Laws and Statutes of sufficient force and validity to bind the Colonys and People of America Subjects of the Crown of Great Britain in all cases whatsoever.

The Stamp Act had been passed in the previous year with the simple purpose of raising £100,000 annually. In England it was accepted passively, but from America objections were heard. There was much argument about George's use of the world *bind*. What were its definition and implications? Mr. Pitt was asked to state his views. The Great Commoner (but greater, some said, as actor) did so:

"Let the sovereign authority of this country over tne colonies be asserted in as strong terms as can be devised, and be made to extend to every point of legislation whatsoever; that we may bind their trade, confine their manufactures, and exercise every power whatsoever, except that of taking their money out of their pockets without their consent."

Mr. Pitt's sonorous phrases failed to soothe the angry and suspicious Americans. So that was it, eh? The Whigs led by Pitt would continue, through Navigation Acts, to compel American exports to be routed through England, to the great profit of English traders and bankers; they would continue to restrict American manufacturing enterprise to those articles which would not compete with English-made goods; while George III and his Tories would continue to insert taxing tubes into American pockets to pay for the Seven Years' War.

American traders, shippers, exporters, growers, and fishermen turned over the word *bind* in their thoughts and resolved that it must disappear from the British government's vocabulary. The Benjamin Franklins tried to remove it with diplomacy; the Patrick Henrys with threats. Tea imported in the English East India Company's vessels was dumped overboard. Other English goods were boycotted. English politicians backed and filled, ran to and fro, proposed compromises. George III was steady. He summoned his twin reliables, firmness and resolution, and his army captains to do their duty. They took measures against the rabble in America just as they would take, had taken, measures against the rabble in England. They fired, and got fired back at. It was a war.

## IV

In England it was at first a popular war.

The merchant and manufacturing classes favored it because it would destroy American competition; the Tory landowners favored it because it would compel the Americans to help bear a tax that otherwise would fall heavily on property. And George III and his court favored it because it would justify Firmness and Resolution.

In America it was not less popular. New England shippers and traders favored it because if successful it would give them the unhampered privilege of shipping to and trading with all the world. The merchants of the middle colonies favored it because it would free them of multitudinous debts to British firms.[3] Others favored it because they admired what they understood to be Liberty and hated what they understood to be Tyranny. But thousands mourned to be cut off from George III and all English connections, and those who did not remain royalists and loyalists obeyed the orders of a Continental Congress with the hope that it would be a short and inconclusive war. They had their counterparts in the English army. English commanders often fought half-heartedly and without expecting to enjoy success even if won.

## V

The war, as all wars do, disappointed everybody. George III had solemnly asseverated that he would never, never consent to American independence. Never is a long word. One summer day in 1785 George III was seated in St.

---

[3]Thomas Jefferson declared that in Virginia "these debts had become hereditary from father to son, for many generations, so that the planters were a species of property, annexed to certain mercantile houses in London." —Schlesinger, *The Colonial Merchants and the American Revolution*, p. 36, N. Y., 1918; Jefferson, *Writings* (P. L. Ford ed.).

James's Palace when Lord Carmarthen ushered in an individual who was probably as welcome to the king as a crocodile. It was John Adams, minister plenipotentiary from the United States of America, who was as English as George III himself and was of the same bull-like traits. Adams, whom no man surpassed in correctness, paused inside the door and made a profound bow. He advanced a few steps and made another bow. When arrived before the royal presence he bowed again. And then he began to speak.

It had been scarcely two years since George had written to Charles James Fox: "As to the question whether I wish to receive a Minister from America, I certainly can never express its being agreeable to me. . . . I cannot help adding, that I shall ever have a bad opinion of any Englishman who would accept of being an accredited Minister for that revolted State."

But those close to the king knew that he was no longer the man he had been. Affliction had beset him, especially in that family circle where he could solace himself for the disappointments of official life and where he was constantly the devoted father and husband. The Prince of Wales, after a long series of episodes that had humiliated his father, had confessed that he owed a sum equal to $800,000 in gambling and other debts, and had then brought his erratic career to a climax by a secret marriage to Mrs. Fitzherbert, belonging to that Roman Catholic faith which George abhorred. The king's brothers and sisters were often involved in scandals.

Not only disgrace but death had brought mourning

to the royal house. The king's youngest son, Prince Alfred, had died, and a few months later came the death of the little Prince Octavius, whom his father adored. "Many people," he wrote, "would regret that they ever had so sweet a child, since they were forced to part with him. That is not my case; I am thankful to God for having graciously allowed me to enjoy such a creature for four years."

The war in America had been in some of its phases directed by him personally; he had studied maps, selected commanders, and outlined campaigns, and the final defeat of Lord Cornwallis at Yorktown by a ragged assortment of Continental soldiers, assisted by the French, that people whom George associated with inefficiency and levity, had weighed heavily upon him.

Nevertheless, as the short-necked, square-set American confronting him began to speak, George braced the frame that in recent years had become a little sagging and corpulent, summoned his British dignity touched with a Hanoverian hauteur, and listened attentively.

What was this truculent Yankee going to say—words of emptiness, defiance, or insult?

Referring to the States from which he had just come, Adams said distinctly and slowly:

"I have the honor to assure your majesty of their unanimous disposition and desire to cultivate the most friendly and liberal intercourse between your majesty's subjects and their citizens."

George nodded his head, but with a look of incredulity, and Adams went on:

"And of their best wishes for your majesty's health and happiness, and for that of your royal family.

"I shall esteem myself the happiest of men if I can be instrumental in recommending my country more and more to your majesty's royal benevolence, and of restoring an entire esteem, confidence, and affection, or, in better words, the old good-nature and the old good-humor between people who, though separated by an ocean, and under different governments, have the same language, a similar religion, and kindred blood."

It was now evident that the king was wholly won. He no longer tried to hide his emotion as Adams concluded:

"I beg your majesty's permission to add that although I have sometime before been intrusted by my country, it was never in my whole life in a manner so agreeable to myself."

George needed a moment to collect himself and then in a voice full of a barely mastered emotion, mingled with the old Georgian dignity, he said:

"Sir, the circumstances of this audience are so extraordinary, the language you have now held is so extremely proper, and the feelings you have displayed so justly adapted to the occasion, that I must say that I not only receive with pleasure the assurance of the friendly dispositions of the United States, but that I am very glad the choice has fallen upon you to be their minister."

His voice cleared and he continued:

"I will be very frank with you. I was the last to consent to the separation; but the separation having been made, and having become inevitable, I have always said, as I say now, that I would be the first to meet the friendship of the United States as an independent power."[4]

It was a manly and sporting speech and word of it got quickly outside; the occasion was considered a triumph for both king and American, so that when Adams emerged from the audience room the master of ceremonies greeted him smilingly and escorted him through the apartments while rows of flunkeys parted respectfully and important voices roared: "Mr. Adams's servants! Mr. Adams's carriage!"

## VI

After the failure to subdue the American revolutionists, those committees of business men who ruled Britain made it plain to George that they could get along without him, and he seemed content to withdraw gradually from political hurly-burlies and to immerse himself in private affairs. Resuming his rôle as Farmer George, he followed with deep interest the attempts of Arthur Young to commercialize and increase the yield of agriculture, and even contributed to Young's agricultural journal under the title of Ralph Robinson. He patronized artists, scientists and reformers, and to some of them he gave bounties and pensions, notably Herschel the astronomer. He was even willing to give a pension to Jean Jacques Rousseau, who belonged to a bitter and hasty nation, but Rousseau refused it and went back to France and to loneliness and derangement.

In the evenings George was never so content as when he could rest in the bosom of his family and kindred, and

[4]Adams's letter to John Jay.

listen to Handel's music. He was fond of operas and plays. And when he discussed them his old animation and vigor returned. Indeed, his discussions ran into garrulity and his vehement monologues sometimes ran into half hours and then longer, and his attendants adopted devices for checking his garrulity before he should exhaust himself.

He liked particularly to invite people representing music and the stage out to Windsor, and one evening when Mrs. Siddons, the actress, was his guest, he handed her with an impressive air a sheet of paper and invited her to cast her mind on *that*. The paper contained his signature at the bottom, but above it was blank. Mrs. Siddons at a convenient moment whispered to the queen, and the queen whispered to the royal physician, who called his colleagues into consultation.

George had been for several days hunting assiduously, and his doctors came to him and advised him to rest before he overtaxed himself. "I am certainly weak and stiff," said George, "but I am certain air and relaxation are the quickest restoratives." His chancellor came and persuaded him to go to bed. From his pillow George looked up and said:

> You, too, then, my Lord Thurlow, forsake me and suppose me ill beyond recovery. But whatever you and Mr. Pitt may think and feel, I, that am born a gentleman, shall never lay my head on my last pillow in peace and quiet so long as I remember the loss of my American colonies.[5]

The Prince of Wales came to see him, and the king sprang up, pushed him violently against a wall, and informed him he was going to speak out. He then spoke in

[5]Malmesbury, *Diaries,* IV, p. 21.

a whisper. The queen's chamberlain came up and led him back to bed. There he lay talking deliriously for hours, but, as the chamberlain afterwards remarked, his feverish reflections were "never accompanied by the slightest impropriety of expression." At length, in a lucid interval, the king cried aloud: "I wish to God that I might die, for I am going to be mad!"

He was removed to Kew, that he might look out upon its gardens. There he had two doctors. One, Doctor Willis, was identified with the court party. The other, Doctor Warren, became known as the doctor of the Opposition. A disputation arose and an official inquiry was held, in which Doctor Willis was accused under three heads, viz.: that he had permitted the king to read Shakespeare's *King Lear;* that he had permitted him to use a razor and scissors; and that he had permitted him to talk with the queen and his children.

Doctor Willis had a convincing defense. He explained that the king had asked for *King Lear,* but that he had substituted a volume of comedies by George Colman. Unfortunately Colman's adaptation of *Lear,* which his accusers called most improper to be put into the king's hands, was contained in this book, but the fact was not discovered until too late. As to the toilet implements, they had been introduced because the king's hair and beard had grown to an inordinate length.

"I could not," added the doctor, "apprehend any harm, having the firmest reliance on his majesty's sentiments of piety, which, even in this dreadful crisis, never altered."

To having admitted the queen and the royal children to

fifteen-minute interviews with the king he pleaded guilty, but he offered proof that the effects had been beneficial to the patient.

Gradually the king's sanity returned and he was able to comment with his usual vigor on the revolution among the French—"that most savage as well as unprincipled nation." Once more he resumed the royal reins, but only for a few years. Although England went to war with revolutionary France and tried to draw a sanitary cordon about the fermentation there, its effects spread and George was again the victim of attacks and of threatening letters. But he only remarked he hoped whoever should attempt to take his life "will not do it in a barbarous or brutal manner."

And then his malady returned and remained with him until the eighteenth century was gone and a new century had come, bringing with it the victories of Napoleon and of machinery and the industrial revolution and of a middle class everywhere fostered, increased, and strengthened by flowing profits, heightened rents, and accumulated interest. He lived beyond the eighteenth century for twenty years, but was only dimly aware of the turbulencies of the nineteenth.

In 1811 he rode a horse through the streets of Windsor, led by an attendant, for the king was blind. Then darkness fell upon his mind as well as upon his eyes, and the last eight years of his life were passed in an unwittingness to everything, sitting in a single room, a skull cap upon his head and his long white hair streaming over his shoulders.

## CHAPTER NINE

# ENTER AN ECONOMIST

### I

IN 1764 an acute Scotchman, a subject of George III, led a younger and duller man to the Continent on one of those tours deemed indispensable to the education of the sons of noble British families.

The older man, then aged forty-one, was Adam Smith, recently a professor at Glasgow University. The younger one was the Duke of Buccleuch. Tutor and pupil first went to Paris where they visited Smith's friend, David Hume, who as a philosopher had won conspicuous popularity in the salons and had become intimate with a scintillant circle of thinkers. Hume was then laying the foundations for that admiration for French writers which afterwards induced him to invite Rousseau to England.

After a few days with Hume, Smith and the young duke went south to Toulouse, then a provincial capital with its own parliament and university. The duke had come here to learn the language, but in five months he failed to meet even one Frenchman, and so narrow and confining was the life of pupil and tutor that Smith wrote dolefully to Hume, "The life which I led at Glasgow was a pleasurable dissipated life in comparison of that which I lead here at present. I have begun to write a book in order to pass away the time."[1]

The book which was thus begun in order to relieve the tedium of a Scotchman immured in a French provincial town was *An Inquiry into the Nature and Causes of the Wealth of Nations.* Twelve years were required to complete it. It was published in March, 1776, four months before the Declaration that broke the amorphous lump of the American colonies away from the vast and expanding bulk of the British Empire. (Smith had shown an anxious interest in the quarrel, but the historian Hume had written him: "My notion is that this matter is not so important as is commonly imagined.")

## II

Smith's book had not to wait for attention. Although published in two large quartos and priced at thirty-six shillings, it was almost immediately popular and remained so.

For the praises heaped upon it not only in its own century but in the nineteenth and twentieth centuries there were good reasons. Just as Bayle rationalized and justified the pursuit of learning, just as Montesquieu rationalized and justified systems of government, and just as Blackstone rationalized and justified current concepts of law, so Adam Smith rationalized and justified the nascent institution of industrial capitalism. His book ruled the economics of the ensuing century and shaped the politics of the governing

[1]Hirst, *Adam Smith,* N. Y., 1904, p. 123.

classes. It stamped the life out of mercantilism and other outmoded theories. It was a part of the eighteenth century's effort to rid itself of the vestigial débris of feudalism and the Middle Ages. It was replete with the eighteenth-century spirit of rationality, with its search for and correlation of facts, its canniness, and its anti-mysticism.

Smith's teachings were, in the main, a complete justification of the *laissez-faire* or let-every-man-alone policy first advocated by the French Physiocrats, with whose writings he was familiar.[1] There must be no restrictions upon, no interference with, the right of each man to get ahead in the way most suitable to him. The individual must be free (1) to choose his own occupation; (2) to enjoy free trade in land; (3) to exchange goods freely with his fellow countrymen; (4) to trade freely with foreign countries. All duties, taxes, bounties, and prohibitions upon both local and foreign trade should be removed. This was welcome doctrine to those British merchants and manufacturers who throughout the century had suffered from the interferences of governments inspired by mercantilist ideas and from the monopolies granted to or seized by the great chartered companies fostered by the Stuart and Hanoverian kings in England and the Bourbon kings in France.

[1]There was also a remarkable similarity between some of Smith's economic ideas and those of Boisguilbert, the seventeenth-century Frenchman. Boisguilbert was a Norman magistrate who took it upon himself to offer to Louis XIV's ministers, particularly Chamillart and Desmarets, proposals by which the state of French finance might be rectified and the ruin of the producing classes averted. He had definite and well thought-out ideas regarding money and credit, value and price, land-use and rent, and he wore himself out trying to induce the court to consider them. He was at last ordered to be silent and when he would not, he was exiled. See Roberts, *Boisguilbert: Economist of the Reign of Louis XIV,* New York, 1935.

Smith's views as to the status and functions of labor were no less novel and startling to a world that had been quietly drifting along under George III. The only real *measure* of wealth, he said, was labor (he did not say *source*).

"Labor," he said in his first chapter, "was the first price, the original purchase money that was paid for all things"; the individual "must be rich or poor according to the quantity of labor of other people he can command or which he can afford to purchase."

The vast wealth or "opulence" which had come upon England he attributed to the division of labor. He wrote:

It is the maximum of every prudent master of a family never to attempt to make at home what it will cost him more to make than to buy. The taylor [*sic*] does not attempt to make his own shoes, but buys them of the shoemaker. . . . If a foreign country can supply us with a commodity cheaper than we ourselves can make it, better buy it of them with some part of the produce of our own industry, employed in a way in which we have some advantage.

The mercantilist theory of production as well as monopoly was cast aside in these words: "Consumption is the sole end and purpose of all production; and the interest of the producer ought to be attended to, only so far as it may be necessary for promoting that of the consumer."

But what gave most delight to the commercial classes of his own and subsequent periods was Smith's two pronunciamentoes:

1. That profits were as normal to the capitalist as wages were to the workman.

2. That every man in seeking his own advantage somehow promoted progress and the public good. "The study

of his own advantage naturally, or rather necessarily, leads him to prefer that employment which is most advantageous to society" and he is "led by an invisible hand to promote an end which was no part of his intention."

## III

None of these things was entirely new, since Smith owed much of his substance to his friend Hume and his teacher Hutcheson, and something even to men so seemingly unrelated as Hobbes and Locke and Mandeville; Smith also was indebted to the Frenchmen Quesnay and Turgot, Gournay and Condorcet; but the *Wealth of Nations,* despite its defects, was a success because it was a clear analysis of an outmoded system and an able synthesis of one better suited to the times, and because it dealt only a little with abstractions and much with men. It married sociology to economics and produced a lively and readable offspring.

The *Wealth of Nations* owed its greatest success, however, to its timeliness. It appeared on the very eve of the Industrial Revolution and supplied a chart by which sagacious and enterprising men of the middle classes might override the last hampering restrictions of a crumbling feudal system planted on the ownership of land.

It pointed the way by which the individual might be either "rich or poor according to the quantity of the labor of other people he can command or which he can afford to purchase."

It prepared a path for competition, showing at the same time that a man had only to follow his own interests to minister to the general welfare.

All the conditions were miraculously ripe for such a chart as the *Wealth of Nations*. For while Enclosure Acts were driving the masses off the land and herding them into the towns, inventions were perfecting the means by which the focal center of life might be removed from the land to the nascent factory.

In 1769, birthyear of Napoleon and of Wellington, James Watt presented his steam engine, first used for pumping water from mines. In 1770 Hargreaves patented the spinning jenny, by which many threads could be spun at once, increasing production eightfold. In 1771 Arkwright introduced his "water frame," an improved spinning machine. In 1777 Crompton combined certain features of the spinning jenny and the water frame into a device which, because it was a hybrid, was called a mule. It made possible the operation of 12,000 spindles by one man. In 1785 Doctor Cartwright patented a power loom to do for weaving what Crompton's mule was doing for spinning. In 1785 Watt's engine was hitched to a cotton-spinning device, and it became Year 1 of the machine age.

An act of parliament had already been passed, under pressure from the woollen manufacturers, forbidding the importation into Britain of cotton prints from India. In 1774 England prohibited the export of tools and machinery used in textile manufacture, also the emigration of textile artisans. In the same year it used 4,000,000 pounds of raw cotton, in 1790 it used 31,000,000, and a few years after Englishmen had exchanged the silk knee-length breeches of the eighteenth century for the tubular pantaloons of the nineteenth, their cotton mills were consuming

56,000,000 pounds. The old hand-spinners and weavers, once so independent with spindles and looms installed in their own cottages, were now dependent. Hand-tools had become power-driven machines and were housed no longer in cottages, but in factories where the will of the owner was more to be dreaded than statute law. Manufacture had become monarch, and George III was of small account beside the mill-owner upon whom men were dependent for work and bread. In short, politics was being superseded by economics.

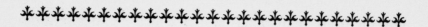

## CHAPTER TEN

# SQUIRE IN BLUE

### I

IN 1770 Arthur Young, to whose *Annals of Agriculture* King George was a contributor, was a young Suffolk squire who went around dressed in blue, embroidered with silver, and carrying a bag and sword.

As landlord and farmer he had made many failures, but in the *Annals* he began to find himself. His well-composed articles dealt not only with agriculture, but with trade, prices, monopolies, and taxation. Since the world was hungry for light on these subjects, he was soon regarded as an authority, and young men came from the Continent to sit at his feet. Among them were three young Russians, sent to him by the Empress Catherine II, and not a few Frenchmen who hoped to discover why England was so prosperous while France was so racked with poverty. Their questions so interested Young that he resolved to visit France and travel over her provinces and survey them with a farmer's eye. Nobles and rich men often travelled, he had observed, but farmers never. In the summer of 1787 he landed at Calais with his mare and from there rode her into the heart of those adventures which he afterward described in *Travels in France*.

## II

Louis XV had died of smallpox thirteen years before, and although inoculation and Doctor Jenner had begun to overcome this malady, the French people ever afterward retained a marked gratitude toward it. In their relief they turned joyfully to the new king, Louis XVI, and to his queen, Marie Antoinette, ninth child of the Austrian empress, Maria Theresa.

From this young couple their subjects expected great things. But Louis XVI showed himself cold, fumbling, and inept, and the strictly reared Marie Antoinette, once she had realized the great power forced into her hands, became giddy and extravagant, bringing upon herself scandals that fetched her brother, Joseph II of Austria, hurrying to Versailles to remonstrate with her. Her gambling debts, which Louis XVI paid for her, brought upon her the name of *Madame Deficit*.

Monsieur Deficit was a name which might better have been applied to the king; for upon his administration fell all the burden of the financial disorder that had been accumulating ever since the days of Louis XIV. This disorder was deeply offensive to the middle classes, who had to pay exacting taxes despite the government's outmoded restrictions upon trade and foolish regulations of industry, while the nobility and clergy were exempt.

The French middle classes were by now, in fact, disgruntled to the point of exasperation. They wanted to be free as England's middle classes were free—free to buy and sell, free to trade and manufacture, free to become equal with the nobility and the clergy. To quiet their murmurs, Louis XVI took a step that brought him encouraging applause. He appointed as Controller-General of Finance the reformer Turgot.

Turgot had been intendent, or civil governor, of the province of Limoges, one of the poorest in France. There he had made a reputation by improving the distribution of taxes, by taking the government's hands off the trade in grain, and by relieving the peasantry of some of the worst oppressions inherited from feudalism. To Louis XVI he outlined this program drawn partly from physiocratic doctrines: "No bankruptcy, no increase of taxation, no more borrowing; fostering of commerce, agriculture, and industry."

Toward these ends he labored diligently, obtaining relaxation meantime in the salons of Paris, particularly in that of Mme. Helvétius, whom he loved and to whom he owed a friendship with Benjamin Franklin, then the American envoy at the court of Versailles[1] and a frequenter of the Helvétius home.

But Turgot, affable as he was in social life, was a strict official, and his tight grasp on the treasury offended Marie Antoinette, while his regulations outraged the nobles and clergy. Together they procured his dismissal. That was in 1776, the year that the American colonies announced their

---

[1] It was for Turgot that Franklin wrote one of his masterpieces: *The Cause and Cure of Smoky Chimneys.*

independence of England. This was an event that delighted the court at Versailles and caused it two years later to sign an alliance with the Americans, in the hope of winning back the prestige and those markets which had been lost in the Seven Years' War.

The dismissal of Turgot and the loans and gifts made to America were two of the first steps in the descent toward Avernus. The various governments under Louis XVI yawed, veered, experimented, wabbled, and stumbled. At last the creaking structure, so top-heavy with a useless nobility, a parasitic clergy, and a fatuous monarchy, began to crack. At last it became plain that partial reforms, such as those attempted by Turgot, would no longer suffice, but that there must be a fundamental revision of all France's institutions. Taxes took away half and sometimes two-thirds of what the peasants could earn in a year, while compulsory statute labors on roads and public works cut down the time they could give to their own fields. At last the peasants in certain districts could no longer feed either their families or themselves and they began to draw together in angry demonstrations.

Riots were not displeasing to the commercial classes, for they wanted to see the dues, the tithes of produce, payments in kind, and other feudal exactions, paid by the peasants to the land-owning nobility, abolished in favor of a system in which all transactions and payments would be made in terms not of wheat or chickens but of money. In short, the middle classes saw an opportunity to overturn an enfeebled but still effective feudalism, but they could not do so without the help of the masses of the people. They therefore stood aside and let the masses break into granaries and bakeries.

An uneasy but not yet frightened king replaced Turgot and his reforms with Necker, whose one idea of saving the state was to raise more loans, although the deficit was being added to by enormous annual increments. But Necker's measures failed to allay the riots in the rural villages; indeed, the peasants, learning of the success of the American revolutionists, not only continued their pillaging but at length refused to pay their taxes.

There followed a new crisis and the minister Calonne convoked the Assembly of the Notables at Versailles early in 1787. When it did nothing, Calonne was replaced by Lomenie de Brienne, Archbishop of Sens, whose severe measures only threw fuel into the spreading fire of disorder. It was obvious that despotism must be relaxed. But how? That was the situation when Young and his mare landed in France.

## III

The first thing Young observed was the contrast between the destitution of the countryside, where the land-holding seigneurs reigned, and the luxury of the towns where the merchants and manufacturers grew rich on monoplies, even in the midst of the turbulencies of revolution. In Brittany there was only *"landes, landes, landes* (waste, waste, waste)—a country possessing but privilege and poverty." At Bordeaux he noted that "the mode of living that takes place among merchants is highly luxurious. Their houses and establishments are on expensive scales. Great entertainments and many served on plate; high play is a much worse thing—and the scandalous chronicle speaks of merchants keeping the dancing and singing girls of the theatre at salaries which ought to import no good to their credit." There were many new houses. "What a satire," wrote Young, "on the government of the two kingdoms (England and France), to permit in one the prejudices of manufacturers and the merchants, and in the other the insidious policy of an ambitious court, to hurry the two nations for ever into wars that check all beneficial works."

At Barbesieux he wrote that "the quantity of waste land is surprising. . . . Whenever you stumble on a Grand Seigneur, even one that was worth millions, you are sure to find his property desert." At the Benedictine abbey of St. Germain, the richest in France, he found that "the abbot has three hundred thousand livres a year. . . . I lose my patience at such revenues being thus bestowed." At industrial Lille he made this note: "The cry here for a war with England amazed me. . . . It is easy enough to discover that the origin of all this violence is the commercial treaty, which is execrated here as the most fatal stroke to their manufactures they ever experienced. These people have the true monopolizing ideas; they would involve four-and-twenty millions of people in the certain miseries of a war, rather than see the interest of those who consume fabrics preferred to the interest of those who make them. The advantages reaped by four-and-twenty millions of consumers are lighter than a feather compared with the inconveniences sustained by half a million of manufacturers."

At Lot in southern France he observed that "all the

country-women and girls are without shoes or stockings; and the plowmen at their work have neither sabots nor feet to their stockings. This is a poverty that strikes at the root of national prosperity; a large consumption among the poor being of more consequence than among the rich; the wealth of a nation lies in its circulation and consumption."

This last observation reveals to what extent new ideas of wealth, similar to those of Adam Smith, were taking possession of the middle-class mind; the older mercantilist concepts had taught that wealth lay in production, not consumption, and in the hoarding of gold and silver, not the circulation of them.

Below Orleans he first encountered the French share-cropper called the *metayer* and wrote: "The poor people who cultivate the soil here are *metayers,* that is, men who hire the land without ability to stock it; the proprietor is forced to provide cattle and seed, and he and his tenants divide the produce; a miserable system, that perpetuates poverty and excludes instruction." South of Beziers he notes that at an inn "we were waited on by a female without shoes or stockings, exquisitely ugly, and diffusing odours not of roses."

On the Marne he met a woman who told him "they had but a morsel of land, one cow, and a poor little horse, yet they had a *franchar* (42 lbs.) of wheat and three chickens to pay as a quit-rent to one Seigneur: and four *franchar* of oats, one chicken, and one shilling to pay to another, besides very heavy tailles and other taxes." She and her husband had seven children. The woman was only twenty-eight years old but broken, and he noted that in France hard work often destroyed "all symmetry of person and every feminine appearance." It was only the children who preserved any beauty. At Montauban in Brittany he found some who were "terribly ragged . . . as to shoes and stockings they are luxuries." He noted one "beautiful girl of six or seven years playing with a stick and smiling under such a bundle of rags as made my heart ache." By 1789 this prevalent poverty was no longer so passive and at Nangis, near Paris, he wrote: "The perruquier that dressed me this morning tells me that everybody is determined to pay no taxes, should the National Assembly so ordain . . . no, sir, never: — be assured as we are, that the French soldiers will never fire on the people; but if they should, it is better to be shot than starved."

At this town Young noted that by order of the magistrates "no person is allowed to buy more than two bushels of wheat at a market, to prevent monopolizing. It is clear to common sense that all such regulations have a direct tendency to increase the evil, but it is in vain to reason with people whose ideas are immovably fixed."

At Cherbourg he found the best inns full and was compelled to resort to "a vile hole, little better than a hog-sty; where for a miserable dirty wretched chamber, two suppers composed chiefly of a plate of apples and some butter and cheese, with some trifle beside too bad to eat and one miserable dinner, they brought me in a bill of thirty-one liv."

Next to the poverty Young complained most of the absence of information and communication. At country inns, even those near Paris, few or no newspapers were to be had and, except for an occasional carriage, few vehicles were to be seen upon the roads. These stigmata of poverty depressed him no less than the discovery that the masses of the people had been almost completely deprived of access to the land, three-fourths of which belonged to the nobles and clergy. Young thought this situation pregnant with evil. "Give a man," he wrote, "the secure possession of a black rock and he will turn it into a garden."

At Chambéry, Young wandered off the main road to visit Charmettes, the house of Mme. de Warens, who had sheltered Rousseau. He could not resist a sentimental interest in this lady who had been already immortalized by Rousseau's pen. "There was something so deliciously amiable in her character," he wrote, "in spite of her frailties —her constant gaiety and good humor—her tenderness and humanity—her farming speculations—but above all other circumstances the love of Rousseau has written her name among the few whose memories are connected with us, are ties more easily felt than described." He found the house, a small one, and "viewed it with a degree of emotion." He was escorted by a young physician of the neighborhood, but Young "was sorry to find that he knew nothing more of the matter than that Mme. de Warens was certainly dead."

At this place he encountered something that horrified him by contrast. It was the *carcan,* or seigneural standard, to which a chain and heavy iron collar were fastened, "as a mark of the lordly arrogance of the nobility, and the slavery of the people."

Young asked why it had not been burned, seeing that the people were poor and ill at their ease. He was told, *Because there are seigneurs everywhere.*

"What a vice it is," commented Young, "and even a curse that the gentry, instead of being the cherishers and benefactors of their poor neighbors, should thus, by the abomination of feudal rights, prove mere tyrants. Will nothing but revolutions, which cause the châteaux to be burnt, induce them to give to reason and humanity what will be extorted by violence and commotion?"

## IV

In the spring of 1789 Louis XVI, by now thoroughly frightened, summoned an assembly of the States-General, intending through them to make certain concessions without unsettling his crown. It was composed of 308 representatives of the clergy, 285 of the nobility, and 621 of the Third Estate or Commons. The nobles had not yet realized their peril. In Paris, Young wrote these notes:

The nobility, with the principles of great lords that I converse with, are most disgustingly tenacious of old rights, however hard they may bear upon the people; they will not hear of giving way in the least to the spirit of liberty, beyond the point of paying equal land-taxes, which they hold to be all that can with reason be demanded.

Not only their obstinacy but their frivolity amazed the young English squire who, after dining with the Duke of Liancourt and a party at Versailles one evening, wrote:

There were not, in thirty persons, five in whose countenances you could guess that any extraordinary event was going forward;

more of the conversation was indifferent than I should have expected. Had it all been so, there would have been no room for wonder, but observations were made with the greatest freedom, and so received as to mark that there was not the least impropriety in making them. . . . They eat, and drank, and sat, and walked, loitered and smirked and smiled, and chatted with easy indifference that made me stare at their insipidity. Perhaps there is a certain nonchalance that is natural to people of fashion from long habit, and which marks them from the vulgar, who have a thousand asperities in the expression of their feelings, that cannot be found on the polished surface of those whose manners are smoothed by society, not worn by attrition. . . . The duc d'Orleans' presence might do a little, but not much; his manner might do more; but it was not without some disgust, that I observed him several times playing off that small sort of wit and flippant readiness to titter, which, I suppose, is a part of his character, or it would not have appeared today. . . .

## V

The nobles at Versailles had had as yet no cause for alarm. The rioting had been confined almost entirely to the countryside. The peasants who had attacked town offices and shops were acting as consumers, not producers. When the price of bread was lowered, they became quieter.

In April, 1787, however, occurred a thing that brought the working people of Paris into the ferment. Some 300 employees had gone on strike against Reveillon, a paper manufacturer and stainer. They wanted a raise in wages sufficient to meet the price of wheat bread. Reveillon laughed at the notion that they were entitled to eat wheat flour. "The workingman can live on black bread and lentils." When told Reveillon had made this remark, a crowd went to his factory and began to plunder his warehouse. Troops fired on them and the battle resulted in death or wounds to 500 people. The soldiers lost 12 killed and 80 wounded.

An instant reaction took place throughout Paris, and a feeling of solidarity sprang up between country peasant and city workman. After that the coals of revolution began to smoke not only in the provinces but in Paris and even in Versailles under the very windows of the royal palace.

Three months later the Bastille, standing at the entrance to the Faubourg Saint-Antoine, the working-class quarter, which was not only a prison but a fort, was rushed and taken.

A few days later a committee of the National Assembly, after reading over the Declaration of Independence written by Thomas Jefferson in 1776, prepared a "Declaration of the Rights of Man and of the Citizen."

In the following October Marie Antoinette's bedroom at Versailles was broken into by a mob that had marched from Paris. It was headed by women who cursed her for a bitch. It was said afterward that Marie was entertaining there a *beau Suedois,* a handsome Swede named de Fersen. But only a few of the palace servants knew his name or position. Who was he?

## CHAPTER ELEVEN

# HANDSOME SWEDE

### I

ONE DAY in January, 1774, Count de Kreutz, ambassador of Gustavus III of Sweden at the court of Louis XV, stepped nervously from his carriage before the palace at Versailles and assisted a slim young man to alight. At sight of the youth, fair and beautifully dressed, the waiting crowd, held back by soldiers, murmured its admiration. Instantly de Kreutz sensed that the present occasion was going to be a success, and, as he escorted the youth toward the palace doors, he arched his chest and smiled with relief. He had come on an errand of high importance, for he was bringing to Versailles for the first time a young countryman, a protégé of King Gustavus, that he might be introduced to the Dauphin and the Dauphine.

The Dauphin was subsequently Louis XVI. The Dauphine was Marie Antoinette. The youth, then only nineteen years old, was the Count Jean (or Hans) Axel de Fersen, son of the Swedish senator and field marshal, Count Frederick Axel de Fersen, and of his wife, the former Countess Hedwige de la Gardie.

De Kreutz's presentiment did not fail him, for he was able afterward to write delightedly to his king:

His male beauty drew attention no less than the charm of his physiognomy and the perfect distinction of his manners.

Marie Antoinette was then only *la petite rousse*—the little red-head—fresh from her mama's apron strings in Austria. At Versailles she passed the time trying to forget among frivolities her boredom as the wife of the Dauphin, who, when not hunting boars, was spending his spare time in his private forge in pursuit of his chief hobby—the manufacture of locks.

What impression young de Fersen first made upon Marie Antoinette is not known; the throng was pressing, the time for each presentation short; but it can be surmised, for when she saw him the second time, August 26, 1778, more than four years later, Marie, then queen, gave a little exclamation.

"Ah!" she said. "Here is an old acquaintance."

Those members of the royal family who were present could not have been pleased by this display of interest, for the count was compelled to confess to his father that they "did not say a word to me."

By this time the young man had developed rapidly under the care of de Kreutz, who wrote joyfully to King Gustavus: "With the handsomest face and much intelligence, he could not fail to succeed in society, and he has done so completely." Marie did not permit another four-year absence to intervene. As queen she was enjoying privileges that were impossible when she was only the Dauphine;

and she used them. November 19, 1778, found the young count writing this to his father:

The queen treats me with great kindness; I often pay her my court at her card games, and each time she makes me little speeches that are full of good-will. As some one had told her of my Swedish uniform she expressed a wish to see me in it. I am to go Thursday thus dressed, not to court, but to the queen's apartments.

## II

Even the birth of her first child, the Princess Marie Thérèse, in December, 1779, failed to draw Marie's attention to domestic affairs more than temporarily, and soon she was playing recklessly at cards again, giving fêtes, and keeping de Fersen at her side as much as court rules would permit. It was considered that the friendship between the queen and the young foreigner was quite platonic; but there were persons to whom Marie's openly exhibited admiration for the Swedish nobleman caused unease. A queen, in public, at least, must be careful. Any partiality, however harmless, for any person, might have political consequences; and in the case of foreigners, the danger of indiscretion was double. Whispers arose in corners and were wafted into corridors. Marie had never been popular at best; her tongue and unconventional conduct had offended many influential persons; she had made enemies who were ready to rear a structure from a straw.

Even de Kreutz was disquieted. His young countryman's social success had gone far beyond any dreamed-of bounds. It was all very well for the count to be highly regarded at Versailles; thus was reflected luster upon the king who had sent him, and credit upon de Kreutz himself who had sponsored him; but to be drawn close to the throne by silken threads woven by royalty itself. . . . He considered whether he should lay the situation before the Swedish king; but on further thought decided to keep still and wait, at least for the present. A statement to the king concerning the circumstances might be construed as a confession of his own failure as a diplomat and as a young man's guardian. Instead, he resolved to drop just a word, at an appropriate moment, into the ear of the young man himself. He did so, and de Fersen listened gravely. The young count then offered a piece of information which caused the diplomat's eyes to open. He announced that de Kreutz need feel no undue alarm, because he had decided to go to America to fight for liberty.

### III

De Kreutz, submerged beneath duties, had given only passing notice to the progress of the rebellion in a remote English colony somewhere on the other side of the ocean, and since he belonged to an older generation, was unaware of the thrills and stirs going on in the bosom of Young France. Three years previously Lafayette's example in sailing for America to fight under Washington had set the hearts of aristocratic young Frenchmen a-smolder with envy, and when Lafayette returned to Paris with laurels of exotic combat upon his brow and demanded that France send to America not only ships but an army which should give meaning to the recently concluded alliance with the infant republic, these young men echoed his demand with cheers. They instantly besieged the ministry of war for appointments and commands in the French regiments and in ships destined for that romantic land overseas.

"All France," wrote Count Ségur in his memoirs, "was filled with an unbounded love for humanity," and was inspired by "those exaggerated general maxims which raise the enthusiasm of young men and which would cause them to run to the world's end to help a Laplander or a Hottentot."

Among those who won their desire were Frenchmen who afterwards, for one reason or another, became famous — the Marquis de Chastellux, the Duke de Lauzun, the Count de Ségur, the Baron Cromot-Dubourg; Mathieu-Dumas, afterwards minister of war to Joseph Bonaparte at Naples; Duportail, afterwards war minister under the Constituent Assembly; young Talleyrand, brother of the statesman; young Mirabeau, brother of the orator; Saint-Simon, founder of the Saint-Simonian sect; Bougainville the explorer, Custine, Berthier, La Perouse, La Touche-Treville, Barras, and the Marquis de Bouillé, who was later to fail his queen under dramatic circumstances. Conspicuous in the list was de Fersen. He had been definitely promised an appointment as aide to Lieutenant-General Jean Baptiste Donatien de Vimeur, Count de Rochambeau, who was to lead the French army going to the rescue of Washington.

De Kreutz, on hearing this news, whistled, but came away easier in mind. Before the young count's departure he wrote to Gustavus III in Sweden a letter in which pride

in the achievements of his young charge struggled with relief at de Fersen's decision to take himself out of the way:

I ought to confide to Your Majesty that the young Count
Fersen has been so well received by the queen that this has given
umbrage to several persons. I own that I cannot help thinking
that she had a liking for him. I have seen too many indications
to doubt it. The conduct of the young count has been admirable
on this occasion for its modesty and reserve, but above all, in the
decision he made to go to America. By thus departing he avoids
all dangers; but it needed evidently a firmness beyond his years
to surmount that seduction. The queen's eyes could not leave him
during the last days, and they often filled with tears. I entreat
Your Majesty to keep this secret, for her sake and that of Senator
Fersen. When the courtiers heard of Count Fersen's departure
they were delighted. The Duchess de Fitz-James said to him,
"Why, Monsieur, is this the way to abandon your conquest?" "If
I had made one I should not abandon it," he replied. "I go freely,
and unfortunately I leave no regrets behind me."
Your Majesty will agree that that answer shows a wisdom and
prudence beyond his years. In other respects the queen behaves
with much more reserve and wisdom than formerly.

## IV

In the spring of 1780 de Fersen sailed from Brest with
Rochambeau's expedition of 5500 men. He resolved to keep
a journal of his American experiences. He began it in
Paris. There despite the memory of Marie Antoinette's sad
eyes, he could not repress this exhilarated entry on March 2:

"I am so glad I do not know what to do with myself."

Rochambeau, however, could have been in no such joyful mood. Well advanced in years—he was seven years
older than Washington—and a veteran of the Seven Years'
War, he had been called from a peaceful hearth and contented family life, to conduct an army of illusioned young

men to a land filled with savages, across seas patrolled by a vigilant English fleet. His fleet of thirty-six transports, convoyed by seven ships of the line and two frigates, got away after many delays and after he had packed men and gear so tightly that he had to leave his own two battle-horses behind. The Frenchmen were two months and ten days at sea. The voyage was distinguished by much rough weather, an outbreak of scurvy, a brush with a force of English vessels, and considerable sea-sickness.

On July 11, 1780, Newport, Rhode Island, was reached, which town celebrated the event by firing thirteen rockets, putting lights in the windows, and ringing its single bell till midnight. The Rhode Islanders were relieved to find that their guests were orderly, courteous, and prompt to pay.

"It is difficult to imagine," wrote the Abbé Robin, chaplain to the French host, "the idea the Americans entertained about the French before the war. They considered them as groaning under the yoke of despotism, a prey to superstition and prejudices, almost idolatrous in their religion, and as a kind of light, brittle queer-shapen mechanisms, only busy frizzling their hair and painting their faces, without faith or morals."

William Channing, however, apparently found no prejudicial methods of hair-dressing among the visitors; he wrote to Ezra Stiles, president of Yale College:

The French are a fine body of men, and appear to be well-officered. Neither the officers nor men are the effeminate beings we were heretofore taught to believe them. They are as large and likely men as can be produced by any nation.

De Fersen's first American letter, dated August 5, 1780, was sent to his father from the French fortified camp at Newport, which had been promptly blockaded by the English fleet under Admiral Graves. "We wish," he said, "to join General Washington, who is only twenty-five miles from New York." That port at the time was firmly held by the British, and Washington was hoping that the French reinforcements would help him drive them out.

On September 8 de Fersen wrote again in cheerful style. Boasting of the good behavior of his associates, he said:

Nothing is taken from the inhabitants except by their free will and for ready money. We have not yet had a single complaint against the troops. Such discipline is admirable, and astonishes the inhabitants, who are accustomed to the pillage of the English and even their own troops.

But even among such gay reflections there were bound to be a few thorny thoughts, and suddenly there was a change of subject:

You know Frenchmen, my dear father, what are called courtiers, enough to judge of the despair of our young men of that class, who see themselves obliged to pass the winter tranquilly in Newport far from their mistresses and the pleasures of Paris; no suppers, no theatres, no balls. They are in despair. Nothing but an order to march on the enemy could console them. We have had excessive heat throughout the month of August. I have never felt the like in Italy. Now the air is cooler, the climate is superb and the country charming. . . . The general went upon the mainland a week ago. I was the only one of the aides-de-camp who accompanied him. We stayed two days and saw one of the finest regions in the world—well cultivated, situations charming, inhabitants prosperous, but without luxury or display. They content themselves with mere necessaries, which in other lands is the lot of the lower classes. Their clothes are simple but good, and their morals have not been spoiled by the luxury of Europeans. It is a country which will surely be very happy if it can enjoy a long peace.

By October 16 the complete immobility of the French army, due to the blockading British fleet, had made its effects felt and de Fersen wrote despairingly:

We vegetate at the gate of the enemy in the saddest and most dreadful idleness and inactivity.

Up to that time General Washington had never met the French visitors or their commander, but a meeting with Rochambeau now became imperative and a conference was arranged, to take place at Hartford. This gave de Fersen his first opportunity to see the American commander-in-chief, who had ridden all the way from his camp in Bergen County, New Jersey, stopping at the Hudson River for an intimate talk with General Benedict Arnold. General Washington was accompanied on this trip by Lafayette and General Knox. De Fersen drew this picture of him:

I went with M. de Rochambeau about two weeks ago to Hartford, which is forty leagues from here. An interview was to take place with General Washington. M. de Rochambeau sent me in advance to announce his arrival, and I had time to see that illustrious, not to say unique, man of our era. His noble, majestic, but at the same time gentle and honest face agrees perfectly with his moral qualities. He has the air of a hero. He is very cold, speaks little, but is polite and civil. An air of sadness pervades his whole countenance which is not unbecoming to him, and makes him the more interesting.

It was on his way back to New Jersey from this meeting that Washington learned, through the arrest of Major John André, of the treachery of Benedict Arnold.

## V

By December 7 of the same year, 1780, some of the young count's first glowing impressions had faded, and he made a note in this disillusioned vein:

M. de Rochambeau has just made a little journey of six days on the mainland. I went with him. We were only three, and we did not see a fine country or pleasant people. They were as a rule lazy and selfish. How is it possible with those two qualities to make them useful in war?

On January 9, 1781, the young Swedish nobleman, who by now was perhaps wondering why he had ever left Marie Antoinette's side for the bleak comforts of an inactive camp, continued in the same gloomy strain:

The spirit of patriotism exists only in the leaders and principal people of the country, who are making the greatest sacrifices. The others, who form the greater number, think solely of their personal interests. Money is the prime mover of all their actions. They think only of means to gain it. Each is for himself, and none is for the public good. The inhabitants along the coast, even the best Whigs, carry provisions of all kinds to the English fleet, which is anchored in Gardner's Bay, and that because the English pay them well. They fleece us pitilessly, the price of everything is exorbitant. In all the dealings we have with them they treat us more like enemies than friends. Money is their god. Virtue, honor, seem nothing to them compared to the precious metal. I do not mean there are no estimable people whose character is equally noble and generous — there are many; but I speak of the nation in general.

But young de Fersen was not the only observer who entertained despondent views of the course of the American revolution. Profiteering, selfishness, short-sightedness, were everywhere prevalent, as the country's morale sank to its lowest point. The commander of the French fleet, the Chevalier de Ternay, wrote the gloomiest letters home to his king; and even General Washington broke out into harsh invective against his timorous and stagnant countrymen. Matters went from very bad to much worse. On January 14, 1781, de Fersen wrote:

There is a coolness between General Washington and M. de Rochambeau. The displeasure is on the side of the American general. Ours is ignorant of the cause of it. He has charged me with a letter to take to General Washington. I am also to inform myself as to the causes of his displeasure and remove them if possible. So you see, my dear father, I am entering diplomacy.

But at last came the order to the French troops to march south to effect a junction with the American forces bound for the Chesapeake, to which Admiral de Grasse was to bring up his fleet from the West Indies in an effort to dispose of Lord Cornwallis. The Frenchmen were delighted. The sickness which had assailed them in camp disappeared on the road. The country and its inhabitants were transformed. All objects caressed the eye as lovely.

"We were waited on at supper," wrote the Marquis de Chastellux, the leading literary figure among de Fersen's companions, "by a most beautiful girl called Miss Pearce." This was at a tavern twenty-five miles from Providence. "This young person had, like all the American women, a very decent, nay even serious, carriage. She had no objection to be looked at, nor to have her beauty commended, nor even to receive a few caresses, provided it was done without an air of familiarity or libertinism."

Unfortunately de Fersen's journals referring further to this march south were burned in France at the outbreak of the Revolution there, but it is known that he arrived in Williamsburg, Virginia, in September, 1781, and in October he witnessed Cornwallis's surrender at Yorktown.

## VI

"The young French nobility," wrote Talleyrand, "having enlisted for the cause of independence, clung ever after to the principle which it had gone to defend."

Upon their return to France not a few of these young men who had walked all the way from Newport to Yorktown helped to overturn the old régime, but de Fersen was not among them. He went back bearing the decoration of the Order of Cincinnatus bestowed by General Washington, and on reaching Paris was appointed proprietary colonel of the royal Swedish regiment sworn to defend the monarchy. He found that Marie Antoinette was no longer the "little red-head," but was being called much worse names by a restless populace. Nor was his further friendship with the queen favored by his watchful father, who had determined that he should marry Mlle. Necker, daughter of the financier. De Fersen seems not to have been enthusiastic at this prospect, and was easily resigned to her becoming the Baroness de Staël, wife of the Swedish envoy at Paris. De Fersen's father had reckoned without the wilful queen, and soon she was again receiving the *beau Suedois,* as he was called, in her apartments. When, due to dangerous developments, they could not meet, they ex-

changed letters. Only one of Marie Antoinette's letters
written during this period has survived:

> I wish to tell you that I love you, and that I have time for
> nothing else. Let me know to whom I should address the letters
> that I am able to send you, for I can no longer live without that.
> Adieu, the best loved and the most loving of men. I embrace
> you with all my heart.

## VII

De Fersen's duties compelled him to spend much time
in Sweden, and he travelled back and forth until January,
1790, when he returned to Paris to remain more than a
year. Marie Antoinette had dire need of comfort. A few
months before had occurred the attack of the Bastille, the
march of women on Versailles, and the removal of the
royal family to the Paris Tuileries as virtual prisoners.
Since Marie had a poor opinion of Lafayette, then leading
the Moderates, de Fersen urged her to accept the counsels
of Mirabeau, who was willing to preserve the monarchy
provided it would make concessions. But Mirabeau died
before the negotiations were completed, and Marie, fearing for the lives of herself and her two children, decided
upon a secret flight from Paris. The arrangements for the
escape were made chiefly by de Fersen, assisted by the
Marquis de Bouillé, who, as has been mentioned, had been
a fellow member of the Rochambeau expedition to America. De Fersen spent much of his king's money upon the
preparations, including the luxuriously fitted coach which
was to carry the royal family. He even obtained the pass-
port for the royal couple in the name of Baroness de Korff,
a Russian friend.

In the dark of a June night in 1791, de Fersen, dressed as a coachman, drove the fugitives in a cab to a northern gate of Paris where they were transferred to the coach. De Fersen accompanied them as far as the town of Bondy, but Louis XVI would not permit him to go farther, and his wife's Swedish cavalier then went on to Mons, Belgium, with the intention of reporting to the army of noble emigrants which was to invade France and destroy the Revolution.

At Sainte-Menehould, on the edge of the Argonne forest, the village postmaster, Drouet, recognized the king and gave the alarm. At Varennes, on the road to Verdun, the royal party was overtaken and turned back. Bouillé and his troops arrived too late to rescue them. The return was by way of towns since become doubly famous — Chalons, Epernay, and Château Thierry.

On June 23 de Fersen sent this melancholy despatch to the king of Sweden: "Sire, everything has failed. Sixteen leagues from the frontier the King was arrested and taken back to Paris."

## VIII

The château of the Tuileries became a prison in fact as well as in name. Sentinels guarded all gates and doors, and an aide-de-camp of Lafayette kept Marie Antoinette under constant surveillance, even remaining in her chamber at night, behind a screen.

De Fersen went to Brussels to assist his sovereign in an appeal to European monarchs to come to the rescue. Meantime he and Marie Antoinette corresponded by the aid of a cipher written with prepared water or invisible ink. In June, 1791, she smuggled through to him this brief message:

"Be reassured about us. We live." And again she wrote:

"Be at ease. . . . The Assembly means to treat us gently."

Marie was deceived by the optimistic reports concerning the coalition of Powers which she and her cavalier were sure would yet break open her prison doors. Some of the kings of Europe, such as Gustavus III, were hot for the rescue, but others feared to burn their fingers. Charles IV of Spain thus addressed de Fersen's king:

Monsieur, my brother and cousin: It would be useless to undertake a war against a nation enthusiastic for its apparent liberty and seduced against its monarch. The life of that prince would be exposed to the greatest dangers. Armed conquerors, whoever they be, can only possess the territory they occupy; the people and the misled multitude being their enemies, they must exterminate them and ruin the country.

And Leopold of Austria, Marie's brother, wrote in these terms to the Archduchess Marie Christina:

Do not do anything the French ask you to do. Just show them civility and give them dinners, but don't offer them troops or money. I am sorry for their position, but they only think of their romantic schemes, and of their personal interests and vengeances. They imagine that we must all sacrifice ourselves for them.

The very rumors of a possible invasion by foreign powers united France into a fury of resentment, but neither de Fersen nor Marie Antoinette realized the inevitable consequences of that fury. In February, 1792, de Fersen visited

Paris and obtained a short interview with the imprisoned king and queen. He wrote to his father: "They feel strongly that all negotiations with the rebels are utterly useless and that the only means of re-establishing their authority is by force and foreign help."

Meantime the ferment which was seething through France had spread to other parts of Europe, and a month later de Fersen's own king was shot down at a masked ball.

On January 27, 1793, a note was handed to de Fersen, then at Dusseldorf, announcing the execution of Louis XVI.

On October 20 of the same year another note reached him at Brussels. It announced that Marie Antoinette had died beneath the blade of revolution on the 6th.

## IX

De Fersen returned to Sweden, was appointed grand marshal, and became leader of the Conservative, or aristocratic party. In 1805 Sweden joined the disastrous war of coalition against Napoleon Bonaparte, which left her population impoverished, disillusioned, angry. De Fersen was hated as a reactionary. On June 20, 1810, he attended the funeral of the Swedish crown prince at the capital. He was recognized and dragged out of his carriage. He was denounced as an aristocrat and obstructionist. He broke away, but was overtaken, mobbed, and beaten to death.

## X

There can be little doubt that it was this Swedish lover of Marie Antoinette who, acting under his king's orders, was to a degree responsible for the attempt of European monarchs and nobles to destroy the French Revolution before it should mature; and it was this interference that led to factional suspicion among the revolutionary leaders, to the Terror, and to the rivers of blood that flowed from the guillotine. While he was organizing the royal flight to the frontier, beyond which the armies of the counter-revolutionary coalition were forming, de Fersen wrote to the Baron de Breteuil, one of Marie Antoinette's aides:

Mercy in such cases appears to me extremely pernicious. This is the moment to destroy the Jacobins. . . . We must not hope to win them over by kindness; they must be exterminated, and this is the moment.

And he wrote to his own king:

It should be the common interest of all sovereigns to nip in the bud an evil whose progress is alarming. It is not a simple question of policy, for here the cause of kings is at stake. Without order no society, no security, no property, can exist. Kings are the born depositories of order; they ought to preserve their authority for the welfare of their people.[1]

## XI

Gustavus III probably needed no such incitements, for already he had decided that in his own kingdom there should be no other gods before him. When he had ascended the throne made famous by Charles XII, by Gustavus Adolphus, and Gustavus Vasa, he had found Sweden fermenting with the same brew that had been troubling every land in Europe—the effort of a middle class, invigorated

[1]Klinckowstrom, *Le Comte de Fersen et la cour de France,* Paris, 1877.

by the riches won in commerce, to rise to an equality with a nobility anchored upon feudalism. A war was on between the "Hats" and the "Caps." The Hats represented the nobles, the army, and the land-owning aristocracy. The Cap party included the town burghers and merchants, the lower clergy, and the peasants.

In this war Gustavus threw the royal power on the side of the lower estates, thereby gaining great popularity. But Gustavus had little sympathy with political democracy, and still less with political equality. He supported the middle classes because he intended with their help to tame, as Louis XIV of France had done, an arrogant aristocracy, and bring it humbly around a shining throne. He meant to do in Sweden as Louis XIV had done in France — make himself the supreme power. (Here again we behold the shadow of the Grand Monarch, which spread itself over the whole of the century, deluding kings — and queens — and leading them to abysses.)

## XII

The whole of Gustavus's upbringing had been designed to foster in him egotism and self-will. He had drunk in the liquor of aristocracy with the very milk of his mother's breasts. She was Leonora Ulrica, sister of Frederick the Great of Germany, and more than blood-akin to that gusty monarch. Like her Prussian brother, nature had given her an enormous energy, but unlike him, she could not channel it off into war, state-building, and political intrigue. Hence she made of her domestic circle an empire. Over this she ruled with a savage tyranny. When she could not get her own way by imperious commands, she got it with sulks and tears. She converted her very illnesses into instruments of despotism and throughout a lifetime harassed her son and his ministers with whims and tempers. When at last, to Gustavus's relief, she lay dying, she converted the very death-bed interview into a scene. Death itself approached her with trepidation, and it would not have been strange to hear that she had found fault with a nervous Charon all the way across the river Styx.

Like her brother Frederick II, she had dipped into Voltaire and Pierre Bayle, and the liberal ideas thus obtained she mixed with the most reactionary instincts. It was her notion that princes should not perspire in the vulgar fashion of the common people, and she prevented the child Gustavus from playing at too active games. Lest gross food should dull his mind, she fed him on soups, creams, and vegetables.[2]

Above all, she dreaded, like most monarchs of the period, the boredom that sits in palaces, and she would not have her son sit before tasks that required thoroughness and mastery. She banished from his curriculum all philosophy, religion, and mathematics and all languages except French. Gustavus grew up under a régime of perfect "self-expression." He was versatile, but he could not concentrate. He was facile, but he was not learned. He was wilful, petulant, and filled with a high conceit of himself, but fortunately he was, when not crossed, good-tempered and truthful, and his people, so long accustomed to being ruled by

[2]Bain, *Gustavus III and His Contemporaries,* Vol. I, p. 15.

strong-armed boors, were charmed to have as king a little synthetic Frenchman, having the amiability of Louis XV at his best and the imperiousness of Louis XIV at his worst.

The one passion with which Chancellor Tessin, his chief tutor, succeeded in filling Gustavus was a love for imaginative literature and drama. He wrote plays when in his 'teens, and when he was ten he could stand up in his bed and recite long dramatic passages, making head-dresses and trains of sheets and towels. It is recorded that he was especially fond of enacting female rôles.[3] Indeed, the prince's nature revealed conspicuous feminine strains. He could take in the details of a dress from a corner of his eye, and he was fond of dressing up his subjects in costumes now anciently Swedish and again modernly French. Balls, receptions, masques, routs, ceremonies—whatever brought color and glitter upon the stage of life—for these he had a passion. In short, he was a romantic, and he rejected whatever was prosy and usual in favor of ornament and fantasy.

## XIII

Yet withal he was often practical and canny, and viewing his subjects and their lives as material to be molded into agreeable forms, he strove to remake mediæval Sweden into something modern and very French. He abolished the prison tortures inherited from the Middle Ages and, responsive to his merchants and bankers, he reformed and stabilized the currency and encouraged the filling of the north seas with Swedish ships. He founded an academy of arts and letters. The middle classes, strengthened by his

[3] *Idem.*

energetic measures, saw him as godlike, but the aristocracy regarded him with a more saturnine eye. To the nobles he was a disturber of ancient privileges and they followed him with sullen feet.

Among his antagonists none was more resentful than the Marshal Axel de Fersen, descendant of an immigrant Scotchman named MacPherson, and Sweden's richest man and most arrogant landowner. The marshal sometimes quarrelled fiercely with Gustavus and called him a wrecker, but Gustavus countered by seducing his son Jean (or Hans) away from him and making him his secret agent at the court of Louis XVI and Marie Antoinette. Gustavus had reason to keep an eye upon Versailles, for from the French treasury he drew enormous subsidies as the Bourbon ally in the north and as watchdog of Russia on the one hand and England on the other.[4]

## XIV

The French Revolution was Gustavus's touchstone. He feared its every manifestation not only because its contagion might threaten the whole guild of European monarchs, but because it might cut off his steadiest source of revenue. Without that the Swedish throne would be poor; for the aristocracy, largely consisting of great landowners, had always been reluctant and evasive payers of taxes, and he dared not too greatly tax the trading classes on whose sup-

[4]Sweden between 1772 and 1788 received 32,200,000 livres, according to Akeson, the Swedish historian. The subsidies paid to Gustavus and the loans made to the American colonies during Louis XVI's reign were largely responsible for the disorder in French finances, and thus promoted the Revolution.

port he was politically dependent. The French subsidies, begun in Louis XIV's time, not only maintained his expensive court, but paid for the romantic glitter with which he surrounded himself—the theatrical representations, the balls and masques, the costuming of his courtiers, the grants to poets and other literary men, even the production of his own plays.[5]

Moreover, Gustavus had been brought up on French literature and had done his best to introduce into his native land a Swedified French culture; his mother and his uncle Frederick II of Germany had made him an ardent reader of Voltaire and the Philosophes, and their ideas had helped him to shape himself into the image they held up before him—a benevolent, liberal, and enlightened despot.

Certainly Gustavus III meant to do well by his people; he also meant to do 'well by Gustavus III and the race of kings.

## XV

When the French Revolution began to develop Gustavus lost all patience with the Baron de Staël, his envoy at Versailles, for his failure to check it, and selected as his agent at Paris the young de Fersen, commissioning him to find a way to restore the monarchy.

"So long as there is a Paris," he remarked, "kings cannot exist in France." He outlined to de Fersen a plan by which the royal family was to be rescued from the Tuileries and a

[5]Gustavus III was the author of such dramas as *Gustav Adolf's Adelmod, Helmfelt, Siri Brahe,* and *Natalia Narishkin,* once regarded as the masterpieces of the Swedish theatre.

provincial congress was to be set up which should deal with all rebels as traitors. While de Fersen was having built, at a cost of 6000 livres, the flight-carriage in the name of the Baroness de Korff, Gustavus hurried to Aix where he received the hosts of fleeing aristocrats, keeping an open table for them and entertaining them lavishly. But contact with the emigrés produced disillusions.

"You have no idea of their exaggerated notions on all subjects," he wrote home. " 'Tis certainly curious to hear them, but it is melancholy too."

When the Varennes flight failed, Gustavus sent a note to all the Powers urging them to form a coalition army to invade France and wipe out the rebels. He strongly pressed Catherine the Great of Russia to send 6000 Russians to match 6000 Swedes which were to descend on France from the north while an army of Spaniards and Sardinians attacked from the south. He advised that all these armies be under "a supreme chief of sufficient rank and disinterestedness," and left it to be plainly inferred that this supreme chief was to be himself.

But amidst countless quarrels and intrigues the scheme came to nothing, and at length the invasion was started from Prussia under the muddle-headed Duke of Brunswick, whose deeds and proclamations produced as their major fruit the Terror.

## XVI

The attention Gustavus gave to foreign affairs meantime left openings of which his enemies among the nobility at home took advantage. They were already incensed by the loss of ancient privileges and by the favors shown to members of the lower estates; and when Sweden's financial system, strained by wars with Russia and all but wrecked by the loss of the French subsidies, began to waver, they proclaimed Gustavus to be an incompetent ruler and revived their old effrontery. They even withdrew their women from attendance at court diversions and perfected a social boycott that so unnerved Gustavus he passed the winter of 1791–92 in seclusion, dropping his old gaieties and turning his thoughts to religion. At last the government was scraping the bottom of the treasury and could pay off its army officers only in depreciated paper; while the navy, once the special pet of Gustavus, grumbled so loudly that at Carlscrona a mutiny all but came to a head.

To the army officers the drop in their pay was unendurable, and certain among them united with a few nobles to rid the country of Gustavus and to set up a monarchy of the old style, in which the nobility and the army would be supreme over the other estates and even the throne would be subservient. The conspiracy grew until it included almost half of the Swedish aristocracy.[6] It comprised General Pechlin, a careerist; Baron Bjelke, of an old family; Count Ribbing, an ex-guardsman; Count Horn, a military dude; Captain Liljehorn, a former court page; and Captain Jakob Johan Anckarstrom, a quarrelsome landowner.

These men raised an agitation which forced Gustavus to call a meeting of the Diet, although he despised parliaments and other semblances of political democracy. Before a secret committee of the Diet it was revealed that the gov-

[6]Bain.

ernment, due to the last military encounter between Gustavus and Catherine II of Russia, was virtually bankrupt; that nevertheless it was considering interfering in Poland to prevent its partition; and at the same time the king was building in Haga Park a palace which was to rival Louis XIV's château at Versailles.

All this news made a bad impression even on the estates that had so far supported the king, and for a moment it seemed that Gustavus had no friends. He became despondent, and when it became evident that his enemies were increasing, he said:

"If I am to die a violent death, I pray that it may be publicly, on the scaffold, not by the hand of a Damiens or a Ravaillac."[7]

On March 16, 1792, the last masquerade ball of the season was arranged at the showy opera house, built by Gustavus himself, and Gustavus, to show himself at ease and to defy those members of the nobility who scarcely any longer showed him respect, decided to attend. In the evening he attended a performance of *Les Folies Amoreuses* at the French Theatre and then went to the ball.

At the opera house a messenger brought him a letter written in an affectedly rude hand and tone. It advised the king not to attend the masquerade that night and cautioned him to mend his ways. Gustavus showed the note to his chancellor, laughed, and dressed for the ball. He put on a tricorne hat, a Venetian silk mantle, and a half mask. He left his breast glittering with decorations. After watching the dancers for a time, he walked out on the floor. Two

[7]Bain.

groups of black dominoes then came together so as to catch the king between them.

Count Horn had been selected as the finger-man. He tapped the king on the shoulder, and when Gustavus turned, Anckarstrom shot him in the back. The army officer had provided himself with two muzzle-loading pistols, loaded with bullets, slugs, and nails, and carried a sharpened butcher-knife. From this wound Gustavus died. He was forty-six years old and had reigned twenty-one years.

After the attack Anckarstrom had dropped his pistols to the floor and, protected by the confusion, had mingled unconcernedly with the throng on the opera house floor. But he was traced through the locksmith who had repaired his pistols. His right hand was cut off and he was then beheaded.

The assassination of Gustavus put an end to the whole Gustavian epoch. The aristocratic party came back to power, ruled with a high hand, and involved the country in the Napoleonic wars. But it was too late for the restoration of the rule of feudal lords. The submerged classes revolted against them and pulled them down, and de Fersen, once Gustavus's secret agent and Marie Antoinette's secret lover, died among the dying nobles.

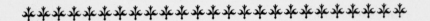

## CHAPTER TWELVE

# END OF VASSALAGE

### I

AFTER the execution of Marie Antoinette and Louis XVI, the Revolution in France went on, backing and filling and fumbling and hesitating, but keeping its sense of direction until at last on July 17, 1793, the Convention in Paris took a step that instantly cut off the past as if with an axe: it issued a decree, abolishing all the rights and privileges of the feudal lords:

*All dues formerly seigneurial, feudal rights, both fixed and casual . . . are suppressed without indemnity.*

The results were apparent within a relatively few years. Famine, which used to afflict some part of France every year, so that one-third of the country was perpetually hungry, was stamped out. Feudalism and famine—these sisters and twins—went out together. The eighteenth century was well acquainted with them; the nineteenth knew them less.

But even before royal absolutism and feudal rights were abolished by decree, the Revolution had caused a convulsive

reaction elsewhere in Europe. It appeared that all possession, whether of thrones or property, was threatened, and
monarchs and statesmen, incited by the de Fersens and
Gustavuses, drew together to crush the menace in France,
and, while it was weak, to dismember it. The spearhead of
the attack was formed of Prussians led by their emperor-
king, Frederick William II, successor to Frederick the
Great. The Prussian army was joined by several corps of
Austrians and by a few thousand French *emigrés*—those
nobles and the sons of nobles who had deserted Louis XVI
and fled to Germany, accompanied by squads of servants
and battalions of mistresses. Before ordering the march
against France, the Duke of Brunswick, commander of the
allied army, issued a proclamation in which this clause appeared:

> *Their Imperial and Royal Majesties render personally respon-
> sible for anything that may happen, under peril of their heads,
> and of military execution without hope of pardon, all members
> of the National Assembly, the Municipality, the National Guards,
> the Justices of the Peace, and all others whom it may concern.*

The proclamation further declared that if the Palace of
the Tuileries or the persons of the royal family suffered
the least violence, the allied monarchs would take *"an ex-
emplary and never-to-be-forgotten vengeance by giving up
the town of Paris to military execution and to total sub-
version, and the guilty rebels to the death they have deserved."*

This invading army was halted and stood off by a French
army of so-called "tailors and cobblers" at Valmy. Among
those who looked on as the Prussian attack disintegrated

was the young German provincial, Goethe. He went away and wrote this to himself in his diary:

From this place and this day dates a new epoch in the history of the world, and you will be able to say, I was there.

## II

The Duke of Brunswick's proclamation accomplished far more than his army. It produced the Terror.

Thomas Carlyle and other romantic and prejudiced writers have made it appear that the French Revolution was the work of a rabble composed of monsters, sub-human and demoniac. Actually its leaders and orators were members of the respectable middle class. Robespierre was a college graduate and lawyer. Marat was a former court physician. Danton was a lawyer who had married a rich wife. In the National Convention sat 215 lawyers and 379 men who had been office-holders or professional men. The Committee of Public Safety, that governed France between September, 1793, and July, 1794, was composed of twelve men; seven were lawyers, two were engineers, one was a Protestant pastor, one was an actor, and one was a law student, the son of a retired army captain.

When the guillotining of Louis XVI brought Pitt and English money into the circle designed to crush the Revolution, and when threatening insurrections were stirred up in provincial cities, the leaders of the Revolution began to fear that the old régime was to be re-imposed on them. They had already had their quarrels, chiefly over property and whether it was to be public or private; they now began

ROBESPIERRE

*Who sounded the ideals of Rousseau
in the French Revolution*

LORD CHESTERFIELD

*Anatomist of Georgian society in
England*

GENERAL ROCHAMBEAU

*Leader of the French forces in Amer-
ica who made possible Washington's
victory at Yorktown. From the painting by Peale*

GOUVERNEUR MORRIS

*American envoy to France and friend
and protector of royalty. From the
painting by Sully in Independence
Hall, Philadelphia*

FURNITURE DESIGN UNDER LOUIS XVI

*Characterized by daintiness and formality reacting from the extravagant and rococo designs of Louis XV. Secrétaire of Marie Antoinette designed by Riesener. From the Morgan loan collection in the Metropolitan Museum of Art*

to suspect each other of dealings with the enemy and then to accuse each other of betraying and selling out the Revolution. They saw reaction and royalty getting stronger; they saw monarchy marching back over the French borders; they saw themselves being saddled once more with the exactions, interferences, and taxes of an interlocking nobility, clergy, and throne. The Convention proclaimed that "the tyrants are still threatening us," and Robespierre declared that these tyrants were dangerous only because they had "accomplices inside the country." He demanded the "stifling of the enemies of the Revolution, within and without." So rose the Terror.

It lasted until 1795, when a decree put an end to the revolutionary tribunal, and a reaction set in, which forbade even the official use of the word "revolutionary." After that came the Directory, Napoleon's whiff of grapeshot, and the victory of the bourgeoisie both over the royalists and the communards.

## III

The French Revolution ended in a triumph for the middle classes not made complete, however, until Napoleon came. Its immediate and most impressive effect was the liberation of the land and of the people who lived and worked upon it. No longer was it possible for an estate-owner to make serfs of the peasants, who at last, in theory at least, were equal to other men in the eyes of the law. Vassalage disappeared from French soil in so far as it gave the landlord control over the person of the laborer. Whatever politically democratic institutions were established by the Rev-

olution were partly stamped out under the ensuing Directory, the Consulate, the Empire, and under the restoration
of the Bourbons, and reaction brought back emperors and
kings to restore thrones and dictatorships; but not even the
cæsarism of the Napoleons was ever able to restore feudalism. Its institutions were so outmoded, its exactions were
so obstructive, its forms were so hollowed out by decay,
that not even a Bonaparte, or any other man on horseback,
could have re-imposed it.

The impression made on the world was enormous.
Feudal serfdom began to retreat elsewhere in Europe, but
was not lifted by official decree in Prussia until 1884 or in
Russia until 1861. Nevertheless, absolutism, whether in
courts or palaces, or in meadow or field, was on the de-
fensive throughout the nineteenth century. Only in industry, as yet embryonic, was it left unmolested.

## IV

The French Revolution was only in a small degree social-
istic or communistic, as those terms are understood today.
There was a body of agitators who wished to see the land
given to the people as a common possession, but they were
in the end suppressed, and the estates of the nobles were
divided and sold off to those able to buy them. There was a
distinct emphasis on property rights. The Declaration of
the Rights of Man, made in August, 1789, was firm in its
insistence that property must be safeguarded. "The aim of
all political association," it said, "is the preservation of the
natural and imprescriptible rights of man. These rights are

liberty, property, security, and resistance to oppression."
And it repeated: "Since property is an inviolable and sacred
right, no one shall be deprived thereof except where public
necessity, legally determined, shall clearly demand it. . . ."

"I defy you to do away with poverty altogether," exclaimed Saint-Just, friend and lieutenant of Robespierre,
"unless each one has his own land."

It was this view that prevailed and France became a nation of small proprietors — small owners of land and of
commercial enterprises — each to work out his own salvation and somehow in the ensuing competition to contribute
to the general good, as taught by Adam Smith and his
school at a time when it was not yet seen that competition
could only end in monopoly and the suppression of competition. It was these thousands of small proprietors of
whom Napoleon afterwards wrote:

It is to their labors and to their blood that we shall owe a general peace, tranquillity, flourishing commerce, and the advantages
of civil liberty. [and again he wrote:] The emperor's decrees
have re-established commerce on the left bank of the Rhine. Our
manufacturers are improving, although the mercenaries subsidized by the British government vaunt, in their empty declara-
tions, her foreign trade and her precarious resources scattered
about the seas and in the Indies, while they describe our shops as
deserted and our artisans as dying of hunger. In spite of this, our
industries are striking root in our own soil and are driving English commerce far from our shores. Our products now equal
theirs and will soon compete with them in all the markets of the
world.

Soon Napoleon was declaring the whole of England
under blockade and was trying to close all of Europe's
markets to English goods.

"So it happened," wrote Pasquier in his *Memoirs,*[1] "that through the most persevering and at times the most ingenious efforts, by the aid of a succession of decrees, and with the help of that strange invention of licenses which were nothing but organized smuggling, continental industry, or rather French industry, backed up with a million bayonets and with an auxiliary force of coast guards, succeeded in meeting a tremendous competition and in deriving large profits."

Nationalism and militarism were the fruits of the Revolution no less than the destruction of feudalism and the liberation of the land. It was Napoleon's mission to complete this destruction in his forays backwards and forwards across Europe.[2] He was the effective agent of that middle class which had been struggling against the cords of a hampering feudalism ever since the opening of the century. At first this struggle was silent and subdued, as under the frown of Louis XIV; as the middle of the century was passed it became more vigorous; and then at last it broke into the triumphant cheers of the Revolution which Napleon shaped into a dictatorship.

[1]Robinson and Beard, *Readings in Modern European History,* Vol. I, p. 350.

[2]For example, Napoleon decreed in 1808 the abolition of feudal rights and monopolies in Spain, declaring "it shall be free to every one who shall conform to the laws to develop his industry without restraint." He also abolished the tribunal of the Inquisition and reduced the number of monastic orders as interfering "with the prosperity of the State." Finally he decreed that "the barriers existing between the provinces shall be suppressed" and ordered the custom houses to be removed to the frontier.

## CHAPTER THIRTEEN

# BUBBLES OF REACTION

### I

ENGLAND reacted against the French Revolution not only by hurling men, ships, and money against it, but by the pursuit of Englishmen suspected of sympathy with it. In the winter of 1795–96 Parliament passed two statutes, the first of which provided punishment not only for treasonable acts, but for speaking or writing in such a manner as to incite hatred of the government; the second prohibited all large public meetings except by special permission and placed lecture-rooms, where political discussions were held, in the same class as disorderly houses.

These suppressive enactments were fostered by the speeches of public men like Burke, who could encourage an American revolution but could not stomach a French one. Oppressed men, he declared, must look to "the final proportions of eternal justice." He was replied to by Thomas Paine, who denied that man had any rightful property in man; "neither has any generation a property in the generations which are to follow." Burke was also answered by Mary Wollstonecraft, who exclaimed, "Security of property! Behold, in a few words, the definition of English liberty!"

English writers and other intellectuals exhibited a reaction scarcely less marked than Burke's. Wordsworth, who in his early years had warmly greeted the Revolution and in the burgeoning of hope had written that "to be young was very heaven," withdrew in his old age from political agitation and retired to the lakes and mountains and solitude. Southey, who in his youth, to show his sympathy with the Revolution, had worn his hair unpowdered and undressed, lived to look upon Shelley with wonder and to exclaim, "He was just like I was in 1794."[1] Coleridge, who in 1789 had written poetry rejoicing in the fall of the Bastille, drowned his disappointment in human nature by resorting to laudanum and opium. William Godwin, who in his youth wrote *Political Justice,* lived to scorn universal suffrage and to become dependent on a Whig government's bounty. Robert Burns, who in a burst of enthusiasm had sent a present of guns to the Convention in Paris, was reduced to inaction by his employers of the Dumfries Excise Board, but could not be estopped from singing:

> It's coming yet for a' that,
> That man to man, the whole world o'er,
> Shall brithers be for a' that.

William Hazlitt was compelled to confess he "little dreamed . . . the sun of liberty would turn to blood or set once more in the night of despotism." William Blake, who once wore a red cap in the streets of London and called

[1] Dowden, *Life of Shelley,* Vol. I, p. 211.

*From "Georgian England" by A. E. Richardson*

STATELY INTERIOR OF A GEORGIAN HOUSE

*Dining room at Holkham, England. The white finish came in
under Queen Anne*

GEORGIAN ART AND COSTUMING

*Portrait of Mrs. Carnac by Sir Joshua Reynolds in the Wallace Collection*

himself a "liberty boy," was tried for treasonable utterances and thereafter contented himself with oblique prophecies.

## II

These men placed upon the relatively narrow shoulders of the Revolution more than it could bear. They saw in it the release of all mankind from physical, mental, and spiritual bondage, and not the simple act of a class rupturing its binding cocoon. We can look now upon the Revolution as a stage in an evolutionary process; they regarded it as final; and when it showed itself not to be final, their world turned black. They did not perceive that around them was developing a revolution second only to the French upheaval, although lacking in violence and dramatic spectacle.

It is usual to speak of what occurred in England in the latter years of the century as the Industrial Revolution. But before there was an industrial revolution there was an agricultural one; there was a shifting of forces on the land before there was one in the workshop. Up to this time the fields of England had been "open" ones. The ownership was separate, but the cultivation was done by common agreement and the meadows and pastures were held in common. The tenants grouped themselves into villages in accordance with the manorial system planted and fostered by William the Conqueror.[2]

The great landowners contended this system, now 700 years old, was slothful and inefficient. The fields were cultivated in strips, often widely separated; weeds and erosion

[2]See the author's book, *William the Conqueror*, N. Y., 1934.

developed; and farm animals, due to sparse and haphazard winter grazing, were improperly fed. Arguing for organized methods and greater yields, the landed proprietors brought pressure upon Parliament, which passed Enclosure Acts that bound separate strips into compact holdings, wiped out the common pastures, and required each enlarged farm to be enclosed with hedges that would check weeds, prevent erosion, and act as boundary lines. This was the origin of those hedges that are now such a feature of the English rural landscape. They are the counterpart of the walls that surround the castles and manorial houses, testifying to individual ownership and emphasizing it.

Thus was the English village broken up. It lost the communal character it had had since the middle ages and no longer existed as an organism and social center. Its passing put an end to what was left of Merrie England, with its leisurely life and jocund diversions, and its sense of security.

In the American colonies the village, with its strong community sense, fastened itself and survived only in New England. In the rest of the country it took root feebly or not at all. In the middle and southern states the pioneer, with his eagerness for the large tracts of land and elbow-room that had been denied him in the Old World, had no patience with villages. Those that sprang up were trading-posts, not centers of tillage or social life. And so the small-holding American farmer developed as a frontiersman, isolated and individual, rarely combining with his fellows except for defense against the Indians and having small sense of social union with them except through the country church.

## III

In England the enclosing of the common lands under great proprietors forced agricultural workers and landless men into the towns where lack of occupation induced dejection and drunkenness. Arthur Young, whose acute eyes could survey the English as well as the French countryside, wrote just as the century closed:

> Go to an ale-house kitchen of an old enclosed country, and there you will see the origin of poverty and poor rates. For whom are they to be sober? For whom are they to save? (Such are their questions.) For the parish? If I am diligent, shall I have leave to build a cottage? If I am sober, shall I have land for a cow? If I am frugal, shall I have half an acre for potatoes? You offer me motives; you have nothing but a parish officer and a workhouse! Bring me another pot.[3]

## IV

The Industrial Revolution occurred just in time to give employment to those families that had been swept off the land. But the inventions that rose in the closing years of the century did not introduce the machine age; improved and complex tools had become so common even in the early part of the century as to attract the attention of an intellectual like Diderot in his encyclopedia. What happened was the linking of machines to steam power. So James Watt's steam engine introduced not the machine age, but the power age.

Watt's engine was developed just as the American peoples, freed from British restrictions and with energies re-

[3]Quoted in *English Economic History:* Select Documents, p. 536.

leased to work upon limitless resources, began to pour upon Europe a wealth of metals, minerals, and raw materials, at the same time absorbing the Old World's unemployed. England, with deposits of coal and iron closely juxtaposed, was in an extraordinarily fortunate position to take advantage of a highly favorable economic position. Her triumph over Napoleon, completed by 1815, enabled her to complete the conquest of Europe's markets through the enhanced production derived from power-driven machinery.

If the eighteenth century be regarded as a hundred years of struggle between England and France, there is no question of England's victory. Watt's engines completed what William III began, and with America absorbed in her own vast self, England went on to the conquest of one-fifth of the world's land and one-fourth of its peoples. Superior wealth and superior tools did it. And with English arms and textiles went English culture.

ADAM SMITH                                    TURGOT

*From a photograph in the Otto Bettmann Collection*

PIERRE BAYLE                          WILLIAM PITT, THE ELDER

*They shaped some of the ideas that governed the eighteenth century*

SALESMAN FIRST

*Talleyrand, who swam the waves under four different régimes. From an engraving by Desnoyers after the painting by Gerard*

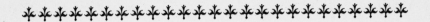

## CHAPTER FOURTEEN

# *MASTER SALESMAN*

### I

I T WAS Napoleon Bonaparte, with his dream of con-
quering all the world and its markets for France, who
became the supreme agent of the merchant state; and with
feudalism dead, with royal despotism destroyed, and with
the power of the nobility gone, a new figure walked out
upon Europe's stage. It was the salesman. Ministers, diplomats, and even emperors and kings became salesmen, trading in territories and peoples and angling for national
advantage. And if in their deals, they made something for
themselves, was it any more than their due commission?

Among the master salesmen of the period no figure was
more impressive than that of Talleyrand. He was active
in the Revolution, in the ensuing Directory, in Napoleon's
Consulate, in the Empire, and in the restoration of the
Bourbons to the throne of France, serving them all, surviving them all, and somehow turning them all to his own
advantage. So greatly did he triumph over the obstacles
that formed what a later century called "sales-resistance"
that Mme. de Staël, who knew him very well, once said of
him with mingled exasperation and admiration:

"He sold the Consulate, he sold the Empire and the Emperor, he sold the Restoration; he sold everything; and he will not cease to sell until his last day everything he can sell and even everything he cannot."

It was the fashion at one time to regard Talleyrand as an enigmatic and even a sinister figure; so great was his reputation for wickedness, so great was the awe of him, that once when he was a visitor in London crowds hastily parted to make a lane for him, gazing upon him as if he were Satan. Such a reception was not displeasing to Talleyrand and he could not resist showing a little professional pride in his reputation as an enigma. "There is something inexplicable about me," he once said to Louis XVIII, "which brings ill luck on the governments that neglect me."

This was no boast. There were persons and institutions that sometimes ill-treated Charles Maurice Talleyrand-Périgord, but he retaliated with no vengeful counter-attacks, for he had learned how to make even Time work for Talleyrand.

## II

Fate itself imposed on him an early handicap. When he was a child a fall injured his right foot. It healed imperfectly so that it resembled a horse's hoof. His parents, ambitious and pushing courtiers, believed that this injury would unfit him for aught but an ecclesiastical career and they placed him in the hands of the church. His theologic days were passed in a miserable solitude,[1] from which he

[1] Talleyrand said to Mme. de Remusat: "You see, situated as I was, I had either to die of distress or to toughen myself so as not to feel the lack of what I could not have."

rescued himself by associating himself with influential personages, especially those women who were so powerful in eighteenth-century France. One day Louis XVI appointed him Bishop of Autun. He joined the Free-Masons and constantly enlarged the circle of which he was the radius, also the center. In this circle were many women with nothing to do, and Talleyrand amused them by making love to them, respectfully if required, disrespectfully if not. He ended his letters to them with "I love you with all my heart," varied by "I love you with all my soul." These women, although they saw through him, were often his agents and promoters; it gave them something to do.

With men he was less successful. His little overtures of friendship made them suspect his motives or repelled them. For example, he once gave to Gouverneur Morris, the American envoy at the court of Louis XVI,[2] a little book which Morris found repugnant. It was called *L'Histoire de Dom B., Portier de Chartreux* and pretended to deal with the adventures of a priestly amorist. Morris could not stomach it, and afterwards could never relish Talleyrand's company which was already distasteful to Morris, who had

[2]Morris, one of the drafters of the United States Constitution, was sent to France by President Washington as successor to Franklin and Jefferson. In Paris he allied himself with the aristocracy and during the Revolution placed his house and services at the disposal of the counter-revolutionists. When Louis XVI saw the crisis coming he placed his cash funds with Morris for safe-keeping, and there is evidence that Morris was in the plot with de Fersen and others to rescue Louis and Marie Antoinette. In the War of 1812 he was on the side of England against the United States and long before the Civil War, he was an advocate of New England's secession from the Union. "He was an American through and through," said Theodore Roosevelt. See his *Gouverneur Morris*, N. Y., 1899, p. 317.

sought the favor of a Mme. de Flahaut, only to find that Talleyrand had already won it.[3]

Of the Paris society in which Talleyrand swam so easily Morris wrote to President Washington:

Everybody agrees that there is an utter prostration of morals—but this general position can never convey to the American mind the degree of depravity—an hundred anecdotes, and an hundred thousand examples are required. . . . There are men and women who are greatly and eminently virtuous. I have the pleasure to number many in my own acquaintance, but they stand forward from a background deeply and darkly shaded. It is however from such crumbling material that the great edifice of liberty must be erected.[4]

## III

In the early days of the Revolution Talleyrand was a representative of the clergy in the States-General and Constituent Assembly. In 1792 he was sent to London on a concealed diplomatic mission. He was coldly received by George III and his ministers, but, having no taste for the tumult of the Revolution, he lingered in England until expelled by the passage of the Alien Bill, which Parliament had enacted in an endeavor to cut England off from any possible revolutionary infection.

Not daring to return to France Talleyrand sailed for America, intending there to construct for himself a new life and make a fortune. "It is not necessary," he once said, "to be a poor devil." He carried letters of introduction, but

[3]Morris once wrote concerning a visit to her: "Madame being ill, goes into the bath and when placed there sends for me. It is a strange place to receive a visit, but there is milk mixed with the water, making it opaque."

[4]Walther, *Gouverneur Morris*, N. Y., 1934.

although he was cordially welcomed by Alexander Hamilton, President Washington declined to receive him. This was partly due to fear of offending the French government, with which Talleyrand was on ill terms; but perhaps mostly due to a private letter from Gouverneur Morris, who concerning Talleyrand spoke of "the variety and the publicity of his amours, his passion for gambling, and above all, his *agiotage* [speculation in money exchange] under the ministry of M. de Calonne."

## IV

In America Talleyrand remained just over two years, during which he visited Philadelphia, New York, Albany and Boston. At Boston he was pleased with a Mme. de Gouvernet, wife of an emigrant noble, and wrote of her to Mme. de Staël:

She speaks the language well, she has simple manners, and what is highly praised here, she sleeps every night with her husband; they have only one room. Tell this to Mathieu and Narbonne; tell them this is an article essential for a good reputation in this country.[5]

In his letters home he made other observations concerning life in the infant American republic, for example: "Don't speak to me of that country where every man you meet wants to sell you his dog. . . . In that country the business of every one without exception is to make a fortune. Money is the sole and universal cult; the measure of all distinctions."

[5]Lacour-Gayet, *Talleyrand*.

How careful a man ought to be in making criticisms, for in so doing he may be delivering verdicts upon himself. At the very time Talleyrand was commenting upon the all-pervading materialism in America he himself was trying to speculate in land and writing letters to Holland and Germany to induce his *emigré* friends to join him in promotional schemes that would bring him quick and easy fortunes.

Speculation in land was one of the institutions let loose by the revolutions both in France and America. In France the breaking up of the feudal estates of the nobles provided opportunities for buying and selling of which the commercial classes took full advantage. In America the destruction of French outposts and the retreat of the Indians had opened vast territories beyond the Alleghenies and the great rivers, and as the population pushed steadily westward, grandiose land companies were organized to buy up tracts ahead of the settlers and when they arrived to sell to them at profits which were sometimes enormous and sometimes otherwise. Not a few of the founding fathers took a hand in these speculations and Robert Morris (not related to Gouverneur Morris), the Philadelphian who gambled on the effects of the American Revolution, ruined himself with them.

Talleyrand's attempts to procure funds from abroad for similar enterprises were not successful; nevertheless his efforts led him into a study of economics by which he became convinced that, due to increased transatlantic trade, England had benefited enormously by the separation from America, and that France, if it was to prosper as a merchant state, must share in this trade and must find and establish colonies.

## V

When in 1794 he was permitted to return to Europe, by way of Hamburg, he was ready to begin the career that made him one of the most imposing figures on a continent running with rivers of intrigue. He was forty years old. He had lost the peachbloom complexion that had caused him to be described as having "the head of an angel and the spirit of a devil," but his faculties were matured and his wit was at its keenest. The Revolution was over and the Directory was in charge of French affairs under the direction of Barras.

It was just a moment for a careerist to step in, and when Mme. de Staël went to Barras, wept over the poverty of Talleyrand and told Barras that he, Barras, alone could now save France, Barras made Talleyrand minister of foreign affairs. Legend says that Talleyrand went to his new post murmuring the words, "an immense fortune, a fortune immense."

If indeed he intended now to feather his nest, he was not long about it. He had scarcely settled himself in his office before the three American envoys, Pinckney, Marshall, and Gerry, arrived in Paris to open negotiations concerning an indemnity from France for American ships seized in the struggle for commercial advantage being waged back and forth across the Atlantic ocean. They were kept waiting for several weeks during which they were visited by a woman, a Hamburg banker, and three agents of the Foreign

Ministry. At length it was intimated that if they would subscribe to a loan of 32,000,000 Dutch florins being raised at Hamburg, and would make to the Directory a little good-will present of $250,000, besides a *douceur* for the intermediaries, a way would be opened to negotiations. The three Americans reported the incident to President John Adams at Washington and indignantly went home.

Talleyrand never explained this incident except to say he could not be held responsible for the conduct of secret agents, and when Mme. de Staël asked him about it he put her off.[6]

## VI

Long before Napoleon came to power, Talleyrand had paid court to him, and when the Corsican crowned himself first as dictator and then as emperor, Talleyrand remained with him as foreign minister. He served Napoleon some fifteen years and made himself useful by curbing some of his whims and wilder ambitions, only to draw this denunciation from Napoleon in their last interview:

"You are a coward, a traitor, and a thief. You do not even believe in God. You have betrayed and deceived everybody. You would sell even your own father."

[6]Talleyrand, who was much indebted to her, was not ungrateful to Mme. de Staël and when Napoleon returned from Egypt, he procured her an interview with the conqueror, who was cold where she was ardent and pressing.

"General," she said, "who is the woman you would love the most?"

"My own," said Napoleon.

"But what woman would you admire the most?"

"The best house-keeper."

"But with you, who would be the first among women?"

"She who has had the most babies."

(Lacour-Gayet, *Talleyrand*. Paris, 1928, p. 272.)

Talleyrand did not reply or change countenance, but walked away with dignity, went home, and resigned. By then the carapace which had formed over tissues and nerves that probably were once highly sensitive, was almost impenetrable.

One of Napoleon's deals that Talleyrand opposed but was not able to prevent was the sale of Louisiana to the United States. This vast territory with its strategic and valuable port of New Orleans had been ceded back to France by Spain in 1802. Napoleon dreamed of using it as a base for an expedition against England's colonies in the new world, but when English pressure forced him to look to his defenses at home, he ordered negotiations opened with the American government, which, under Jefferson, was terrified at the prospect of the outlet of New Orleans being closed to Americans who used the Mississippi as an avenue of trade. The American envoys, Monroe and Livingston, were willing to pay a good price for the *city,* and were amazed to find that Napoleon was willing to sell them an *empire.*[7] They came prepared to pay ten millions for New Orleans, and for five millions more got the enormous territory extending roughly from the Mississippi to the Rocky Mountains and from the Gulf of Mexico to Canada. The deal outraged Spain, but Napoleon, leaving it to Talleyrand, who wore the expression of a man who has just swallowed a repulsive medicine, to make whatever explanations he could, walked away saying:

"I have just given England a maritime rival that sooner or later will lay low her pride."

[7] See Lyon, *Louisiana in French Diplomacy,* Norman, Okla., 1934.

Thus did the visions of Colbert and Louis XIV come to an end; and with them evaporated all subsequent dreams of French colonies in the New World that would over-shadow Britain's. The deal had more momentous consequences than any of the parties to it could have foreseen. It carried France's attention back to the Old World. It freed England from a dangerous rival in the western hemisphere, and it presented American traders with a gigantic internal market which almost totally absorbed them for the next hundred years.

What Talleyrand thought of the little handful of dollars that Napoleon accepted for Louisiana is not known, but his disgust may be imagined. As for him, he thought and carried on business only in terms of an immense fortune, a fortune immense.

## VII

Napoleon gave Talleyrand the title of Prince of Benevent, but there is evidence that long before the Bourbons were called back to the throne, Talleyrand was preparing to discard Napoleon. The two men not only did not trust each other, but differed on questions of polity. Talleyrand favored the peace and tranquillity under which the merchant and investor could thrive, while Napoleon was consistently for war and conquest. Talleyrand's reward under Louis XVIII was his restoration to the foreign ministry, and when he was equally helpful to Louis Philippe, the latter gave him the post that Talleyrand probably regarded

as the greatest gratification of his career — the ambassador-
ship to London. It was from there that he had once been
thrown out as an undesirable alien.

He was now eighty years old. His full cheeks had sagged
until they sank into his high-standing collar. This collar
had flaring points supported by an enormous cravat. His
shaggy hair fell over his forehead from beneath which
looked out his basilisk eyes, blue and heavy lidded.

In England he carried out his mission, which was to proclaim France's pacific intentions and desire for a good understanding, in the manner which caused Gouverneur
Morris to describe him as "lacking in *fortiter in re,* although abundantly provided with *suaviter in modo*";[8] or
what a fellow countryman described as "a mixture of nonchalance and malignity."[9] Talleyrand had once admired
the English and tried to be like the English gentleman of
legend, haughty and imperturbable. Now as he gazed upon
the nondescript beings milling in the streets of a London
larger and richer than ever, his seigneurial instincts, suppressed during the Revolution, came uppermost and he
wrote to a friend his scorn of crowds.

Louis Philippe pronounced Talleyrand's last mission to
England successful and when he returned to France Louis
arranged a grand reception for him. Talleyrand then retired and when eighty-eight years old died at his country
place as peacefully and as full of years and honors as if he
had never known those three "ures" that Baron de Staël
attributed to him: *"parjure, usure, luxure"* — perjury,
usury, and lust.

[8]Walther.                    [9]Lacour-Gayet.

## VIII

Talleyrand probably permitted himself—he may even have encouraged it—to be painted as worse than he was. In the chaotic, anchorless period that followed the Revolution it was worth something to be known as enigmatic, unscrupulous, and formidable; but he was not incapable of tender sentiments. In his childhood he was placed in care of his grandmother, Mme. de Chalais, who numbered among her ancestors Colbert and Chamillart, and through whom Talleyrand was related to these two ministers of Louis XIV. Of her Talleyrand wrote in his *Memoirs:* "She made known to me a kind of sweetness I had never before encountered. She was the first woman of my family to show me affection, and she was the first also who made me taste the happiness of loving. Blessings upon her!" As he wrote at a later day: "Youth is the time of life when one has the most probity."

It was common to accuse the mature Talleyrand of an insatiable love of money. That was a vice that, as feudalism decayed, seized all classes like an infectious fever and that spread like a cholera when the Directory, after the Revolution, established the middle classes in the seats of power. As feudalism grew old, it permitted goods and services, such as those the peasant owed to his lord, to be commuted into money payments; and at length money, which had been invented as a medium of exchange, became the absolute yardstick and weigh-scale of all values. Before the Revolution a man, provided he had birth and position, and an "estate," however poor and tiny, was, even though he might be penniless, *something;* after the Revolution he was, unless he had money, virtually nothing. He had, however, the comfort of the belief that in acquiring wealth his chances were as good as any other man's, according to the dictum of John Law in 1720: "The gates of wealth are now open to all the world." It was the French Revolution which made this dictum come true. And Talleyrand made it come true for himself.

There is no evidence that Talleyrand got riches by any crude or illegal device. He acquired a fortune by using his various official positions to obtain secret or advance information by which he guided his speculative ventures, chiefly on the money exchanges or the stock market. And he made another fortune through the comfortable pensions paid him by the various governments he served.

He sought money not to display it or to roll in it like a nabob, but to enjoy the power and position it gave him. It enabled him to be at the center of events and to surround himself with *movement,* which he extolled as that thing through which "one manages to fortify one's self enough to be engulfed by the convulsions of the soul."

## IX

Talleyrand left nothing substantial behind him save the recollection of his cynical wit. When it was remarked that Fouché, an associate of Talleyrand under Napoleon, had a profound contempt for human nature, he replied:

"To be sure; he has made a careful study of himself."

Of a member of that feminine circle which was always admiring Talleyrand and constantly promoting his fortunes, he said:

"Mme. de Genlis, in order to avoid the scandal of coquetry, always yielded easily."

When a certain politician was spoken of as capable of assassinating any one, Talleyrand remarked: "Assassinating, no! Poisoning, yes!"

When a diplomat remarked that he could not understand why he was called ill-natured, for in all his life he had never done but one ill-natured action, Talleyrand asked: "And when will it end?"

To a friend who defended the behavior of the upper chamber, saying, "At least you find consciences there," Talleyrand replied: "Ah, yes, many, many consciences. Semonville, for example, has at least two."

Once when Mme. de Staël was praising the British Constitution, Talleyrand explained in an aside: "Above all she admires the habeas corpus."

Such witticisms gave him a reputation for brilliance and craftiness which he was supposed to carry into his diplomatic conferences. But in actual sittings he was likely to disconcert rival diplomats by placing all his cards, face up, on the table and by making his proposals simple and plain. He never antagonized, and could not bear heated argument.

"In a room," he used to say, "beyond which my voice is not to extend, the attempt to enforce my opinion against that which another is engaged to adopt obliges him to be more formal and positive in expressing his hostility, and often leads him, from a desire to shine in the sense of his instructions, to go beyond them."

He avoided the appearance of hurry and scorned those persons who were always pleading lack of time.

"One should always," he once wrote, "have time to spare, and rather put off till tomorrow what you cannot do well and easily today, than get into that hurry and flurry which is the necessary consequence of feeling one has too much to do."

In conference he spoke little and only to the point. He reserved his opinions until all the rest had been aired and then often carried the day by an eloquence which rhythmic expression and precise diction made, on occasions, singularly effective.

Of Talleyrand as a thinker Napoleon had a low opinion. "He turns always upon the same idea." Talleyrand's ideas were indeed few. In diplomacy he worked consistently for the preservation of peace and for an understanding with England; in private life he worked consistently for Talleyrand. This latter activity built up a great fortune, but not enough self-respect. He once told Mme. de Remusat that his great defect was that he had "never cared enough about himself."

## X

Talleyrand lived on both sides of the line that divided the eighteenth century from the nineteenth. In him we see the transition man. It is possible that he tried very hard to be a nineteenth-century liberal, but the pull of eighteenth-century aristocracy remained very strong. "The old governments," he wrote, "alone offer repose and happiness to individuals. Constitutions are follies; nations will have nothing to do with them, because they have the conservative instinct."

In Talleyrand's almost every utterance we see a mirror of himself. His own instinct, even while he served with revolutionists, was conservative. The Talleyrand mind might roam among the ideas that Napoleon and nineteenth-century innovations had introduced, but the Talleyrand body and spirit craved the cushions of the older way. And so he wrote, "He who did not live before 1789 has never tasted the sweetness of living."

## AFTERWORD

### I

So ENDS the chronicle. It is chiefly a chronicle of the great and highly placed; necessarily so, since it is mostly with personages, and not with people, that the records are concerned. The annalists of the century show us that Louis XIV shaped its manners and Voltaire its ideas, but with humbler folk they rarely deal. For the lives of the obscure we have resorted to Rousseau and Arthur Young, and to the story of Damiens, the assailant of Louis XVI, as told by Michelet.

The historians have not much helped us. They are preoccupied with kings, dynasties, and battles. Historians love war. With peace they are easily bored, not seeing that the plowshare may be as dramatic as the sword; indeed more dramatic, for the sword has remained what it was, while the plowshare has evolved into the power tractor—a symbol of those engined mechanisms that are admired by men because they point the way by which the Adamic curse of overwork may be relieved; but which are feared also because these mechanisms, as owned, take work away from men, and so take away their lives.

315

Historians having such special loves and fancies, we have sought a balance for them in the gossips. Among great gossips the Duke of St. Simon is chiefest. Experiencing a disappointment at the hands of Louis XIV, this small, neat man sought revenge, after being at court all day, by going nightly to his chamber and recording in meticulous detail all that went on in the corridors of Versailles. He makes plain the beginnings of those processes that culminated in the French Revolution.

This was the event for which the entire century, in France, was a preparation. We see its shadow long before the thing itself appears. And we see its dust hanging over the world long after the volcano has subsided.

In England, where there were great possessions, the fright it produced was worse than that in France, determining the manners and morals of the entire century that followed. Victorianism itself was a product of the reaction against the French Revolution, mixed with sober elements drawn from the lesson of the American revolt and from the necessity of strict attention to business induced by the third revolution of the century — the industrial one.

It may be seen that the necessities of the situation have compelled us to give most attention to England, France, and America. It was in those three countries that the salient events took place; and it was in them that the major forces at work best reveal themselves.

Until the Louisiana Purchase took place, the United States were a part of Europe. The states hemmed between the Alleghenies looked across the Atlantic for their trade, their interests, their culture. But when Napoleon sold the Louisiana Territory to Thomas Jefferson, thereby liquidating the last of the great French possessions in the New World, he gave America an empire. The taking up and digestion of this empire totally absorbed it for almost the whole of the nineteenth century. In fact, America did not walk upon the world-stage again until 1898 in the Spanish war, and more emphatically in 1917 when it entered the World War, thus uniting the two hemispheres in a single convulsive struggle that signalled the approaching birth of a totally new arrangement of human strata.

## II

No extensive bibliographic list need be given here. Beside those works referred to in footnotes, the following may be consulted for the details of atmosphere, social modes, and background:

Mowatt: *England in the Eighteenth Century.*
Botsford: *English Society in the Eighteenth Century.*
Roscoe: *The English Scene in the Eighteenth Century.*
Sydney: *England and the English in the Eighteenth Century.*
Turberville: *Englishmen and Manners in the Eighteenth Century.*
Traill: *Social England* (Vols. IV and V).
Lecky: *History of England in the Eighteenth Century.*
Lecky: *History of the Rise and Influence of Nationalism in Europe.*
Bowden: *Industrial Society in England toward the End of the Eighteenth Century.*
Mantoux: *Industrial Revolution in the Eighteenth Century.*
Lockitt: *Relations of French and English Society, 1763–1795.*
Ducros: *French Society in the Eighteenth Century.*

Green: *Eighteenth Century France.*
Shorr: *Science and Superstition in the Eighteenth Century.*
Knight, Barnes, and Fluger: *Economic History of Europe.*
Osgood: *The American Colonies in the Eighteenth Century.*

# INDEX